Helen Dillon

ON GARDENING

**TOWN
HOUSE**
DUBLIN

First published as articles by the *Sunday Tribune* 1992–5
This selection first published in volume form in 1998 by

TownHouse, Dublin
THCH Ltd
Trinity House
Charleston Road
Ranelagh
Dublin 6
Ireland

www.townhouse.ie

This edition published by TownHouse in 2005

ISBN: 1-86059-243-0

Cover photograph by Jonathan Hession
Cover design by Sin É Design
Typeset by Typeform
Printed by WS Bookwell in Finland, 2005

To Grub, Rum and Mr Reginald

Acknowledgements

With special thanks to Val Dillon, Marie Heaney, Siobhán Parkinson, Charles Nelson, Mary Davies, Roslyn Dee, Mary Rowe and her sister-in-law Mary Rowe, Diane Tomlinson, Rose Mary O'Brien, Feargus McGarvey, Assumpta Broomfield, Melanie Eclare and May Carmody.

The publishers acknowledge the kind assistance of the *Sunday Tribune.*

Editorial Note

This is a selection of articles that appeared in the *Sunday Tribune* between April 1992 and September 1995. The majority of the pieces that appeared in the newspaper over that period have been included and have been retained, by and large, in their original form. Since the policy has been to respect the integrity of the articles as written, repeated information has not in general been deleted. Deletions have, however, been made where data was too topical or specific to be of interest to today's reader.

To make the book easy to use, the articles have been arranged month by month rather than year by year, and within each month the pieces are in chronological order of date rather than year. So for example all the pieces relating to early June appear together, followed by mid and late June, regardless of what year they were written in.

For details of nurseries and sources of plants mentioned in the articles, please refer to *The RHS Plant Finder* (Dorling Kindersley).

Contents

Introduction

If I met somebody at school, and I then see them again fifty years on, I find that if I liked them then, I still do now. It's exactly the same with plants. Glancing through this book almost a decade after it first appeared, it's remarkable how much I agree with myself. I still love lilies and cyclamen, peonies and clematis, primroses and *Solanum jasminoides* 'Album' and I still hate *Houttuynia cordata* 'Chameleon' (of course, I had to look up the correct spelling of its name). I still think the bully of the garden is the lawn. But I have at last got the better of it. I dug it all up. A canal set in Irish limestone has taken its place. A gravel garden has taken over from the smaller oval lawn. And there's still no satisfactory answer to the 'moss on lawn' question. Clematis still wilt. Slugs munch on. Weeds proliferate. Excitement is still generated by so-called 'new' plants, and then you find that they've been in cultivation for hundreds of years. Admittedly, I've gone off some plants, roses 'New Dawn' and 'Madame Grégoire Staechelin' for example – both for being leafless by August due to black spot – and I've got bored of dahlia 'Bishop of Llandaff'. Dahlias 'Murdoch' and 'Hillcrest Royal' are top choice at the moment.

The garden here has changed greatly over the last decade, as I've acquired the courage to practice what I'm forever telling people to do. I realised, after coming home from many garden advice appointments, having waved my arms enthusiastically about, entreating the clients to 'Simplify, simplify…' that when I returned home to my own front garden I would find a stupendous muddle of plants, accumulated over the last thirty-three years. Now, in place of all their hectic growth, is a grove of birch trees. Serenity reigns. Long may it remain. I'm becoming ever more committed to ruthlessness. Once I've made the decision that a plant must go, go it must, preferably today, before those little guilty thoughts come wheedling along.

A huge change has occurred in gardening, especially over the last five years. Plants that were only grown in specialist conditions are easily found in supermarket-style garden centres. All plants are available to all people. How wonderful that the snobbish element of gardening, the 'I've got it you haven't', no longer survives. When you can buy just about any plant, the choice becomes all the more fascinating. Also we've had years of mild winters. Old hands like me still don't dare to plant mimosas or bananas without the protection of a wall, but younger gardeners, who've never known anything else, keep gaily planting tender plants. Here's to them.

I find that I no longer want to look after a part of the garden I invented years ago. I want to be a creator, not a curator. The excitement is imagining how the replanted area is going to look, not tending a dated area of planting, constantly wiping its bottom – weeding and tidying, watering and staking. A point rarely mentioned in gardening books is that the longer you garden in the same spot, the more likely it is that there's a

1

build-up of pests and diseases. Young gardeners, working with fresh soil, have a terrific time. Everything is easy to grow. It's later on that you must become a better gardener to overcome the problems if, through shortage of space, you can't operate crop rotation.

However, over the last few years, on the four allotments I've cleaned, dug and installed with raised beds, I have managed to switch the different families of vegetables around. I love cooking and eating and despite having to move allotments regularly, I adore growing vegetables. In the garden here I always grow beans, French and runner, sometimes in rows of dustbins. If I had to write this book again there would be masses of encouragement to cram in something to eat among the flowers: chives and parsley for edging, rocket and mixed salad leaves to spice up ordinary lettuces, bright coloured cultivars of Swiss chard, seakale and delicate fennel for foliage contrast, tarragon in pots, courgettes in the greenhouse – I often go to sleep dreaming of how to cram in more things to eat.

I'm still as bad-tempered as ever – I think it helps in the making of a good garden. I walk past a bit of the garden that needs weeding, deciding I'll leave it until later. I then find myself coming straight back and fixing it. I still believe in feeding plants, with compost, manure, leafmould, or endless cans of liquid feed. I'm still dedicated to the use of the black plastic standard-issue builder's bucket, equipped with secateurs, trowel, string, ties and so on to save trips back to the potting shed. But I no longer spray against greenfly. I'd rather give natural predators a chance to do the job for me. Anyway, in early summer, high season for aphids, one can do a lot of squishing between finger and thumb.

I cannot tell you how many plants I've killed over the years, sometimes through general unsuitability for a Dublin climate, but mostly because I forgot where I planted them and they became shaded out by neighbouring plants. But however much I try to control the habit, I can't resist trying out new plants. And I still think that if my tummy doesn't turn over with excitement when I see a new plant at the garden centre then the moment has come when I should pack it all in.

As with life itself, moving on is important. Since the first publication of this book, some of my opinions have changed dramatically. The use of colour is still the most exhilarating element of gardening to me, but I'm no longer interested in harmonious groupings of allied shades. I'd rather rock the boat than preserve the status quo. Now I like to try out clashes that excite and startle. Yet having somewhere in the garden to sit and think has become more important than ever, somewhere to stay quite still.

Gardening is so many things at once: it is a science, yes, of botany and instruction on all things beginning with 'P' – planting, pruning, propagating, preparation of soil; an art, certainly, of positioning the shapes and colours of plants and then watching how sunlight changes everything; but it's also about moments of calm in a troubled world, breathing fresh air and looking up at your own bit of sky.

January

Tactical Change in War on Slugs

This is the year that I'm going to become horticulturally correct. The killing-shelf in the potting-shed is going to be hidden away behind a curtain. I'm investing in a head torch, the sort coal-miners wear, so insecticide and fungicide can be applied under cover of darkness. Little drops of poison will be dispensed to the weeds at night.

Take slugs. These days we are supposed to erect notices at slug level announcing 'Be my Guest'. At the mention of slug bait, the modern attitude is to become dreamy-eyed, mutter 'poor little things' and then offer slugs a lettuce leaf, half a grapefruit or a saucer of beer. After trapping them, you are supposed to lay them under a hedge in the Wicklow Mountains.

Weeds. Gone are the scorched-earth days of paraquating the lot. If you do use weedkiller, it's not something to mention in public. The green gardener now kills weeds by smothering them with old carpets. (Surely there are logistical problems here – the chance of there being the same amount of old carpets as there are weeds seems unlikely.)

Compost heaps, on the other hand, can be mentioned at the best supper parties. Major bores on the subject abound, and each considers his method of making compost the one and only, and it is his duty to explain it in detail. As a topic of conversation, compost heaps have taken the place of burglaries – remember how everybody in the 1980s had to tell you about their burglary? Each individual story had to be told all around the dinner table. Now we have to listen, way beyond the coffee stage, as everybody expounds on the precise positioning of their grass cuttings.

Now to plants. Beware of mentioning cyclamen or orchids, unless you are certain that the origins of your plants are clean, ie that they haven't been dug up in the wild. Other subjects to steer clear of are Christmas trees (their cultivation destroys the habitats of many different creatures) and opium poppies (which we all have, despite its being illegal to grow them).

Here are some tips for the fashion-conscious plantsman. Ferns of all sorts are top of the chart: there are few pteridologists around to argue

4

with you and ferns have wonderfully intimidating names – try saying *Polystichum setiferum* 'Plumosodivisilobum Baldwinii' a few times to shut other gardeners up. Box, white flowers, green flowers, old roses, seedheads, cow parsley, clematis, herbs, seakale, decorative vegetable gardens, arbours, trellis-work and pergolas are 'in'. Dahlias (except for 'Bishop of Llandaff' and 'Bednall Beauty'), rockeries of all sorts and insectivorous plants should be treated with caution. A little dig here at chamomile lawns. Such 'lawns', in my experience, are a complete nonsense. Lazing around, sipping champagne on a fragrant, herby, carpet is indeed a romantic idea, but any chamomile lawn I've seen to date has been a muddy, weed-infested disaster.

Tips of the week

- Check round roses and support bushes lashed by gales.
- Dig and manure empty ground.
- Under glass, water sparingly and remove any dead leaves.
- Winter prune wisterias by cutting young shoots to within 3 ins of old wood.
- Send the mower to be serviced; clean and sharpen tools.

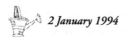 *2 January 1994*

True Grit

My mother makes lists. She got it from my grandmother, who made endless lists in a little red book that lived in the hall. I always knew when my grandmother was heading for the book, as the large bunch of keys attached to her person would jangle her approach through a series of banging doors. Surrounded by an aura of crossness and Mansion floor polish (which was constantly applied to the slidey oak floor) she would start muttering away and writing in the book.

My mother almost certainly makes lists of her lists. When feeling rattled about too many things to do, I've been known to write down things that've just been done, only to cross them off straight away –

very therapeutic for the obsessive list maker (it gives the illusion of work in progress).

Lists of plants in my gardening notes are marked 'Rescue', 'Dump', 'Propagate', 'Replace', 'Move', 'Prune' or 'Give Away'. Desiderata are marked 'Get'.

There are lists of planting combinations in containers that are worth repeating, lists of primroses, irises, violas, snowdrops and when they were divided, lists of good ideas noted on garden visits. As with any other list, some things get moved on to further lists, often remaining in limbo for ever.

On a garden visit in Wales last summer were some brilliantly healthy pot plants. Gardening note number 825 gives the recipe for their potting compost, which came originally from Tony Hancock, head gardener at the National Trust's Powis Castle, renowned for its marvellous containers. I've found the mixture so good I use it now for all pot plants. It consists of one bucket of Shamrock potting compost; half bucket of homemade garden compost (well rotted good and rough); quarter bucket of coarse grit. Osmocote fertiliser is added according to the directions on the packet.

'Grit' is complicated to explain to beginners, who imagine anything between the grit at the bottom of the budgie's cage to the stuff they put on roads under the tarmac. Vita Sackville-West was a great believer in grit: 'Grit, grit, lots of grit, the sharper the better.' I agree (except 'sharp' also needs explaining now).

We use granite grit, about 5–10mm in diameter, which is whitish in colour. To test grit to see if it's sharp enough, squeeze a handful together – the stones should protest with loud scrunching noises. Grit is essential if, like me, you're an inveterate over-waterer – the drainage is so good you get away with it. To confuse matters, grit is sometimes synonymous with chippings.

God knows where note number 785 came from —'Tomato fertiliser protects clematis against wilt and increases flower size' (sounds like something written on a banner being paraded up and down Grafton Street) – but I intend to try it anyway. Incidentally, I find tomato fertiliser excellent for pot plants – it contains a lot of potash to encourage flowers. Many fertilisers contain too much nitrogen, which encourages growth and leaves at the expense of the flowers.

In an artist's garden in Wales I noted an original idea for containers – three wooden tubs filled with globe artichokes. I'm forever waffling on about how sensational artichoke foliage is, and how the great arching silvery leaves look so wonderful in winter. Don't spoil them with other plant clutter, leave them to their stately selves.

In the same garden was a ravishing plant association: *Rosa glauca*, dark velvety crimson sweet williams and, quite new to me, a delectable dark black-maroon cornflower. I've been looking through 1995 seed catalogues for this and it *might* be the one in Thompson & Morgan's catalogue, listed under *Centaurea* 'Black Ball', but there's no illustration so I can't be certain. Anyway, they'll send you a catalogue free of charge.

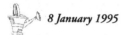 *8 January 1995*

Another Role for the Toilet Roll

This week I must tell you about six essential items for your garden shed: empty loo-paper rolls, wire coat-hangers, banana skins, used yoghurt cartons, clear plastic mineral bottles and bubble-wrap.

Up until now, I'd never found a sensible role for an empty roll of toilet paper, but I've just seen some put to brilliant use. If you've ever tried to force hyacinth bulbs for Christmas, you'll know what I mean. No sooner do the shiny fat snouts emerge from the soil, than they display a frantic desire to reach the light. They insist on growing at an angle of 45 degrees. Nothing on earth, bar an individual cardboard paper holder placed over each snout, will control this unseemly behaviour.

Wire coat hangers (the sort clothes come back from the cleaners on) are invaluable in the garden. Garden labels, you may have noticed, are seemingly mobile. Apart from human interference with labels, the main culprit is usually magpies. To deter the avaricious gleam in a magpie's eye, there's nothing better than a coat-hanger. Using pliers, cut the hanger in two. Straighten it out. Make a neat loop at the top, attach the label, and tighten the gap with the pliers. Sink into the soil beside the plant.

I've only just discovered about banana skins. I'm told they contain some element infinitely beneficial to roses. Apparently you eat as many as possible, buy a rose and then put the skins in the bottom of the planting hole.

Yoghurt cartons are a useful source of extra flowerpots. It helps if you're also a smoker. The tip of a lit cigarette, applied to the base of the carton, makes a drainage hole of just the right size.

Any clear plastic mineral water bottle with the top cut off makes an instant mini garden frame for placing over seedlings and outdoor cuttings and as a protection against slugs. Silly of Coca-Cola not knowing about this – their bottle is the wrong colour and doesn't let enough light in.

But the bubble-wrap can be made into a mini-greenhouse in a few minutes. Drive four stout wooden stakes into the ground, nail bubble-wrap neatly around it, place some more over the top. This would form excellent protection for a tender shrub. You can also make a sort of plant duvet, any shape you want, by attaching bubble-wrap to wire netting.

One last tip for the frugally minded: never throw away old garden hose. Most tree and shrub ties, even the expensive ones, eventually cut into the bark. By cutting a section of the hose, and running a piece of thick wire through it, you can make a tie that will never chafe.

In the course of digging in this garden for the past twenty years or so I've unearthed many potsherds – broken pieces of Dublin delft, bits of Chinese porcelain from the late eighteenth to the twentieth century, assorted blue and white pottery, mostly English *c* 1830 and the odd bit of lustreware. I have dug up quantities of oyster shells, marbles, clay pipes, horse shoes, bottles *ad infinitum*, mostly undamaged. I rebury all these things – one must leave something for future archaeologists.

But I once dug up a small dwarf. He was made of lead, and very appealing. I had him attached to an arch at the end of the garden. Would the person who stole him kindly return him?

 *9 January 1994*

A Gardener's Refuge

The garden shed, the one you see pictures of in gardening books, is equipped with clean tools, gleaming tidily from their hooks, stacks of flowerpots, graded according to size, and an immaculate potting bench. Reality is somewhat different. The most versatile structure you can buy, the garden shed can be adapted to any use. Apart from being the last refuge for smokers these days, an extra bedroom in an emergency, a dump for anything and everything that seems too good to throw away, for me its most brilliant attribute is as a private place in which to escape from the world.

For a start nobody knows exactly what you are doing in the shed, but obviously you're very busy, and shouldn't be disturbed. It should be sited out of hearing distance of the telephone or doorbell. At the sound of approaching footsteps, rattle the flowerpots, so as to give the impression of work in progress.

The immediate reaction of most gardeners on the arrival of a new shed is to tuck it away in some gloomy corner. But a different approach is to turn it into a garden feature in its own right, for its sides offer instant scope for more climbers. Southern aspects are always in short supply, and the south side would be just the right spot for a lobster claw (*Clianthus puniceus*), say, or a passion flower (*Passiflora caerulea*). Or you could drape it in roses, honeysuckle or clematis. The rose 'New Dawn' with scented, blush-pink flowers would be about the right size for a small shed, when allowed to drape itself over the roof. By choosing *Clematis alpina* (blue, spring, no pruning) you would have room for several other climbers, but for a wonderful jungle effect try the vigorous *Clematis montana* or *Akebia quinata* (semi-evergreen, chocolate coloured flowers, vanilla scent). The little yellow starry flowers of the winter jasmine (*Jasminum nudiflorum*) would be suitable if you don't want to smother the shed – it isn't exactly a climber but a shrub which likes something to lean on.

In a shady situation, I would clothe the shed completely in ivy, planting the same cultivar all the way round, up to five plants on each side. Clipped once a year, this would eventually become a complete house of ivy. A living sculpture that forms the ultimate retreat from the annoyances of life – what more do you want?

 *10 January 1993*

About Those Bloomin' Daffodil Bulbs

Spells never work for me, except the ones to do with the weather. I reckon that as soon as I write about the exceptionally mild season, winter will start showing its teeth. Then my life will stop being seriously interrupted by people telling me about their daffodils and tulips, and asking me what'll happen to all the bulbs poking their noses above ground prematurely. (They simply stop growing in cold weather, and wait for things to improve.)

Incidentally, I once read (with apologies for forgetting source) that it has been scientifically proven that in the case of certain bulbs, the nose is perceptibly warmer than the rest of the bulb, enabling them to push through frozen earth. Why are we all feeling so peculiar? Because last summer's plants are still pottering on and there's been no killer frost, so you see the ridiculous juxtaposition of tobacco plants flowering with snowdrops, Christmas roses with argyranthemums, and roses forming masses of promising buds. My ever-foolish tree peony even has visible flower buds.

I have no doubt that nature will adjust the scales; extra sun in November invariably means a deluge in February, or icicles in March. What we need is a few cold nights to freeze the whiskers off the greenfly. I can't tell you precisely what'll happen, but as my astrologer says, 'Expect the unexpected' (a useful saying which covers every eventuality).

Dealing with pot plants you were given for Christmas

Azaleas are easy to keep going for many years, provided you remember that the plant must never dry out. I once saw azaleas being grown commercially, and the plants were kept permanently sodden. Move the plant to a greenhouse (or outside in sheltered gardens) as too long in a hot sitting-room will cause leaf-drop. Repot occasionally using an ericaceous compost for lime-hating plants, and don't use too large a pot. (This is known as over-potting, and means that surplus compost becomes stagnant and inhospitable to roots.)

Cyclamen you can forget, unless you are very economical with the watering can. These are best watered sparingly from below. All dead remains of leaves and flowers should be carefully tweaked away from the corm to prevent fungus diseases. Once the leaves start to turn yellow, allow the plant to dry off completely. After two to three months' dormancy, water moderately to encourage growth.

Hyacinths, planted outside now in unimportant places, will give many years of flower; the flowerheads may be small until they settle down after being forced.

Deliciously scented **white jasmine** (*Jasminum polyanthum*) does well as a long-term pot plant. Give it a major prune after flowering. Indoors, fed often and repotted occasionally, it makes a living, flowering curtain, if you train it around and over a bright window. You could also plant it out under glass (or at the foot of a sunny wall, in the warmest parts of the country).

Poinsettias – I can't pretend to like these, but here are the official instructions on how to deal with them. Reduce water in late winter and after leaf drop cut back stems by half. Place in a shaded position at 10-15°C. Water only to sustain life. Repot in early summer and increase temperature to 18°C, keeping plant in bright, indirect light. Flower initiation occurs as nights lengthen to 12 hours and longer. Commercially grown poinsettias are treated with regulators, so your home-grown specimen is bound to be leggy. (The idea of treating plants with dwarfing compound is only disgusting.)

 *15 January 1995*

Winter Shrubs:
The First Flush is the Greatest

Daphne bholua, the most heavenly shrub of the garden, is in full flower at the moment. The clusters of flower are pale pink, suffused rosy-purple. So sublime is its winter scent that it makes you think of giddy summer days; delicious wafts are dispensed for yards around, to be sniffed half a garden away. Flowers appear for two months or more, but the first flush is the greatest.

From the Himalayas, common in the valleys round Khatmandu, the bark of this daphne is used for paper-making and rope manufacture. Rare among daphnes, it seems remarkably easy to grow, doesn't suffer from mysterious die-back, and is not fussy about soil. My plant, the evergreen form, now reaches to 10 feet on a warm wall. Sometimes suckers appear from the root, which form an easy method of propagation, so I'm trying one out as a conservatory plant. If you live in colder parts of the country, try and find the deciduous cultivar, 'Gurkha'; this has richly-tinted buds and an equally intoxicating fragrance. I'm told 'Jacqueline Postill' is also good.

Jasminum nudiflorum is a true plant of winter. One of the great survivors, long loved in gardens, you sometimes see it flowering happily away on the walls of derelict houses, its slender drooping stems and dark green trifoliate leaves illuminated by little yellow flowers. Graham Stuart Thomas describes this as 'one of the six best shrubs', in his book *Ornamental Shrubs, Climbers and Bamboos* (John Murray 1992). Praise indeed from this great plantsman. The winter jasmine is a sprawling shrub requiring some support – mine is trained to wires on a wall. Prune immediately after flowering.

'In any garden large enough to hold two plants *Iris unguicularis* should be the first…' remarked E A Bowles in *My Garden in Autumn and Winter* (T C & E C Jack, London 1915). The Algerian iris must have the warmest, sunniest position going, at the base of a south-facing wall, for example. The lavender flowers with delicate veining are ethereally beautiful. Pick them in bud and watch them unfurl in the warmth indoors – they have a gentle perfume, hard to put a name to.

The best possible reason for increasing your overdraft facility has just been published – a most elegant book, *Trees of Ireland*, by Charles Nelson, with illustrations by Wendy Walsh (The Lilliput Press, Dublin 1993). We can be proud that this book, a stylish celebration of Ireland's trees, equals the highest international standards, both in its writing and in its art. This is a book accessible to all. You can browse through the book looking at the exquisite paintings, or learn about the history and folklore of trees. It is scattered throughout with charming and inform-ative quotations. Charles Nelson and Wendy Walsh are to be greatly applauded on their meticulous work.

 *16 January 1994*

A Truly Glorious Beast

Think of scruffy hedges and privet springs to mind. Common not only by name *Ligustrum vulgare* – privet – is a Cinderella among shrubs, its dusty grey-green leaves and sickly scented off-white flowers usually found only in dark corners where little else will grow.

But a free-range privet is quite another matter. A flourishing, well-fed specimen of golden privet *Ligustrum ovalifolium* 'Aureum', given its head and allowed to grow untamed, is a truly glorious beast. I saw one yesterday in a garden near Bray. There were beautiful winter shrubs in this garden – witch hazels (*Hamamelis*), including the infinitely desirable 'Moonlight', its ethereal, crumpled, pale lemon petals on leafless twigs perfectly displayed against a background of evergreen. There were fragile cream bells of *Clematis cirrhosa* var. *balearica* draped over a tree, its pale colouring totally a-tune with winter, little yellow stars on winter jasmine, lemon bobbles on mimosa and the bare branches of cornelian cherry (*Cornus mas*) were prolifically covered in promising buds. (Incidentally, for those of you who find witch hazels difficult, this cornus is a pretty, easy, February-flowering shrub – it will eventually get large but does not mind being pruned.)

However, even among this cream of winter shrubs, the golden privet held its own, making a patch of pale gold shining in the late afternoon gloom. Some yellow and green variegated foliage appears irritatingly brash in winter, gold-variegated euonymus for example; not so this privet. A most suitable complement was a group of *Euphorbia characias* subsp. *wulfenii* growing nearby, adding a cool touch of blue-grey foliage.

Privet is easily rooted from cuttings. Young plants would make a cheerful background planting for a winter window box (not, please, with bright pink winter-flowering heathers), or try one in a container to brighten a shady courtyard, even in the dustbin department. When the plant outgrows its pot, let it out of captivity into the garden to provide good foliage for cutting throughout the year.

Privet is notoriously greedy and will rob neighbouring plants of food and moisture. To curb this, the roots of privet hedges can be chopped annually with a sharp spade, two feet or so from the centre of the hedge. Follow up with a general fertiliser and a mulch of manure or garden compost. Hedges should be clipped twice or three times in the growing season, but if you are thinking of a major cutting back of an overgrown hedge, April is the best time, thus giving it the whole season to recover.

The aristocrat of the privet family is undoubtedly the Chinese *Ligustrum quihoui*. Every time I see this plant, which, when mature, has more the appearance of a graceful small tree than a shrub, I make a note 'must get' and am only restrained by the fact that it eventually reaches 10 feet. It is one of the few late-flowering shrubs, blooming from August to October. The fragrant flowers are creamy-white with a hint of green like a mint ice-cream, and the airy panicles of flower are reminiscent of lilac – to which indeed privets are related. The leaves are a lustrous dark green – almost in the camellia class.

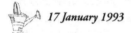 *17 January 1993*

Get Dug into that Therapeutic Dirt

Throw the Prozac out of the window, chuck the Mogadon down the lavatory and get out the spade. If people did more digging, drug companies would be out of business and counsellors would all be living in cardboard boxes (if there were any left that is, after all the therapists had their pick). Digging is the only treatment that works equally well for the alcoholic, chocoholic, potatoholic and/or sex fiends. Even members of the dirty mackintosh brigade would be instantly reformed. Bus them out to allotments, say I, and cool their ardour with a spade – after one day's digging, they wouldn't have the energy to unbutton the mackintosh, let alone anything else.

I adore digging, the most therapeutic of occupations. Thumping headaches fade, ghastly worries take wing, and my ever uncertain temper is calmed. But the problem here is that there isn't any room to do much digging, so stuffed is the garden with plants. More space would help imminent withdrawal symptoms over the Terry's All Gold.

The rhythmic motion of the experienced digger (accompanied by a little hum) takes practice to get right. First attempts are best unobserved – ensuing expletives might frighten the robins. If you're using the short, English type of spade, stand right on top of it and push it down straight into the soil – inserting it an angle causes instant back-ache. When using the longer traditional Irish spade you can stand back more from it. At this point I should like to have given a discourse on the subject of left-footers and right-footers (I understand that the way spades were used was the origin of these terms) but unfortunately I'm not certain of the facts.

Start by making a trench, about 60cm wide, and barrow the soil up to the far end of the area you're about to dig. Break up the soil in the bottom of the trench with a fork. This is the bit that really helps, for roots immediately have a whole new area in which to forage for moisture and nutrients. Throw in as many bucketfuls of organic matter (manure, compost or whatever) as you can spare – books say one bucket per square yard – I say up to three. Stir around with the fork. Dig a similar trench to one side, using the excavated soil to fill up the first trench.

Curiously enough, exactly the same treatment – winter digging plus the incorporation of any organic stuff you can get hold of – improves any type of soil. It lightens and aerates heavy soils and it also enriches thin, poor soils, greatly helping them to retain moisture.

My doppelgänger (with me, this takes the form of a dirty black crow who lives on my shoulder just out of ear-shot) has been troublesome of late. The other day he got so excited he nearly fell off, he was squawking so much with laughter. The reason for his mirth, rude bird, was that I have a plague of larvae of the swift moth. Take heart, those of you who have vine weevil. The larvae (underground caterpillars) of the swift moth are three times more voracious and three times the size, with creamy-white segmented bodies and shiny brown heads. They have catholic tastes, enjoying the roots of an alphabet of plants, starting with aster and auricula. Needless to say, Murphy's Law decrees that their favourite plants are also mine, ie hellebores and peonies. My friend Finola Reid found a book which said these caterpillars are 'mostly seen in weedy or neglected ground'. It was this remark that the doppelgänger found so funny – so much for the immaculate Dillon garden.

Adult moths fly at dusk during June–August and release eggs while in flight. Probably the best available method of control, now that chemicals such as Bromophos have been taken off the market, is deep and thorough digging. Cultivation exposes the caterpillars, providing caviar for the robins, who will rush up and buzz by you flapping their wings as soon as you start digging. The way a robin deals with such an outsize meal is interesting to watch: swoops down and grabs caterpillar by the head; flips it over and chomps the tail end; with a natty movement of his beak, makes little nips down the length of the body; gobbles it up; flies off triumphantly.

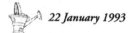 *22 January 1993*

Blooming Wintertime

I don't like summer's impostors on the winter scene. I don't want roses with their frozen petals struggling on or the silly foxglove and a couple of pinks attempting to flower in this garden now. No, I want plants that give a cheerful account of themselves, even when a Siberian wind sweeps down over Ireland.

In the front garden you need plants that give a comfortable, well-furnished appearance at this time of year. *Arum italicum* subsp. *italicum* is related to the wild arum, or lords-and-ladies, but the glossy green spear-shaped leaves are beautifully marbled in silver. The spring flowers are nondescript greenish-white, followed in autumn by fat little stalks with orange-red berries atop. I have several groups interplanted with hostas. As the hosta retires below ground in autumn, up pops the arum – *vice versa* in spring.

Much of my winter front garden depends on the contrast of leaf colour and texture. Polished silver spikes of New Zealand daisies

(*Celmisia semicordata*), grey felt of *Lavandula lanata*, acid-green spears of aciphylla, turquoise-green of rue, copper-bronze of epimedium and plum-purple of *Mahonia nervosa*. Splashes of daffodil yellow are provided by the foliage of *Valeriana phu* 'Aurea' and *Tolmiea menziesii* 'Taff's Gold', a form of the pickaback plant with lime-green leaves mottled in yellow. There are bergenias aplenty, best of all being *Bergenia purpurascens*, with shining, leathery, deep crimson leaves, which turn back to green in spring.

Golden privet, golden Irish yew (*Taxus baccata* 'Fastigiata Aurea') and a holly, 'Golden King', are some of the shrubs. I love their cheery winter look (although this patch in summer must be restricted to a mainly yellow colour scheme, including roses 'Graham Thomas' and 'Yellow Wings', *Cytisus battandieri* and *Phormium* 'Cream Delight').

Plant of the week has to be *Helleborus foetidus* also known, somewhat unfairly, as stinking hellebore. The contrast of palest green clusters of flowerbells against the black-green, deeply divided leaves is quite superb. An invaluable plant for the depths of winter, it will flourish and seed itself around in dry shade. Another plant that you have to buy only once.

For the patio there are some potted treats: well-budded camellias that will flower within the next two months – remember to use a lime-free mixture. Pots of bridal wreath (*Francoa ramosa*) look good throughout the year. Both these plants will do well on shady paved areas, but they will need regular watering, even in winter.

 *23 January 1994*

As Pure as the Driven Snow

I admit to being a galanthophile – *Galanthus* is the Latin name for snowdrop, while 'phile' means 'lover of'– but there's nothing sinister about collecting these demure little flowers of spring. Their modest white flowers are the very symbol of purity. Snowdrops are natives of western Europe to the Iranian Caucasus and the Caspian Sea. There's no garden too overcrowded to fit in yet another one; early in the year there's little else to distract, and fascinating discussions may be had with other galanthophiles on the minute differences between one snowdrop and another (invisible to the non-snowdrop fancier), making good diversions for an unsocial season.

Last February I spent an enjoyable day with Mrs Ruby Baker from London, who visited Ireland specially to see snowdrops. She herself looked rather like one – pretty in a wan and wintry way, in her pale grey coat. The enamel pin on her collar, needless to say, depicted a snowdrop.

If you love great sheets of the common snowdrop, *Galanthus nivalis*, its pure white flowers and blue-green leaves radiant under a low spring sun, the next stage is to be captivated by the niceties of some other species and cultivars.

I grow 54 different snowdrops, but if I could grow only one, that would have to be 'S. Arnott', a snowdrop of singular quality. As the petals open in the sun or a warm room, they are voluptuously curved, symmetrical, beautifully poised and faintly fragrant of honey.

'Magnet' can be immediately recognised by its unusually long, graceful flower stalks, so the flowers virtually quiver in each little breeze. 'Tiny' is indeed very small. The outer petals of 'Viridapicis' are washed in green at the tips – this is an easy snowdrop compared to 'Pusey Green Tip', a double that refuses to flourish. Other doubles include the old *G. nivalis* 'Flore Pleno', a pleasant enough little bulb, but the Irish double, 'Hill Poë', is superior by far, having engagingly plump flowers with five outer petals (three is the norm) and a tightly frilled green and white middle. 'Lady Elphinstone', a troublesome double, is quite special when thriving, as her inner petals form yellow petticoats, but if she's in a sulk, these are green. Search also for 'Cordelia' and 'Jacquenetta', two scarce doubles with immaculate central rosettes of green. 'Merlin', considered by some to be a hybrid of *G. elwesii*, is a snowdrop as magical as its name: beautiful large flowers open to display inner petals almost entirely green, rimmed with a neat white picotee.

The species *G. elwesii* itself, a native of the Balkans and West Turkey, is distinguished by its very telling leaves, light blue–green and up to an inch wide. Gardening books seldom mention how decorative broad swathes of snowdrop foliage can be on naked earth, particularly for places unnoticed in summer, such as the back of the border. *Galanthus ikariae* subsp. *ikariae* from the Aegean Islands, Turkey and the Caucasus, is distinctive with broad, shining, bright green leaves; a good snowdrop for starting a collection, as the foliage makes it instantly recognised.

Of oddities, 'Mrs Backhouse's Spectacles', an elegant snowdrop with extra long, slender outer petals, must be grown for its name alone. 'Boyd's Double' is a miffy monstrosity, apparently in the last stages of virus disease, whilst 'Virescens', in which the petals are nearly all green, is nice and healthy looking. Sadly my 'Mighty Atom', aptly-named because the flowers are very large for the size of the plant, seems to have disappeared for good. 'Scharlockii', by no means a strong grower here, is a dear little thing: each flower has two long, erect bracts that look just like donkey's ears.

Snowdrops must be transplanted 'in the green', ie in full leaf. Dry bulbs are difficult to establish. In flower or just after is ideal. Moist but well-drained, humus-rich soil in dappled shade is preferred. You can fit them in under deciduous trees or among herbaceous plants that are hardly ever moved, such as large clumps of hostas.

Lastly, you must try snowflakes. *Leucojum vernum*, the spring snowflake, is a close relative of the snowdrop. In bloom in late January, this has nodding flowers, like glistening white little lampshades, and shiny dark green leaves. Each pointy petal has a green spot. The flowers are brilliantly designed to withstand lashing winter rain – raindrops run down the side of the flower, quiver for a moment, and fall off.

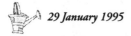 *29 January 1995*

The Lazy Gardener Loses Out

The hopeless gardener feels the first idle flickerings of interest about the beginning of April. Vaguely noticing the daffodils and tulips, he congratulates himself thereon, and rushes back indoors. There will be no further sign of him until the first sunny Saturday in May, when frequent sightings are guaranteed at the local garden centre. He has one idea in his head: plants must be bought without delay, it doesn't matter which ones, provided they're in full flower. Finally he grabs his chance, collars one of the salespeople, bombards them with questions, doesn't listen to the answers, and, chequebook flapping, stuffs as many plants as possible into the car.

The annual migration of the hopeless gardener is thus explained: the last tulips have faded, the wallflowers are on their last legs and there's very little in flower. The garden is mostly green, albeit forty shades thereof. This recognised phenomenon is known as the May Gap.

Any hopeless gardener who has read this far gets a star for effort, so we'd better suggest some easy plants for starters. *Euphorbia griffithii* 'Fireglow' is such a one, with orange–red 'flowers' on three foot stems with attractive whorls of leaves that have orange mid-ribs. It will ramp around in sun or partial shade and looks most beautiful when combined with green only or in a hottish colour scheme with purple foliage.

Globe-flowers (*Trollius*) are like luxuriant giant buttercups, with beautiful globular flowers and glistening petals, in lemon or orange, reliable perennials which prefer their soil nice and moist. They invariably bloom in the first week in May. A lovely, cottagey effect is given by columbines or aquilegias – my May garden cannot do without these charming old-fashioned plants. There'll only be a few flowers in year one, but after that they'll fatten up and self-seed everywhere. You'll start off with sophisticated specimens with two-tone petals, decorated by long spurs, but their offspring will show their wildling blood, and you'll soon have the fat little many-petalled flowers of the true grannies' bonnets.

Other early perennials to look out for now are brunneras, camassias, dicentras, Solomon's seals, smilacina, lily-of-the-valley and dwarf bearded irises. Lupins are usually in flower by the end of May, as are *Geranium* × *magnificum* and *G. pratense* 'Mrs Kendall Clark'. And don't forget two biennials – honesty and sweet rocket. (None of the above remarks apply if you've got lime-free soil – May should be your best month for rhododendrons, azaleas, camellias and so on.)

The eyes of the hopeless gardener are starting to glaze at the mention of so many names, so I'll only mention two shrubs. *Ceanothus arboreus* 'Trewithen Blue' has dense clusters of tiny, rich blue flowers. Unless in a coastal garden, this must have a 20-foot sunny wall. It's a very large evergreen – 'arboreus' means tree-like. And anybody can find room for *Clematis alpina* 'Frances Rivis' – an easy late-spring-flowering clematis with heavenly blue flowers. I've never known it to suffer wilt and it will grow in shade.

Needless to say, the hopeless gardener didn't realise that spring bedding (wallflowers, stocks, bachelor's buttons, forget-me-nots etc) should have been planted last autumn. If he could bear to leave the television/golf course/pub for an hour he could buy some winter pansies and potted primroses, and make little patches of colour in obvious places.

 *30 January 1994*

Finding the Most Social Climbers

When new to gardening I used to pester everyone I met with the same question: which climbing plants did they grow on their best, south-facing sunny wall? The answer to this is far more complicated than it appears, for the list of plants suitable for such a position is full of delicious temptation; should one plant wisteria, Banksian rose, *Clematis armandii*, passion flower or campsis to climb up the wall? And which to choose from the multitude of tender shrubs – carpenteria, fremonto-dendron, or mimosa for example? Gardeners love a bit of speculation: if the catalogue states 'only for the mildest areas' or 'very tender, only for a south wall' they cannot resist having a go.

Just to let you know a few snags in connection with the plants mentioned above, the Banksian rose (*Rosa banksiae* 'Lutea', evergreen with clusters of buttery yellow rosettes in early summer), was one of my first choices. With a glorious vision in my head of the house bedecked in roses in May, I planted it in a large bed at the base of a south wall. By the end of its first summer long arms of new growth waved in every direction, smothering all nearby plants, leaving no room whatsoever for sitting in the sun and other niceties of terrace life. We can't have this, I thought, and promptly gave it a severe pruning. There were no flowers the following year. This I couldn't understand, until I learned that it

only flowers on the wood produced the previous year. I have just looked it up in five worthy gardening books; they all state that it is a vigorous climber (up to 30 feet), but fail to mention the vitally important fact that the more you prune it, the less it will flower. So unless you have space to allow it to bulge out as much as 10 feet, choose something else.

To continue the theme; I tried a campsis (trumpet vine); it didn't flower, there isn't enough sun in Dublin to ripen the wood and induce good flowering; same story with the passion flower, masses of growth and barely a flower to speak of (usual problem – most books are written from southern England); *Clematis armandii*, the evergreen, spring-flowering clematis, is a success, but insists on going round in bare legs – for the first 8 feet from the ground it has unsightly naked stems – I have got round this be planting *Tropaeolum pentaphyllum* and a double calystegia to wind their way up the clematis. Fremontodendron – sorry to carp, but I don't care how beautiful its individual flowers are (large golden saucers), if it doesn't have the grace to drop its deadheads, to me it always looks a mess. I love the carpenteria for its clusters of crystalline white in midsummer, but its deportment is none too good and its leaves look distinctly tatty at the end of winter.

But *Solanum jasminoides* 'Album' I could never tire of – even if you hack it to the ground it will produce its lovely white potato flowers for many months in autumn – it will twine its way through neighbouring plants to charming effect. A variegated myrtle (*Luma apiculata* 'Glanleam Gold') has proved a success and looks especially pretty in spring when veiled in blue by *Clematis alpina* 'Frances Rivis'. Other plants which have passed 20 years of review and still warrant a place are *Hebe hulkeana*, a prostrate form of *Coronilla glauca* which starts to flower before Christmas, *Melianthus major*, perhaps the king of foliage plants, and *Acacia pravissima*, the hardiest of the mimosas.

The plant most deserving of a place at the foot of your best sunny wall is neither shrub nor climber. It is *Iris unguicularis*, the Algerian iris. Throughout winter it produces exquisite fleurs-de-lys, each fragile lavender-blue petal delicately veined and feathered, with a faint scent of primroses. You will be disappointed when you first acquire this plant – it takes a year or more to settle down, during which time it will just be a mass of untidy leaves. But once established, you should be able to pick flowers every day. (Gather the flowers whilst still in bud, by pulling rather than picking, so they come cleanly from the base. They gradually unfurl in a warm room.) Never transplant it and keep constant guard against slugs.

 *31 January 1993*

February

Letting the Garden Do All the Work

All my ideas about gardening have been turned upside
down after yesterday's visit to a garden in Blackrock. I
was invited there to discuss design. I had been fully intending
to give its owner, Bernadette, my usual lecture about pulling the place
apart, digging in mountains of manure, the charm of box gardens, the
necessity for focal points. With a family, let alone so many other
interests, she wouldn't have time for my grand schemes.

The approach to the front door was marked by a row of standard
modern roses that had seen better days, their trunks gnarled with age.
We discussed getting them professionally pruned by somebody with
strong hands to cut out the dead wood. But I then began to think how
unsuitable such roses were for somebody with a busy lifestyle, with their
endless demands for pruning, feeding, spraying, deadheading and
staking. Much better value (and no work) could be had by planting
quite different roses, such as *Rosa glauca* (heavenly mauve-grey leaves,
small pink flowers, lovely hips), *Rosa moyesii* (much taller, arching habit,
soft scarlet flowers, lovely hips), any of the hybrid musks (repeat-
flowering, hard to choose between them they're all so good) or any of
the rugosa roses (tough as a boot). All these roses, well planted initially,
will give many years of beauty with *no care whatsoever,* except a little
admiration as you drift past them in a dressing-gown early on summer
mornings.

From the sitting-room window across the patio was a view of a
wooden summer house. As so often happens with garden buildings, it
had become a general storehouse. I suggested cladding this with cheap
wooden trellis, painting the whole thing dark green, and then
encouraging climbers to ramble over it. The purple-leaved grape vine,
Vitis vinifera 'Purpurea', *Akebia quinata* or *Clematis montana* would do
the trick – even better if the climber could be trained to continue along
the house wall to the right.

A long, narrow bed the length of the garden would look much better
if it was considerably wider. (It often doesn't occur to people who have
inherited existing gardens how much better they'd look if the beds were
widened.) I bullied Bernadette into agreeing to enlarge it (and turn the

wiggly bit at the end into a sweeping curve). The other thing she promised to do in the future before planting *anything*, was to try and find out whether the plant preferred sun or shade. This makes for easier (less bother with sulking plants) and infinitely better gardening. For example, one end of the garden under a large cherry, should be planted with things that flourish in dry shade – *Euphorbia amygdaloides* var. *robbiae*, *Geranium macrorrhizum*, periwinkles, honesty, bluebells, London pride, bergenias, epimediums and the inestimable Japanese anemones. Then in her best, sunny bits of garden, she'd have more room for sun-loving delphiniums, roses, lavenders, pinks and so on.

I noticed several clumps of *Geranium endressii*. This is a brilliant plant – flowers for months, grows anywhere, divides easily at any season. It prompted the idea of what was the best advice that I could suggest: here is a delightful person, who loves gardening just as much as I do, and is particularly good at feeding and watering plants. But time and strength in large quantities are required to emulate the beautiful pictures you see in gardening books (there was a big pile of these in the sitting-room). What about planting masses of the wild fuchsia to mask the modern concrete walls, lots of *Alchemilla mollis* to form great, frothy pools of lime-green, *Campanula persicifolia* (like Canterbury bells but perennial), foxgloves, hardy geraniums, easy shrub roses, and let the whole thing turn into a magical sort of wilderness? Please, Bernadette, make big groups of the *same* plant, and let the plants seed about and do the gardening for you. Lastly, I thought of planting lots of hydrangeas, such as 'Annabelle', 'Madame Emile Moullière', and *H. paniculata* 'Grandiflora' (all creamy-white) in the front garden (provided watering is easy there). Please remember to divide the hemerocallis into seven bits and plant them randomly along the length of the newly widened border – there's nothing better than repetition for bringing a border together. Thanks for the tea.

 *5 February 1995*

Thinking of Turning Japanese

'Yet they are not very frequently seen in good condition,' states W J Bean in *Trees and Shrubs Hardy in the British Isles*. Quite. Japanese maples (cultivars of *Acer palmatum* and *A. japonicum*) are refined relations of the sycamore. Nothing can stop you falling for these on sight, regardless of price (usually hefty). They are quite impossible to resist, even more so if dissectum is part of their name. Their exquisite, finely-cut foliage is especially appealing as the tender young leaves unfold in spring.

They like bright light, but dislike strong sun. They are highly susceptible to late spring frost and cold east wind. They prefer lime-free soil, nicely moist at the root. They particularly resent drying August winds. By late summer the more delicate forms present a heart-breaking sight, their fragile leaves disfigured and shrivelled by wind. I tried them in pots and out of pots, trundling them around from place to place. But a sufficiently sheltered spot was not to be found, and the plants were eventually given away.

Now for an exception. *Acer palmatum* 'Sango-kaku' (formerly 'Senkaki'), the coral-bark maple, has been a major success. Its leaves, somewhat tougher than the other Japanese maples, are light green and prettily cut, turning to soft yellow–orange in autumn. After 15 years it is now a little tree about 12 feet tall. The young stems are beautiful coral pink, especially pronounced in winter, gleaming from the distance on a dull day. It is underplanted with the spring snowflake (*Leucojum vernum)* with February flowers like white satin crinolines.

Apart from 'Sango-kaku', I felt more a murderess than a gardener in my dealings with Japanese maples, and didn't risk buying an acer of any kind for years. I was then disgusted to discover that one of the most beautiful of all small trees, namely the Chinese *Acer griseum*, would have been perfectly happy all along in my dryish, limey soil. Many years had thus been wasted. *A. griseum* is the paperbark maple, so called because the old bark flakes and curls back to reveal the glossy, red-brown bark beneath. Until recently this lovely tree has been all too scarce, due apparently to the low germination rate of its seed. But 18-inch specimens are now quite readily available, from garden centres such as Johnstown Garden Centre, Naas, Co Kildare and Murphy and Wood, Johnstown Road, Cabinteely, Co Dublin. At the moment my small specimen seems like a little orphan plant marooned in a sea of soil, but it should eventually become one of the best trees here.

The common sycamore, *Acer pseudoplatanus*, is a stalwart warrior, one of the few trees capable of withstanding salty, coastal gales. Its winged seeds, twirling like little tops, disperse on autumn winds, colonising the vacant spots of all our suburbias, seeding into walls and eventually rending the stones apart. Sycamores are capable of growing 10 feet or more in a season, so unless they are urgently required for screening purposes, pull out the seedlings when young. Nevertheless, the sycamore is unsurpassed for an exposed site.

A final snag for the unwary: *Acer pseudoplatanus* 'Brilliantissimum'. Another plant guaranteed to sell on sight, I've seen its leaves variously described as 'a beautiful pinkish hue' and 'glorious shrimp-pink'. But 'dirty smoked salmon' is nearer the point. It is a man-made plant, grafted on to a tall stem, in effect a lollipop. After its brief, all-too-flamboyant spring display, the leaves turn a grubby, yellow–green for the remainder of summer. I can live without it.

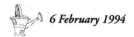 *6 February 1994*

The Cost of Ignoring Your Mistakes

Most of us gardeners get along quite well by using the ostrich method, ie simply refusing to notice any mistakes. You drift round the garden allowing your eye to land only on the plants that are doing well, pausing only to admire. A common problem (the sort one ignores indefinitely) is that of two plants growing in a space where there is only room for one.

A friend asked me recently what she should do about an ivy (in this case *Hedera colchica*, 'Sulphur Heart', more often know as 'Paddy's Pride') and the climbing rose 'Handel'. These two plants are now imprisoned in the gardening equivalent of a narrow single bed. Whilst the marriage began in harmony, below ground their roots are now fighting like mad for food and moisture, and their stems do likewise above for light and air. Ivy leaves splashed with gold intermingled with rose petals washed in shocking pink is an uncertain colour combination and the only happy outcome of the union is that greenfly find the resulting mass of leafage a nice breeding ground.

The ivy and the rose were originally planted to grow over a little outhouse, built of stone, which forms a focal point to one side of the garden. The ivy was chosen to give a pleasant, clothed evergreen effect in winter, and the rose to satisfy the desire for summer flowers.

To start with all went swimmingly. The ivy crept slowly up the wall and the rose duly produced its flowers each summer, but in middle age they are now locked in unholy embrace. They no longer even keep up appearances, for the true character of each plant has come out – the ivy is rampaging around the roof of the outhouse, flinging its leafy arms in every direction, whilst the rose's inherent fault (a too-stiff habit with a propensity for producing flowers only at the very top) has started to show.

I used to grow 'Handel' – in fact I had no less than three specimens. On the plus side is good foliage and freedom of flower. Bred by McGredy in the late 1950s, you can just imagine 'Handel' decorating the drawing-rooms of the period, in a cut-glass bowl suitably placed upon a cream lacy mat – altogether too refined a rose to keep company with flashily-dressed ivies such as 'Paddy's Pride'. So, apart from practical matters of overcrowding, one of them has got to go. The ivy contributes much more to the garden scene throughout the year than the rose and it is so easy to make an ivy do exactly what you want it to do, ie mask the outhouse without smothering it. Half an hour's thoughtful clipping would do the job. So the rose is for the chop.

If you are going to get rid of a rose, do it as quickly as possible – it's no use leaving it a few weeks more, for the buds will burst into fresh spring growth, new shiny leaves will unfurl, your heart will melt and the idea will be abandoned.

'Paddy's Pride' is one of the large-leaved ivies. If you prefer silver-variegated leaves choose *Hedera canariensis* 'Gloire de Marengo'. Fast-growing, decorative and ideally suited to a high garden or house wall, it would be my first choice for one facing north. Do not make the same mistake as I did and plant two or three different ivies on the same wall. It would have been far more visually pleasing if I'd used the same

cultivar all the way along. Ivies are self-clinging climbers, which should
have young growths trained in the right direction until the wall is
covered. Thereafter they should be kept neatly clipped to the wall
(spring is the recommended time, but you could do it now if
necessary).

Ivies will not damage a wall that is in good condition in the first
place, but will soon sink their aerial roots into soft, old mortar. This
shouldn't matter on an old garden wall provided you prevent the plant
becoming top-heavy, by pruning it regularly, so it cannot act as a sail in
high winds.

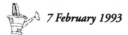 *7 February 1993*

Shedding Life's Multiple Irritations

Window panes filmed with cobwebs, the scrunch of broken flower-pots
underfoot, seed packets depicting fading flowers and the all-pervading
smell of earth – to me there's nothing move evocative than an
abandoned old potting shed. One can imagine generations of gardeners
rubbing their callused hands on a cold day, stamping their feet on the
earth floor, painting their home-made wooden labels, and crumbling
up leaf mould before the advent of peat. The modern potting shed may
not have such nostalgic appeal, but there's no better place to hide away
from the multiple irritations of life. Even if you don't actually need a
potting shed, and are quite happy to mess around with plants in the
corner of the garage, a shed is a brilliant private place, provided it is out
of earshot of the doorbell or telephone.

So, rather than build an extension to the house, go for a potting
shed. (Conservatories don't make good retreats, they're too close to
civilisation and its attendant demands.) My ideal potting shed would
have a kettle, a fire, a comfortable old chair (saw one on a skip last
week, my companion was too embarrassed to let me take it), a damp-
proof tin for potato crisps and a Coke dispenser. My existing potting
shed has just been given its annual tidy. Much of the contents consists
of things that might come in useful: the year before last's seeds, odd

lengths of wire, a box of miscellaneous metal things, their original use long-forgotten, and rows of bottles on the killing-shelf, designed to kill everything that flies, crawls or slithers.

Old containers of chemicals should be got rid of, more importantly if the instructions are unreadable. (I admit to not knowing what the safest way to dump them is – drive them out to the tip perhaps?) There is a large pot full of old labels, which make for an edifying read. Like keeping the collar of a much-loved dog, I keep labels of rare and difficult plants, as reminders that they once grew here.

Under the potting bench is a mountain of rubbish, dry bits of vegetation mixed with soil, providing ideal hidey-holes for the adult vine weevil. This must all be tidied. Now is the time to get the mower and other tools serviced or sharpened. For instant revival of rusty or seized-up secateurs, try using WD40 (penetrating oil). Stakes and bamboo canes should be stacked neatly – try standing them in large pots – and take off any attached bits of old string. Wash all seed trays and flower pots. Resolve this year to make up a decent amount of potting compost, and store it in a dustbin ready for action, rather than making it in dribs and drabs.

Parcel up those green paper wire-filled ties. Get in a store of bonemeal, fertilisers, sand, peat, manure. 'What a pain,' you say, but being organised now will save you time when spring starts in earnest. Under glass, first repottings of the year have commenced. If rooted cuttings of verbenas, argyranthemums, penstemons etc weren't potted on in autumn, do them now.

Pelargoniums (indoor geraniums) should have much of their old soil teased away from the roots, to make space for fresh compost. Don't use too large a pot: you can kill them with kindness by providing a soggy mass of unused compost when plants are still growing slowly. Repotting of fuchsias is best left until March. Pot lilies in a rich and gritty mix. If the bulbs look dry and shrivelled, plump them up by plunging them in trays of damp peat and keeping in a warm place for ten days.

If you know the lilies to be stem-rooting (such as *Lilium auratum*, the golden-rayed lily of Japan, or *Lilium regale)* place the bulbs fairly deep in the compost, say three inches' depth of compost above the bulbs. Even if you have a heated propagator, don't be too impatient to

sow seeds: rapid germination may leave you with hundreds of delicate
young plants, and nowhere warm enough to grow them on.

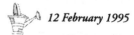 *12 February 1995*

Coping with the Seeds of Hope and Despair

There must be special training colleges for people who write seed
catalogues; the first year is spent learning not to tell the truth, the
second in learning adjectives (with extra marks if you can get more than
seven attached to the same flower) and at the end of the course students
are presented with rose-tinted spectacles which can never be taken off.
Thus you never see remarks in seed catalogues such as 'very unlikely to
come up' or 'easy to germinate, but not worth growing in the first
place'. But you see plenty of 'nothing to match it in the entire flower
kingdom' (applied to a pansy) or 'rich purple flowers which remarkably
transform into scores of translucent silver mirrors' (applied to honesty).
If you are an imaginative gardener and like lying in bed reading about
gardening, rather than doing it, seed catalogues are a marvellous spring
tonic.

But what really bothers me (pinpointed recently by meeting a friend
who had bought umpteen packets of different petunia seeds) are the
instructions found on the back of the packets. To be fair you cannot
expect the seed merchants to know your gardening arrangements (ie
have you got a greenhouse, or only a windowsill for germinating half-
hardy annuals?). If you do have a greenhouse, it is worth having a go at
anything. But, and this is the vital 'but', if all you have is a sunny
windowsill, the problems start. The temperature recommended on the
packet for germination is not all that difficult to find (many seeds will
come up within a week in the hot press) but what about the seeds that
insist on warmth and also light to come up, such as begonias and
petunias? And, as both these plants are extremely frost-tender, what on
earth do you do with the delicate young plants until the middle of May,
when it is safe (in the Dublin area, but wait two weeks more in the

colder midlands) to plant them outside? You may say that they can stay on the windowsill until then, but the chances are that even on the sunniest, warmest windowsill the young plants will get pale and drawn towards the light. So, the packet of a hundred petunia seeds for little more than £1 is not such a bargain as you thought. I wouldn't dream of growing petunias or begonias from seed. I can buy excellent plants, precisely when I want them, without all the worry.

But I do grow nicotiana from seed, because you cannot readily buy the colour I want (the green ones), which are brilliant for picking and do well in shade. Don't make the mistake of sowing too early – April will do on a warm windowsill. Cosmos is another pretty, easy, half-hardy annual (sow in warmth in April, or outside in May). Three feet tall, the daisy flowers and pretty, ferny foliage look appropriate in the mixed border unlike many annuals. Plants in mixed colours are easily bought, but I'm growing some from seed because I adore the one called 'Purity'. Needless to say this is white.

The plants I would most recommend that you grow from seed are those which you only have to buy once, those annuals that seed themselves from year to year, old reliables such as love-in-a-mist, larkspur, opium poppies and alyssum (incidentally, this latter is correctly named sweet alison, not sweet alyssum). All these can be sown outside where they are to flower (make sure to leave some to drop their seed).

 *14 February 1993*

The Fine Art of Making Compost

Yesterday I found a perfectly good tomato on its way out to the compost heap. Typical. Constant arguments take place here as to whether a vegetable is more suitable for the pot or the compost. In the kitchen, noisy discussions ensue as to the exact stage of decomposition of each vegetable. And daily bulletins are received from the warring states (the passage between the kitchen and the yard), as to the current condition of the compost heaps.

My co-gardener has developed compost-making into a high art, and his grumpy comments are to be heard every time I put something on them – he objects to unsuitable material such as prickly rose prunings, cigarette ends, and leaves that take for ever to rot down such as those of phormiums, ferns and all evergreen shrubs. But I have to admit his results are a delicious, crumbly, sweet-smelling substance – absolute dynamite for plants.

Situated in the yard is a series of compost heaps, in various stages of maturity. The great maw of number one, started in November and only half full, gapes at me every time I pass, demanding leafy offerings. Number two, sweetly redolent of last summer, slowly ripens to a rich, humusy, perfection. Number three lies empty, in waiting for spring. All vegetable matter – kitchen waste, stems of herbaceous plants, weeds, lawn mowings, thin prunings – is chopped and mixed into a wonderful homogeneous pie before being put on. The idea is to have a happy balance between grass cuttings and other matter. Too thick a layer of grass cuttings makes a sludgy, silage-like mess, and not enough grass cuttings means the heap is slower to heat up. Winter-made heaps may need a compost activator to speed ripening.

Ideally the heaps should be built directly on the soil, to encourage worms. In this case, simply drive four strong wooden stakes into the ground, and surround them with wire netting or planks of wood. For compost on a small scale, proprietary plastic compost bins are quite satisfactory. It is best to have two or more heaps – one ready for use and another still being added to. Turning a heap by taking out all the compost and throwing it back in again speeds the rotting process – an excellent job for a cold day.

Rolls Royce quality compost heaps are all very well, but the only difference between a compost heap and a rubbish heap is the time it takes to make one. Contrary to all the above instructions, you could easily adopt the lazy-man approach: choose your most unloved corner, make an enormous pile of vegetable rubbish, including evergreen leaves and rose prunings, and leave for two or three years. You may have to pick out some unwanted large roots, stones or bits of wood, but the long-term results will be just as good.

Tips of the week

- Signs of fungus disease on hellebores are black spotting on the leaves and, in bad cases, disfigured flowers. As a prevention, cut off and discard old leaves. Spray emerging young growth with fungicide (I use Roseclear).

- Cut the old leaves off epimediums. If you leave this too late, you can easily cut off the flowerbuds by mistake.

 *14 February 1994*

To the Water and the Wiles

For 22 years I've been making a garden. For 22 years I've been experimenting with water in this garden. Every experiment to date has proved a disaster of the watery kind. Holes have been dug for numerous pools. Holes have been variously lined with concrete, butyl, or polythene. With delicious expectation we have waited for them to fill up with water; champagne bottles have been opened; celebrations have been had; and goldfish, lovingly chosen from pet shops, have been released into their supposedly watery heaven.

First, the case of Albert, an unfortunate fish. The moment he arrived, I noticed a mysterious bulge to one side of his body. This grew and grew until he could only swim in a lop-sided fashion. And as for a watery heaven, Albert's pool went the way of many a garden pool, it became clogged with leaf debris and rapidly turned into a disgusting, slurpy, primeval mud. For years Albert swam bravely on through the gloom, increasingly over-balanced by the bulge, until he resembled a ferry about to capsize. The pool couldn't be cleaned out, for fear of upsetting him. I hadn't the heart to knock him on the head. When the final solution arrived, in the form of a heron, his pool was the first of many to be filled in again.

I've always had notions about formal pools. An immaculate circle or rectangle of fresh, still water, placed to reflect the sky, seems so sophisticated, so reminiscent of grand Italian gardens. Years ago, at considerable expense, a circular pool was installed. Agreed, it was perfectly round, but perfectly level it most certainly wasn't. To gaze too long at a pool that isn't quite level stops you feeling sophisticated and makes you feel slightly sick. At considerable expense, the cement of the pool was noisily bashed up with a jack-hammer and a new one was installed. This time, the level of the water and the level of the pool were in perfect unison. But round it was not. If anything, this was even more annoying. At this moment I can't think straight for the din of the jack-hammer bashing up the concrete yet again. Two fingers to a fate that has decreed that there shall be no formal pools in suburban Ranelagh. I think that unless garden pools are of a reasonable size, are situated in full sun out of the way of fallen leaves, have their liners completely obscured from view, have the right balance of oxygenating plants, water plants, fish and snails to clean up extra vegetable matter, they should be avoided.

Pitfalls abound also when it comes to choosing fountains. To begin with, there was nothing I wanted more than a single jet of water soaring high into the sky. Such elegant simplicity. A powerful pump was duly purchased. But disenchantment set in immediately it was switched on. A Niagara Falls of water noisily crashed down from on high; waves of white water flung themselves onto the lawn. Puddles formed in the flowerbeds. Conclusion: a powerful jet of water is all very well when seen in the distance from a grand hotel, but for a small garden there's nothing more shattering to the peace than the thundering sound of tumbling water.

The obvious answer is to get a smaller pump for a gentle trickle of water. But this too is fraught with problems. You have to consider the trickle factor. Trickles affect people differently, mostly inducing the instant need for a pee. Once again, the peace of the garden is disturbed by people fidgeting and crossing their legs. Myself, I find water with the wrong trickle factor makes me feel inexplicably ratty.

Now for the good news. I recently met an extraordinarily rare species of plumber, a plumber who is actually fascinated by the complications of installing water in a garden. Agreed, he thought for several weeks before coming up with the right solution, agreed the job was by no means cheap, agreed it was meant to be finished by early last month. But the result of his thoughts is brilliant: the new water arrangements not only look marvellous but also the water flows at precisely the rate to inspire soothing thoughts in the onlooker.

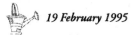 **19 February 1995**

Her Lover's Head in a Basil Pot!

I dimly remember a poem by Keats about a lady who kept her lover's head in a basil pot. Any morbid fancies about the exact condition of the head were always superseded by worrying about the basil. She didn't keep the potted head in a greenhouse, so how on earth did the basil grow? Basil doesn't even consider growing without masses of warmth and sunlight.

This delicious and essential culinary herb is an aromatic annual; it should be sown under glass in spring and planted out in a sunny position in late May. In pots under glass it is invariably prey to greenfly, whitefly and red spider. My gardening dictionary recommends spraying with a pyrethrum-based insecticide, which may well be safe for the basil, but what about the human?

I always felt Keats had taken poetic licence too far, until I visited Morocco last month. Then it all made sense. The basil he was obviously referring to was the perennial basil, altogether a tougher plant, a shrubby little bush, used for cooking and making tea in North Africa (although a cook friend informs me that the perennial basil is nothing like so good for cooking – the leaves are too small and the taste different).

Mint is also widely used in Morocco for making tea. The mint is kept chopped hard back to within a few inches of the soil, encouraging chubby, juicy young shoots. Handfuls of these, plus sugar and boiling water make a refreshing drink. My mint always looks moth-eaten by late summer so from now on I'm chopping it back regularly.

Moroccan gardens calm the spirit. Always enclosed, always formal, they are a shady retreat from the hot dusty world outside. The gentle trickle of fountains moistens the air. Roses, fresh daily, are scattered on the surface of the water. Coolness is provided by alleys of olives and citrus trees laden with oranges and lemons.

One long, narrow rectangular flowerbed was bordered on all four sides by a burgeoning hedge of lavender. Up the centre marched a slender avenue of orange trees. The remainder of the bed was planted entirely with a carpet of nasturtiums, tumbling their flowers over each other, in a vivid array of scarlet and burnt orange and bright yellow, a glorious and effective muddle. Simple and easy to copy, except that in Ireland you'd use another small tree (oranges aren't hardy) for the avenue, such as crab apples or amelanchiers. Another bed, also formal but this time hedged in box, held a profusion of colour and scent, a random mix of marigolds, alyssum, snapdragons, pansies, larkspur, fluffy blue ageratum, cinerarias, roses, godetia, petunias and stocks. Lovely.

Since my visit to Morocco I've given up worrying what people do to basil. But there were an awful lot of oranges there – perhaps I should worry about what people do with them instead?

Tips of the week

- Prune roses. Prune late summer-flowering clematis, *C. viticella* cultivars etc, to three feet from ground level. Prune recently flowered stems from winter jasmine.

- Tidy up flowerbeds, cutting back old herbaceous stems, weeding as you go, but avoid trampling on wet soil. Sprinkle general fertiliser (such as John Innes Base) around delphiniums and peonies and work into the top few inches of soil.

- Scatter slug bait round pinks, violas, alpines and delphiniums.

- Plant lilies as soon as possible. When buying lilies insist on plump bulbs that haven't dried out.

 *20 February 1994*

Take your Courage in your Hands

Have you pruned the roses? If not, why not? Roses are a bit like Rottweilers – they seem to know instinctively whether or not you are frightened of them. So, secateurs in hand, approach the rose in a businesslike way, as if you actually know what you are doing. Start by taking out any dead wood, cutting back to a healthy-looking bud. Then remove any spindly growth. When all that remains are strong healthy shoots, at least as thick as a little finger, stop and study the plant: the aim now should be to keep the centre of the bush open, thus allowing in plenty of light and air. Therefore prune to just above an *outward-facing* bud. All the strength of the plant will go into the topmost bud, and if that is pointing away from the middle of the plant, the chances are growth will set off in that direction.

You are now wondering how far down to cut these shoots? Well, as a rule of thumb: hybrid teas, cut away about a third; species roses and old roses, hardly prune at all, except for weak, dead or damaged wood. In the next few weeks, when the weather warms up, work two handfuls of bonemeal and two of general fertiliser into the soil around the plant, and mulch with one to two buckets of garden compost or well-rotted manure.

Next, what about clematis? Large-flowered clematis fall into two distinct groups. The first comprises those that flower before midsummer on the wood formed the previous year, such as 'Nelly Moser', 'Duchess of Edinburgh', 'Vyvyan Pennell' and 'Lasurstern'. Prune these very lightly (if at all), just removing dead or weak wood down to a healthy pair of buds. The second group of large-flowered clematis, blooming in late summer, *C.* × *jackmanii*, 'Comtesse de Bouchaud', 'Perle d'Azur' and so on, should be pruned to within three feet of the ground. All *C. viticella* and *C. texensis* cultivars are treated the same way. Pruning this sort of clematis is amazingly easy: you don't need to think at all, just chop the whole bushy tangle in a straight line and, with a sharp tug, pull away the floating bird's-nest above. Don't worry about removing all those lovely young buds – if you don't do so, the flowers will be so high up you'll never see them. Don't prune spring-flowering kinds, *Clematis armandii*, *C. macropetala*, *C. alpina* and *C. montana* for example.

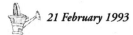 **21 February 1993**

Discovering Tír na nÓg

When it comes to gardening, age rules OK, and ageists may go and jump in the pond. One of the best gardeners I ever knew was a much-esteemed elderly lady in Northern Ireland. Despite the fact that the top part of her body was as right angles to the lower part (she had become completely L-shaped with age and arthritis), weeds seemed to tremble in the beam of her gaze. Her hands, gnarled as a burr-walnut and with skin the texture of an ancient handbag, would whirl in all directions. Snatching at weeds with dextrous tweaks, she would rapidly fill her basket with wilting greenery. But, in praise of age, what a wonderfully convincing argument she represented!

For a long time I've wanted an excuse to write about an unusual front garden, situated beside a main road in Dublin 4. Yesterday, I was invited to lunch by its owner, a lady of 82, who has one new hip and a not-quite healed broken pelvis. Both she and her garden are an inspiration. She's a super cook, and we sat down to a three-course lunch. The puddings (crème caramel and some Hungarian plums she'd bottled herself) were sitting on a table in the room next-door to where we were eating. I was surprised when she picked up the whole thing – table, puddings, plates, cutlery, the lot, and carried it through to where we were eating.

To begin with, her front garden was just a long, bare rectangle of gravel. There wasn't even a surrounding hedge, though it was redeemed by a southerly aspect. One August bank holiday, some 25 years ago, she moved gardens (curious that you 'move house' in the singular and 'move gardens' in the plural). All she did was scrape aside the gravel and provide each plant with two buckets of topsoil and a bucket of water. But despite the shallow layer, there are certain plants that revel in such exceptionally well-drained, hot sunny conditions. Little bulbs of all sorts are specially happy, self-seeding all over the place.

Yesterday *Crocus tommasinianus* was forming iridescent sheets of mauve and pearly lilac, mixed up with snowdrops (*Galanthus atkinsii* and *G. elwesii*), little irises (*Iris reticulata*) and several exciting forms of the Algerian iris (*Iris unguicularis*), notably a unique variegated cultivar that arose in this garden. The owner admits that the conditions are a bit too dry for most daffodils and fritillaries, but dog's-tooth violets (*Erythronium*) flourish in the shadier spots.

The winter cyclamen, *C. coum*, was much in evidence and spring-flowering *C. repandum* was already in leaf, bearing witness to the warm soil. A bay tree, rock roses, sisyrinchiums, and lavenders adore this garden, presumably because the microclimate caused by the gravelly conditions is what they like. There was a handsome specimen of a good, rich blue rosemary. (One of the more annoying facts of horticulture is that the deeper blue a rosemary's flowers are, the more likely the plant is to be tender.)

Over a quarter century, the surroundings of the garden have taken on a life of their own, forming a rambling mass of small trees, shrubs, and climbers, sequestering the garden from traffic and passers-by. Clematis are renowned for disliking dryness at the root, but spring-flowering blue *Clematis macropetala* has been a success (those with dry gardens, take note). Witch hazels are represented by Chinese *Hamamelis mollis* – in the owner's opinion its clusters of fragrant yellow February flowers are far prettier than those of the modern hybrids. Many of the old roses now gracing this garden have lost their names, over the years, but two known favourites are 'Souvenir de la Malmaison' and her daughter 'Souvenir de Saint Anne's'. *Buddleja auriculata*, now two metres tall, grows near the gate. I still regret I didn't take up the offer of a present of this unusual butterfly bush – I've looked it up and see that it is winter-flowering and highly fragrant.

The owner told me that her mother always insisted 'Virtue goes out of your hands with age' (meaning that plants don't grow so well, nor cuttings root so easily). But I entirely disagree after yesterday's visit. By gardening with nature rather than against, by using plants entirely at home on a small, gravelly site in Dublin 4, she has created a magical garden. Her parting remark at the gate was 'I own my garden – it doesn't own me. The great thing is to enjoy oneself.' Amen. (She was too modest to allow her name to be mentioned.)

 *26 February 1995*

Magical Plants that Keep Coming Up Roses

Hellebores are perhaps the most magical plants I grow. I adore them all. Heaven would be a large field of rich, retentive soil, on a north-facing slope, in which to grow their numerous seedlings on to flowering size. But here they must be culled before they smother the parent plants, an almost unbearable operation.

The so-called Lenten roses, *Helleborus orientalis* hybrids, have glossy, evergreen, divided leaves, forming a mound about 18 inches high. Their flowers come in meltingly beautiful colours, ranging from pure white, to the sort of green you see on the walls of 1930s bathrooms, to primrose and lemon, rosy pink, burgundy, claret, numerous variations on the theme of murky purple, and almost blue-black. The darkest have a plum-like bloom.

Their nodding, cup-shaped flowers are remarkably large, some inches in diameter, compared to the usually meek little plants of winter and spring. A further dimension is added when you lift up each flower. They are often exquisitely spotted within, each one unique, sometimes as if with a fine pen dipped in ruby ink, sometimes densely speckled in maroon all over.

From the moment their buds first show colour, often before midwinter, they gradually increase in beauty. Even after the flowers are fertilised, as spring turns into summer, their flowers dim to beautiful understated hues, old rose and mauvey greens, reminding me of faded dowagers.

The Corsican hellebore, *H. argutifolius*, forms extremely handsome mounds of foliage. Semi-woody stems bear handsome trifoliate leaves, edged with prickly teeth, veined in paler green and like cool leather to touch. Great trusses of flower atop three-foot stems are composed of cup-shaped lime-green flowers, luminous from a distance. A native of Corsica and Sardinia, it is best situated in plenty of sun in rich, well drained soil.

Helleborus foetidus is a somewhat shorter plant; it is often treated as a Cinderella among hellebores, as it is willing to thrive in poorer parts of the garden, gracefully furnishing dryest shade. The panicles of flower are set off by palest green bracts, the same colour as the tulip-shaped flowers, which are delicately edged with maroon, in striking contrast to the intense dark green, deeply divided leaves. It is known as the stinking hellebore, but all I can detect is a faint sour smell when the leaves are crushed.

The ultimate hellebore for the picky collector has to be *H. lividus* a refined, much smaller and very lovely Majorcan relation of the Corsican hellebore. Grey-green trifoliate leaves are marbled in silvery green, the underside is smoky-mauve and the central veins are flushed maroon. The apple-green flowers and stems are heavily suffused purple pink.

My plant is from wild collected seed; it is kept in a clay pot in gritty mixture, well away from trouble, for if *H. argutifolius* is anywhere near they will cross-pollinate, and I want to keep the seed pure. The result of a cross between these two hellebores, *H.* × *sternii,* displays features from both parents in varying proportions. The more pink flush to the flowers, inherited from *H. lividus,* the more tender the plant is likely to be. 'Boughton Beauty' is an excellent cultivar, producing a large crop of seedlings, which warrant careful selection.

Hellebores are among the greediest plants we grow. When planting I work in at least two buckets of fresh topsoil mixed with well-rotted manure, garden compost, leaf mould and bonemeal. I used to divide them in early spring. But now I've learnt (from Elizabeth Strangman and Graham Rice's excellent book *The Gardener's Guide to Growing Hellebores*) that the *H. orientalis* hybrids make a lot of root growth in autumn and winter, so early autumn is the optimum moment. Division involves a bucket of water to wash the roots so that you can see what you're doing, and a sharp kitchen knife. Small pieces establish faster than larger sections.

 *27 February 1994*

March

Bringing it All Back Home

G ardeners need an occasional treat. Chelsea Flower Show, held in May, is a major expedition, guaranteeing exhaustion. It's far too exciting and always tormenting because you can't buy the plants (except for a few wilting specimens on the last day). I've just come back from one of the Royal Horticultural Society's fortnightly shows, where you can buy plants then and there, secrete them in ever-increasing heaps in the downstairs cloakrooms, and rush upstairs for more.

Don't let the shoving of crowds put you off. (Manners go out of the window when the English gardener wants to get hold of a plant – many's the time I've been swiped on the shin by a handbag owned by a twinset and pearls.) Last Tuesday, as I was negotiating my place in the queue for a new corydalis, I was startled by the remark 'brazen hussy,' from over my shoulder. 'That one will live to regret my recent sessions in the gym,' thought I, before realising she was only talking about a lesser celandine (the one which flaunts bronze leaves and livid yellow flowers).

Of lesser celandines (*Ranunculus ficaria*) there was a whole stand. This is the little plant of hedgerows and ditches with yellow buttercuppy flowers, which some consider a pestilential weed, whilst others scour the countryside for peculiar forms. These may be double or single, and range from primrose, orange, lemon and white to curiosities, such as 'Tree-Frog Primrose', in which the backs of the petals are brilliant green, to the unromantically named 'Double Mud'. I asked the owner of the stand (Rowden Gardens) to point out his most exciting item of the 60 different cultivars on display. This turned out to be 'Elan' – an exquisite double white, the reverse of the petals gun-metal bronze.

There were stands of camellias, orchids, scented geraniums, shrubs, double primroses, ivies and ferns, but the greatest hum of excitement was around the spring bulbs. Before the recent regulations allowing freedom of movement of plants in EU countries, whenever I asked stallholders if they exported to the Republic of Ireland, the reply was invariably a sniffy 'No,' making me feel very small. Now nurseries are delighted with Irish orders.

Potterton and Martin had a lovely range of corydalis on show. It was also good to see the very scarce *Eranthis* × *tubergenii* for sale. This is a superb winter aconite, much larger and more vigorous than the common one, with large shining, golden yellow flowers. Broadleigh Gardens were showing different forms of *Cyclamen coum*, the hardy winter-flowering cyclamen. Some had leaves that were silvery all over; others were heavily marked. The little flowers, in pink, white or crimson, were appropriately displayed on a background of beech leaves and larch needles. They also had many dwarf daffodils, scillas, the rare and expensive *Tecophilia cyanocrocus*, and a delicious sugar-pink corydalis which I managed to acquire, namely 'Beth Evans'. Roger Skelmersdale, joint owner of the stand, explained to me just how long it takes to get a new daffodil onto the market: 'Gypsy Queen', a tiny lemon daffodil, was a chance seedling that turned up at Broadleigh in the early 1960s. For safety, the bulbs were grown in plastic window-box liners, and it wasn't until 1990 that he had enough to plant out three bulbs in the garden.

Burncoose and South Down Nurseries had a superb display of camellias. 'Mrs D. W. Davies' was irresistible. She had the largest flowers of any camellia I'd ever seen, with semi-double flowers in blush pink of voluptuous proportions. Single, pale pink 'Akebono' (low-growing, suitable for small gardens) might be the choice for gardeners of more modest tastes.

To become a member of the Royal Horticultural Society ring 0044–171–821–3000.

 *5 March 1995*

More to Spring than Bulbs

The gardening nightmare of the year recurs at the beginning of March, when the first serious weeding takes place. Each footstep means potential heartbreak, threatening the tender snouts of trilliums, erythroniums, Solomon's seal, podophyllums, disporums, uvularias; the succulent, uncurling stems of *Anemone nemorosa* and cardamines; and the vulnerable fat noses of hostas. Despite the fact that the positions of plants still below ground are liberally decorated with marking canes, weeding is now more a ballet dance of bad temper than a soothing pastime, as my boot – with a sickening scrunch – descends on yet another juicy, barely visible shoot.

For most of us, spring is synonymous with bulbs. But there are some excellent small herbaceous plants that you should know about. I'm still waiting for the toothworts, so-called on account of their odd-looking whitish, rhizomatous roots, to receive proper recognition. Their Latin name is *Cardamine* (it used to be *Dentaria*) and they are thus refined relations of cuckoo flowers and hairy bittercress (*Cardamine hirsuta*), the beastly little weed that you should be out looking for at the moment. These toothworts are most desirable for their early flowering, not least because their colour range includes pink, mauve and purple, instead of the more usual yellows and blues of spring. They are conveniently fitted in among shrubs or later perennials and they seem happy anywhere except the driest shade, although in the wild they are usually found in damp, mountain woodlands.

Cardamine pentaphyllos has light green divided leaves and clusters of lilac pink flowers on one-foot stems from March to late April. *C. heptaphylla* is slightly taller, with more erect stems and white flowers, whilst *C. enneaphyllos* has creamy-yellow flowers, in nice contrast to the young bronze leaves.

Pachyphragma macrophylla from Turkey and the Caucasus, another member of the same family (the Cruciferae) and perhaps more neglected, has clusters of pristine white little flowers which present a lacy effect above the glossy, bright green, rounded leaves. *Pachyphragma* makes good ground cover for shade, begins to flower with the snowdrops, is still pottering on in May and is especially good planted near deep purple hellebores. Agreed, it's not a major star, but it well deserves a place in the chorus.

Pulmonaria or lungworts are small early-flowering perennials with the typical rough-to-touch leaves of the borage family. *P. officinalis* is the common, well-loved old garden plant, with heart-shaped spotted leaves and pink and blue flowers at the same time. *P. saccharata* and its cultivars are often so spotted they are frosted silver all over. All are easily grown in part or full shade, in moist, humus-rich soil. The moment I plant a new pulmonaria, I'm wondering how soon I can divide it into a large patch – much more telling than one solitary specimen. Look out for *P. rubra* 'David Ward', with beautifully variegated leaves in cream and light green and brick-red flowers, and 'Mrs Kittle', a little doll of a pulmonaria, pale grey–blue, lovely with smokey mauve hellebores.

A second performance of the snout and boot ballet takes place for the very late arrivals on the garden scene, such as *Arisaema candidissimum* which never comes up until June. From its sinister, maroon-mottled snouts arise hooded white flowers, beautifully striped in candy-pink. Large leaves form protective umbrellas over the flowers. Apart from surrounding the patch of arisaema with a stockade of small canes, with little flags attached marked 'Beware of the Boot', one way to remind you of where they are is to plant some early bulbs such as crocuses or snowdrops on top.

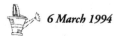 *6 March 1994*

More to Herbs than Parsley

I've just been talking to Jekka McVicar about her book, *Jekka's Complete Herb Book*. 'I hope it inspires people to try out new herbs, and that it answers some of their questions,' she says. Jekka is a bouncy, bubbly person full of jokes, and wildly enthusiastic about herbs and what to do with them. She has been growing them for 20 years and runs a nursery near Bristol. From pictures in the book, this looks an immaculately tidy establishment.

'I'm organic. If you're disciplined, pests and diseases are more easily controlled.' The most fascinating thing she discovered when researching herbs was how long some species have been in use. 'Coriander seed was found in Tutankhamen's tomb, and when the Roman legions marched across Europe, they put cloves of garlic between their toes to prevent foot rot – that's what got me into writing the book. I didn't realise how much astrology was tied into herbs. For instance, Venus and violets go together.' (The growth of violets is governed by the planet.) Yarrow is also under Venus: 'If you want to prove that your lover is unfaithful, wave some yarrow under their nostrils. If they have a nose bleed, they're faithful.' Apparently cheating, by bopping them on the nose, isn't allowed.

Four years ago, at Chelsea Flower Show, she worked on the British Herb Trade Stand. The two questions she was most frequently asked were 'Why is my basil dead?' and 'When do I cut back my lavender?' The answers, respectively, are 'Too cold, over-watering and it's only an annual,' and 'After flowering, but before the frosts.'

On the subject of basil: 'Don't stick to sweet basil, there are some superb basils about, like lemon basil, and cinnamon basil that I've done with stuffed peppers and tomato sauce and a little bit of grated ginger. Gorgeous.' What were her most useful discoveries? 'A crushed leaf of angelica put in the car stops my children being sick. Also, I'm allergic to red ant sting – I don't swell up if I rub on pennyroyal immediately after I'm stung.' Her son always carries some sempervivum (houseleek) in his pocket for nettle stings – 'they're better than dock.' Jekka also found that sorrel was good for banishing ink stains: 'I just pulverise it and let the juice drip onto the stain.'

Jekka stresses that she isn't a herbalist but a herb grower. I asked her which was the most neglected and useful herb (after the obvious parsley, mint, sage etc). 'Savory,' she replied, 'the perennial winter savory for stews and casseroles, and the annual summer savory to eat with beans and pulse dishes – it stops flatulence and tastes wonderful, like a mixture of rosemary and thyme with a hint of pepper.'

'Herbs are not just culinary, not just medicinal, they're the most generous plants I know. Take lemon verbena. If I'm feeling at all uptight or low I make a cup of tea (about 3–5 leaves depending on size), pour on boiling water and drink it at night. It's better than anything to help you sleep.'

Jekka's Complete Herb Book, by Jekka McVicar, with an introduction by Penelope Hobhouse (Gill & Macmillan), is an extremely pretty book and easy to look at, for everything to do with each herb is on the same page – the different species and cultivars, cultivation, medicinal use, culinary use, companion planting, harvesting, maintenance, and advice on growing herbs in containers. If the herb is poisonous, proper warnings are mentioned. 'I've had so much trouble getting this section right – to make people respect the plants and at the same time warn them of the hazards.'

The book illustrates several tempting designs for herb gardens, including one for an aromatherapy herb garden. There's a herb dye chart, and sections on propagation and pests and diseases. This is one of the few books with 'complete' in the title that actually *is* complete. I have no hesitation in thoroughly recommending it.

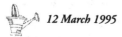 *12 March 1995*

Shady Shrubs in the Background

Just as rooms need furniture, gardens need furnishing plants – the equivalent of the sofa and chairs and dining room table – comfortable background shrubs that behave themselves, and are not subject to mysterious collapse (such as daphnes and large-flowered clematis are prone to).

Ephemeral plants, herbaceous plants, annuals and bulbs, can be thought of more as pictures and ornaments that can be moved around according to whim. We all want dashing new cultivars, the latest in variegated or colour-splashed leaves, the fashionable arrivistes at last year's Chelsea Flower Show: but they mightn't live up to expectations and if you made a garden of these alone, the effect could be rather hectic.

I'm very fond of the old laurustinus or *Viburnum tinus*. You've probably never given a thought to such an ordinary old-fashioned shrub. It has shiny dark evergreen leaves and pinky white flowers at the moment. It has been in cultivation since the sixteenth century. It makes a satisfying bulge, eventually reaching 10 feet, will do in indifferent soil, and will flourish in shade (though you'll have more flowers in sun). 'Eve Price' is a pretty and much more compact form of laurustinus, with pink flowers, carmine in bud.

The Mexican orange flower, *Choisya ternata*, is another nice, bulgy evergreen, also capable of reaching 10 feet but you can keep it down to five feet by pruning, a most enjoyable operation accompanied by the delicious spice scent of the cut leaves and stems. It has clusters of white flowers fragrant of hawthorn. On no account be persuaded into buying the cultivar 'Sundance' – a parvenu indeed – its yellow leaves can turn a harsh gold. (Admittedly I once saw 'Sundance' looking good, but then it had been very skilfully planted by growing it in shade, the leaves had turned a cool lime green and its planting partners were blue-leaved hostas and blue rue, *Ruta graveolens* 'Jackman's Blue'.)

Artemisia 'Powis Castle' makes a lovely mound of finely-cut, silky, silvery leaves. Apart from *Artemisia lactiflora* (a seriously good herbaceous plant, with long-lasting creamy plumes), most artemisias have nondescript flowers, but 'Powis Castle' makes no attempt to flower and is thus your ideal furnishing plant – a sort of sumptuous, large (three feet square) silver cushion. Agreed, the upholstery is looking a little grubby after winter, but by next month it will have put on new leaves and will be back to its shining self. 'Powis Castle' looks marvellous with mauves, pinks and pale blues and will grow on any well-drained soil in sun. Any of the purple-leaved forms of smoke bush (*Cotinus coggygria*) make wonderful background shrubs. Curiously enough, the dusky purple leaves seem to enhance any sort of colour scheme – a perfect complement for the pale shades and also a brilliant enrichment for scarlet and orange; peachy colours also look good against its purple leaves. It will stand considerable pruning and is not particular about soil or position.

Anyone who has been to Sissinghurst comes home with a fixation about weeping silver pear trees (*Pyrus salicifolia* 'Pendula') – now almost a cliché of gardening vocabulary, since it was given a certificate of excellence by Vita Sackville-West. If not pruned correctly you end up with something like a giant bird's nest on top of a stick; keep pruning lower stems back to the trunk, put in a temporary stake to guide the leading shoot upwards: regularly thin out a number of the weeping branches: aim to have an airy tree rather than a congested tangle.

An excellent substitute for the pear is *Elaeagnus* 'Quicksilver'. A small deciduous tree with glistening silver leaves and tiny, fragrant yellow flowers. You can prune it as much or as little as you like.

Rosa glauca (used to be known as *R. rubrifolia*) is madly pretty and has infinite uses as a furnishing plant. Its pale pink single flowers, like miniature Tudor roses, are rather fleeting but its leaves and stems are an exquisite pinky-mauve, with a bloom like that on a plum. In shade the foliage is blushed with glaucous blue. Irresistible. You can treat this entirely as a foliage plant by cutting it to within one foot of the ground each year (now). Give it a generous feed (two handfuls of bonemeal, two of general fertiliser) and a two-bucket mulch of rotted manure or compost to make up.

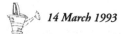 *14 March 1993*

Some Species are Worth the Risk

I often think that the more you know about gardening the less fun it is. Old hands have had their fingers burnt too often. It's 10 years or more since we've had a killer-winter, after which I've never risked tender plants outdoors. And, knowing only too well which plants are said to hate lime, I never risk experimenting with them, much as I'd like to prove gardening books inaccurate.

I was shivering in the greenhouse recently on a foul day, when John Bourke called. He gardens at the Marino Institute of Education in Griffith Avenue, Dublin and he started telling me about the many successes he's had with plants of doubtful hardiness. John Bourke loves taking risks with plants, especially in the courtyard at the Institute, which is surrounded by walls, three of them 30–40 feet high. One such plant is *Grevillea rosmarinifolia*.

This beautiful Australian shrub has always tantalised me, but *Hilliers' Manual of Trees and Shrubs* insists that it is not only lime-hating but also frost-tender. I suspect that slightly limey Dublin soil with liberal additions of peat, plus sheltering courtyard walls, equal a comfortable home for grevillea. The needle-like leaves are dark grey–green and the deep rosy-red flowers are in terminal racemes. John says that his specimen has been flowering all winter on a west-facing wall. Fool that I am, for not trying one!

Cobaea scandens (the cup and saucer vine, usually grown as an annual) has been flowering all winter on a sunny wall. *Lapageria rosea* has reached 12 feet in the shade. A half-barrel of the heavenly, fragrant, reputedly tender *Rhododendron* 'Fragrantissimum' is covered in buds, having spent winter outdoors. John complained of its sprawly habit, so I suggest hard pruning half the stems immediately after flowering. Pruning annually this way you can keep the bush shapely and still leave enough branches to form flower buds.

'A plant that never ceases to amaze is *Abutilon* 'Kentish Belle,' said John. He has it growing beside a sunny wall, in bloom from June to November. Abutilons are fast-growing, usually wind-brittle, tropical or sub-tropical shrubs, very easy from cuttings. (Always grow a back-up plant for emergencies.) They become scrawny-looking by spring, and I suggested pruning the side branches by about half or more in April to encourage bushy growth. Even the hardier *A. vitifolium* needs regular pruning, after flowering and in spring, to encourage wind-resistance. 'Ashford Red', with vibrant soft red flowers, is another beautiful tenderish abutilon worth a try.

Luckily, plant lovers are not so vigilant as the animal protection brigade, or I'd have them after me for cruelty to abutilons. Congestion in the greenhouse forced me to plant a six-foot specimen of *Abutilon megapotamicum* outside in January, albeit beside a warm wall. The plant is now sitting in a puddle, glaring at me through the window. One of the more hardy abutilons, this is usually grown in its rather suspect variegated form (the mottled yellow on the leaves is caused by a virus), but I think the plain green leaves of the species proper show off the little red bellflowers with egg-yolk-yellow underskirts much better.

We started a discussion about *Griselinia* 'Bantry Bay'. I've always been rude about griselinias, being overwhelmed by the plastic green of their leaves. But the Irish-born 'Bantry Bay' is a delightful, slow-growing exception, the leaves variously marked in cream, with cream reverses. John likes it for the bright splash of winter colour it makes in the courtyard.

Olearia stellulata, an Australasian daisy bush, in effect like a shrubby Michaelmas daisy, has been a mass of tiny blue flowers all winter. Another southern hemisphere shrub, *Leptospermum scoparium* 'Red Damask', said to prefer acid soil, is now six feet tall, with double, deep red, long-lasting flowers. Tasmanian *Billardiera longiflora*, grown for its shiny, deep violet-blue berries, is another experiment. The *RHS Dictionary* recommends lime-free soil for this slender climber, but what are rules for, if not to be broken? John Bourke believes that all the manure that he's added to the soil could well have made the soil more acidic and (an excellent tip) recommended pine needles as a mulch for camellias – guaranteed to increase acidity. He feeds his camellias regularly with Miracid and never lets their pots dry out.

After my conversation with John Bourke I felt inspired to try out more risky plants – either of hardiness or of soil preference. (A remark such as this may well pre-empt a killer-spring.)

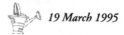 *19 March 1995*

Just Give me Some of them Old-fashioned Primroses

The primrose – *prima rosa* – is the first 'rose' of the year. But if you go down to the woods today, the primroses won't be there. At least they won't be exactly where you remembered them: they will have seeded themselves on to fresh ground, further up the bank, or down the ditch, or into the wood. In the garden, primroses refuse to thrive for long in the same position.

The uncanny thing about them is that even if you change the soil, but replant them in the same spot, they seem to know. They cannot be fooled. In my experience, and this goes for all members of the genus *Primula*, they need regular division (every two years or less) and replanting in fresh topsoil mixed with crumbled manure and bonemeal, in a completely different position.

The most pernickety, needless to say the most enchanting, are the old doubles, such as 'Alba Plena' and 'Lilacina Plena', in white and mauve respectively. I've had square yards of these in the past, and brushed aside all mention of their tricky reputations. You may know the rest of the story: first the plants look a bit pinched, then the group gets smaller, and finally an inexorable dwindle sets in, the only way to stop it being instant removal to a new spot.

The garish modern primroses and polyanthus have none of the charm of old-fashioned plants such as the mauve-pink form of our wild yellow primrose, *Primula vulgaris* subsp. *sibthorpii* from the Balkans; 'Guinevere', raised in Ireland circa 1930, distinguished by purple-bronze leaves and lilac-pink flowers; 'Lady Greer', another old Irish cultivar, a fragile-looking, pale yellow, polyanthus-type; and rare 'Tipperary Purple', a reddish-violet jack-in-the-green, each flower set in a leafy green ruff. 'Wanda' is the easy old primrose you used to see in cottage gardens.

The green primrose, *Primula vulgaris* 'Viridis', with luminous apple-green petals, is an elusive, magical plant which poses a unique problem: they say the fairies will get you if you buy it; it is equally bad luck to be given it.

The cowslip, *Primula veris*, is another plant which likes to move around. The name arose not from 'cow's lip' but from 'cow slip' (Old English *cu* cow, *slyppe* slime), from the notion that the plant would only take root in a meadow wherever a cow lifted its tail. You don't go out and buy cowslips. You wait and see. You are *honoured* if they turn up. Try fresh soil from an uncultivated field and a vintage cowpat.

Tip of the week

• Early March, as the soil warms up, is a brilliant time for dividing herbaceous perennials. Instead of buying new plants, go out and divide your hostas, geraniums, phlox, Michaelmas daisies, agapanthus, delphiniums, kniphofias, anaphalis, sedums, astrantias, lamiums, hemerocallis, catmint, lamb's ears and campanulas.

 *20 March 1994*

'Ballawley' the Best of the Bergenias

Not everyone likes bergenias. Bergenias and gravel; bergenias and paving – we've heard it all before, ever since Gertrude Jekyll recommended them as edging plants. Nevertheless their handsome evergreen leaves do form invaluable bold contrast to the mostly nondescript leaves of other herbaceous plants. And you do have to give

Bergenia crassifolia an extra mark for effort – it's been in cultivation since 1765, and it's the one you see peering from the bushes in derelict gardens in spring, a quiet composition of mauvey-pink and green.

The king of the bergenias is the Irish cultivar 'Ballawley', raised in Dublin before 1950, at Ballawley Park Nursery in Dundrum (the site of the nursery, now built over, is just past Super Crazy Prices, on the right going out of town). 'Ballawley' is a magnificent fellow, with huge leaves, if well fed, and splendid trusses of magenta flowers on crimson-tinged stalks in April. The leaves suffuse red at the first frost and turn green again overnight, chameleon-like, whenever the temperature goes up. I can see it from the kitchen window, so can use it as a thermometer without going outside.

On the other hand, the smaller, more erect leaves of *Bergenia purpurascens* turn gleaming beetroot at the first cold spell in autumn, forming marvellous crimson pools of colour, and remain like that until spring. The contrast between the deep purple of the upper surface of the leaves and the lighter red reverse makes each leaf seem backlit. It looks good with red hellebores – you couldn't get more horticulturally correct than grow these two fashionable plants together.

Among the white cultivars, 'Bressingham White' is excellent. The more I compare it to 'Silberlicht', the better I like it. 'Silberlicht' has white flowers, ageing to pinkish, cupped by attractive crimson sepals, but the ungainly leaves flop about, forming untidy umbrellas which hide the flowers. 'Bressingham White' is altogether neater, slugs permitting, and the flowers much better displayed. Bergenias spread by stout rhizomes which become elongated with time, but 'Silberlicht' seems intent on climbing out of the ground, the result being woody-looking trunks with leaves of flabby leather at the ends. They must be divided and replanted firmly and more deeply, so the leaves of each section are just above soil level.

Bergenia stracheyi 'Alba' is my favourite, a nice diminutive thing, with pure white flowers that fade to shell pink. It looks good leaning on stone in small paved areas. Do you know the hairy bergenia, *Bergenia ciliata*? It has foliage that is extraordinary to touch, being very hairy on both sides; the fleshy stalks are also hairy. The flowers are pale pink with reddish sepals. This bergenia has an unusual way of coping with the cold; it simply acts as if it was deciduous, but some leaves persist through most Irish winters.

If you're ever in a garden where the owner insists that they haven't got vine weevil, take a look at the bergenias. The tell-tale signs of a visit from the 'ticket-collector' (the adult vine weevil) will be there for all to see, in the form of neat bites around the edges of the leaves. (The holes in the middle of the leaves are due to snails.)

A no-nonsense attitude is required towards bergenias. I cut off any damaged leaves around now, to show off the flowers which are just forming. If the clumps haven't been divided recently, a top dressing of fresh soil 1–2 inches deep will conveniently disguise any exposed rhizomes and encourage the plant to make further offsets.

 *26 March 1995*

Bulbs to Light up the Spring

Yesterday somebody asked 'What should I do about bulbs after they've flowered?' Small early bulbs, such as crocuses, snowdrops and dog's-tooth violets die away and should be left where they are to seed about. If you're planning colour schemes for next year move the bulbs in flower or soon after, or you'll forget.

Experiments some years ago at Wisley – the Royal Horticultural Society's garden near Woking, Surrey – showed that daffodil leaves should be left for a minimum of six weeks after flowering to build up the bulbs for the following year. I prefer eight weeks. Don't tie daffodil leaves into knots – it looks horrible and is bad for the bulb. The smaller the daffodil, the less unsightly are its dying leaves. Broadleigh Gardens have eight pages in their catalogue of small daffodils, including the little wild daffodil, or lent lily. This is *Narcissus pseudonarcissus* 'Lobularis', Wordsworth's daffodil.

When should you divide daffodils? The moment the clumps don't have as many flowers as last year, move them. Immediately after flowering, dig them up and discard all but the fattest bulbs. Fork over the soil, and work in well-rotted compost if available (manure is unsuitable for bulbs) and a generous handful of bonemeal per six bulbs. Pop each bulb into a little hole, flood it with water, fill it in and water again.

Long before tulipomania reached its peak in Holland in 1634–7, with fabulous prices paid for special bulbs, tulips had been grown in quantity in Turkish gardens. In 1574 Selim II ordered '50,000 bulbs for my Royal Gardens from the Sheriff of Aziz'. Such extravagance should be imitated albeit on a minor scale and my miserly Scottish heart melts when it comes to buying tulips. They rarely last more than two years on light Dublin soils and I find lifting them once growth has died down isn't worth the effort. The only ones you can count as permanent are small species such as *T. sylvestris, T. batalinii* and scarlet, late-flowering *T. sprengeri*.

Tomato fertiliser (liquid) has had a marvellous effect on my *Trillium sessile*, a choice North American woodland bulb, usually agonisingly slow to increase. Its richness in potash makes it an excellent food for all bulbs. Several doses at weekly intervals starting now will build up energy for flowering next year. I've read several times in gardening journals about 'mulching bulbs with peat'. This is complete nonsense. Damp peat shows off your daffodils to good effect but it will do no good whatsoever to the bulbs, and is a waste of a natural resource.

Fair warning of a 'Tip of the Week' coming in May – it is likely to involve sweat and bad temper, so start the softening up of cross co-gardeners now. If you want to grow good plants in containers this summer, All The Soil Should Be Changed. I use a mixture of six parts fresh topsoil, three damp peat and two horticultural sand.[1] Old soil from containers may be scattered about the flowerbeds, provided it doesn't contain any wriggling white grubs of the vine weevil.

 *27 March 1994*

Keeping the Herb Garden at Bay

I cannot look at borage without thinking of glossy magazines, or remember the 1980s without thinking of herb gardens. So many people

---

1. The potting mixture I'm now using is given on page 6 (under True Grit).

with masses of money and nothing to do except pick borage flowers in order to float them on glasses of Pimm's. No issue of *House and Garden* or *Country Living* seemed complete without yet another example of how to make a herb garden. Herb gardens come under the general heading 'Nostalgia' which also includes such items as cottage gardening, wild flower gardening, sprigged muslins, lavender sachets, country smocks and genuine old milkchurns.

It seems the ethos of the 1980s was one long illusion, from Thatcherism to pot-pourri. The only time I tried making this essential commodity of the new-age drawing room, confusion set in. Should the dew still be on the freshly gathered rose petals? Or should it have just been dried by the early morning sun? The only result was an evil-smelling mess in the hot-press. But I do agree, what more elegant occupation can one pretend to than the making of pot-pourri?

Back to herb gardens. Save a few brilliant examples (notably Darina Allen's at Ballymaloe Cookery School), herb gardens are a disaster. Herbs (apart from being essential to good cookery) are predisposed to being very untidy. The exceptions are rosemary (be circumspect with this one, it is said that where the rosemary flourishes the woman is in charge), sage, bay, lavender and cotton lavender (*Santolina chamaecyparissus*). Parsley, chives and thyme (if kept neatly trimmed) do make nice, low edging plants, but as for the remainder, they are an unruly lot.

Mint will run all over the place. Gardening books recommend that you plant it in a bucket or large pot with holes in the bottom sunk in the ground, but unless you replant it with fresh soil each year, mint will pine away. Lovage (wonderful for soup) will grow to six feet or more, elbowing out its neighbours as it goes, and unless you envisage its eventual bulk, it will quickly unbalance the garden scene. I don't mind how much of a straggly mess French tarragon is, though, because it is so delicious with chicken, but I grow it in a pot in the greenhouse anyway. Insist on proper French tarragon (*Artemisia dracunculus*), for Russian tarragon has so little taste it's not worth growing.

Fortunately, the craze for chamomile lawns has subsided. I'm not surprised – they don't work. I once fell for one myself, but the idea of sitting on apple-scented leaves soon lost its romance when I found that the general effect was more of a hen-run than a lawn. Agreed, fresh horseradish sauce is quite wonderful, but the plant itself, what an ugly customer! Huge, coarse leaves, usually turned into green lace by slugs, sprawl about smothering nearby plants. Be sure to plant it in the right place first time, as it is nigh impossible to eradicate. On the other hand, I'm mad about fennel, specially the purple-leaved form. It makes a graceful accent plant in the flower border, doesn't need staking, is decorative for most of the summer, has leaves of the finest filigree and long-lasting umbels of tiny, lime-yellow flowers.

The answer to herbs is to corral them up. The most successful and aesthetically pleasing herb gardens are those designed as a simple, formal, geometric pattern of beds, intersected by paths; each bed should be surrounded by a neat green edging of box. (You could use lavender or santolina instead, or even rue, but there would be more clipping involved and you would have to replace the plants after seven years or so.) In the smallest gardens, a plain rectangular box-edged bed would suffice. The rampant enthusiasm of most herbs, to flop and sprawl with indecent abandon, can be thus restrained.

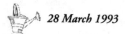 *28 March 1993*

April

The Hostas with the Mostest

A man who keeps dahlias ('Bishop of Llandaff' and 'Twilight Time') under the sofa during the winter turned up here this week in a high state of excitement. He assured me that the tubers of both were 'very dry and very healthy... I'm so enraptured by having been successful with 'Twilight Time' that I'm now proceeding with 'Nuit d'Été'. The idea is to plunge further into the depths of an Irish summer night gloom via dahlias – I breathlessly await the arrival of 'Midnight Chimes'.

'By the way,' he continued, 'I'm afraid it's a cactus dahlia,' no doubt expecting me to faint with shock. Dahlias – bar the Bishop which is acceptable to the sniffiest of gardeners – are usually considered a bit naff. And the conversation veered onto the subject of gardening fashion.

Take the waxing and waning of the popularity of hostas. At one stage I was described as 'hosta-sick' – whenever I saw a new hosta I had to *buy* it. Then the market was flooded with absurdly-named new varieties from America, such as 'Blue Dimples', 'Chartreuse Wiggles', 'Krinkled Joy' and 'Shining Tot'. With 472 hostas listed in *The Plant Finder* there were simply too many to choose from. But they are very fine plants, without which our gardens would be much the poorer.

The thing to remember is that you don't need 472 different hostas, but you do need (1) a good large-leaved blue, such as *H. sieboldiana* var. *elegans* or 'Snowden'; (2) a good white-variegated, such as 'Thomas Hogg' (now listed as *H. undulata* var. *albomarginata*) or *H. ventricosa* 'Aureomarginata' (I know it says aureo-, but in fact the leaves have super white rims); (3) a good, small-leaved blue – 'Halycon' is unbeatable; (4) a gold-variegated – *H. fortunei* 'Gold Standard' (smallish) or *H. montana* 'Aureomarginata' (large). Optional extras would be 'Shade Fanfare' and 'Frances Williams'. When buying hostas, count the number of snouts in the pot – there may be enough to warrant dividing the plant (with a sharp knife) and halving the cost.

Some plants, *Echinacea purpurea* 'White Swan' for example, are being heavily pushed right now. A glance at Thompson & Morgan's seed catalogue entry reads 'often with 14-plus 4-inch blooms out at once.' In seed-catalogue speak 'often' is the key word. There must be some doubt about flowering capacity or 'often' wouldn't be mentioned. My experience of this plant is that the most it ever had was two flowers in late autumn, and they were nearer grubby cream than white. American coneflowers like American sun – damp Irish summers won't do. However, all parts of the plant are used by herbalists and The General Health Food Store (93 Marlborough Street, Dublin 1) told me that tincture of *Echinacea purpurea* is brilliant for giving a massive boost to the immune system.

The enormous influx of plants from South Africa is hot news. Unknown plants are constantly being introduced to cultivation, particularly from the Drakensberg. Plantsmen in the know talk of little else but their next collecting trip.

Daisies abound – felicias, gazanias and osteospermums galore – most of which are tender perennials used as summer bedding plants. With regard to osteospermums, the one called 'Whirligig' can be a trap for the unwary. It has been available for some time, and is guaranteed to be bought on sight. The foliage is greyish and the petals powder-blue. The shape of the petals is enchanting, nipped in the middle, so the flowers look like whirling propellers. But 'Whirligig' only whirls if there's masses of sun and the plant is very comfortably fed and watered. Otherwise it has disappointingly ordinary daisies. Much more reliable, is the quite excellent *Osteospermum* 'Irish Lavender'. Totally hardy in a well-drained sunny position, this has been flowering non-stop for the past four years.

The discussion of gardening fashions led to conifers and heathers, two pariahs which cannot be mentioned singly, so much are they coupled together in unholy visions of designs for 1960s gardens. Individual specimens of conifers, given space to develop full beauty, and planted in appropriate situations – on a broad sweep of grass, in light woodland – can be wondrous plants. But if I see another blue cedar (estimated height of maturity 120 feet) squeezed into a gap beside a garden shed, I shall be ill. Heathers, I love, but only seen as a purple haze in the distance, except for the lime-tolerant winter-flowering sorts (clip these over soon to remove dead flowers and keep the plants compact.)

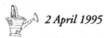 *2 April 1995*

Letting Fly with a Hedge Trimmer

The distant sound of snapping shears or whining hedge-trimmer can only mean that some poor shrub is being 'pruned'. Two images spring to mind. One of a kerria cut into an immaculate cube, another of a poodle-ised juniper, its unfortunate foliage shaped into ridiculous tuffets, forming a series of blobs, connected by branches entirely naked of leaves.

Charlie, a nice enough fellow at heart, with shears in hand is instantly transmogrified into Mr Hyde. 'Needs pruning,' he'd pronounce, a predatory gleam in his eye. No matter which shrub – so far as he was concerned, pruning was essential for the lot of 'em. And pruning, for Charlie, meant chopping bits off, willy-nilly. Chop-chop-chop resounded from wall to wall of the garden. Now and again he stood back and, cocking his head to one side, administered the final artistic tweak. And the victim, unrecognisable as to which species it belonged to, had been turned into an anonymous blob. The results of Charlie's handiwork, often seen in the vicinity of public lavatories, should be inspected before allowing him into your garden. A typical example may be viewed on the corner of Mountjoy Square.

I met a rare person the other day, a maintenance contractor who actually likes plants. We discussed the new gardening horror, entitled 'running amok with the hedge-trimmer' or 'Son of Charlie'. When Charlie was in the garden, at least you could lure him from further destruction with tea and sandwiches, but a young man enthused by a hedge-trimmer is something else. A few lethal swipes and he's taken out his frustration on every shrub in the garden.

Very few shrubs actually need pruning. The reasons for pruning are to keep a shrub vigorous, healthy and well-balanced and to encourage flowers and fruit. So always take out dead, damaged or weak wood. Shrubs that flower on wood formed the previous season – deutzia, philadephus, weigela, forsythia – should have some of the weaker shoots pruned away immediately after flowering. If you don't prune *Buddleja davidii* hard to about three feet now, you get a lanky plant with flowers way above your head.

Hardy fuchsias may be pruned now, to within one foot of the

ground if you like. Grey-leaved santolinas and artemisias may also be clipped hard now to keep the plants compact. You don't have to prune penstemons, but healthy growth from the base will produce better flowers than tattier growth above. Lavateras should be pruned to around three or four feet. If you let them get too big they are easily blown over by wind. Lavateras are not long-lived, so take cuttings now as replacements. Indigoferas, melianthus and *Cestrum parqui* can be pruned now to almost ground level – although they're shrubs, they can be treated as herbaceous plants.

Ceanothus will not stand being cut back into old wood, but a light trim of young finished-flowering shoots is acceptable. Cistus also resents being cut into old wood. Old lavender bushes cannot be rejuvenated by cutting back into old wood – the most they'll stand is clipping back flowered shoots. If your plants look moth-eaten, replace them now – young plants give a much better show.

You need to take time to prune the mop-headed type of hydrangea (*H. macrophylla*). Take out some of the older branches (paler bark) close to the ground. Don't touch the younger branches except for nipping off old flowerheads. But *Hydrangea arborescens* 'Annabelle' and *H. paniculata* flower on wood produced this year, so prune them hard now, to within a few inches of the base of last year's shoots. Generously feed and mulch all hydrangeas.

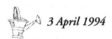 *3 April 1994*

The Legend of the Periwinkle

One of the longest-running gardening myths is that of the existence of the double white periwinkle. Rumours of its discovery in some long lost garden do the rounds at regular intervals. Even Gertrude Jekyll had heard tell of it early this century, but she never actually saw it. But imagine what a nice plant it would be – neat, shining, evergreen leaves and little white double rosettes of flower, like miniature roses. Very desirable. As far as I know – though I would love to be proved otherwise – the double white periwinkle remains only a legend.

I know somebody so mad about periwinkles he would happily cover his whole garden with them. A true minimalist is rare among gardeners, but what a neat idea he has, for this is a plant that will come up smiling in the most inhospitable parts of the garden. No matter how cat-ridden, weed-infested, dank and shaded, the lesser periwinkle, *Vinca minor*, will do the gardening for you. Its larger brother, *Vinca major*, is also a decent, obliging fellow, with somewhat sloppier habits. (Both names remind one of Edwardian books about public schoolboys.)

Periwinkles make new roots at each leaf joint whenever they touch the soil. The young plantlets knit closely together, forming a weed-proof evergreen rug, which in spring is dotted with flowers. These may be various shades of blue, both double and single, semi-double burgundy or pure white (single only I'm afraid). The leaves may be variegated or otherwise.

I may have mentioned *Euphorbia amygdaloides* var. *robbiae* before, but it also deserves a non-stop eulogy as the all-time brilliant plant for dry shade. It has dark, glossy green leaves that remain fresh throughout the year and bright lime-green flowers which last for ages and are excellent for picking. All you must do is remove the spent flower stems in summer. (Some people are allergic to the milky sap of euphorbias.)

Herbaceous plants. You immediately think of summer. Yes, lupins of course, and poppies, phlox, campanulas, let alone the numerous sorts of daisies, Michaelmas and others, the backbone of the herbaceous border. But what about a group of good plants, all in bloom now, the neglected throng of spring-flowering herbaceous perennials that most gardeners, who can think of spring only in terms of bulbs, haven't even considered?

An easy small plant, *Lathyrus vernus*, related to the sweet pea, is in full flower now. Ferny leaves, uncurling from bare soil, support pretty vetch-like flowers that can be any combination of violet, magenta, pink, blue or white. By the time it stops flowering in May, it will be about a foot high, and you needn't give it another thought until next year. A sun-lover by choice, it will also do nicely in shade, provided it is not too dry. It will seed mildly around. If you need to transplant the seedlings do so whilst they are small – established plants have astonishingly tough, wiry roots, difficult to dislodge.

Omphalodes cappadocica is in effect like a particularly good forget-me-not, about six inches tall, with brilliant blue flowers and almost evergreen leaves. Happy in light woodland, the front of shady borders, tucked between shrubs, this is an invaluable spring plant for filling the gaps. Just coming on the market is the new cultivar 'Starry Eyes', which has each sky-blue petal neatly rimmed with mauve-pink.

Lastly, another favourite spring herbaceous plant – *Brunnera macrophylla* 'Hadspen Cream' – for fertile soil that is not too dry. Clouds of blue flowers hover above mounds of heart-shaped leaves, nicely splashed in cream and lovat-green. (The better known *Brunnera macrophylla* 'Dawson's White' is a more delicate plant – slow, miffy and liable to revert to plain green; 'Hadspen Cream' is far superior.) It is a picture at the moment, mixed up with patches of blue scillas, blue and white chionodoxas and pale blue wood anemones.

 *4 April 1993*

The Big Geraniums are Top of the Pops

Geraniums are long-blooming, adaptable, hardy and unbelievably easy plants. Why do people rave about them? Why are there whole nurseries devoted to the many species and cultivars of the ever-popular family? Their common name of cranesbill refers to the long beak-like shape of the fruit. Our native bright purple *Geranium sanguineum*, or bloody cranesbill, occurs in many parts of Ireland, and in particular abundance on the Burren. Flowering from midsummer on, it makes a pretty pathside edging plant. If you're not keen on magenta, you'd prefer pale pink *G. sanguineum* var. *striatum*. In the case of little *G. robertianum*, or herb Robert, some say native, some say weed. The feathery crimson-crushed leaves have a pungent smell. The flowers are deep pink but there are also two white forms, one with bright green leaves, 'Celtic White'.

To slot geraniums into categories, let's start with those for the herbaceous border proper, such as *G. psilostemon*, which has intense magenta flowers with black centres. Blooming at rose time, the flower colour is echoed by that of the pinks and purples of old roses. Give it

light support, such as with a metal hoop. 'Mrs Kendall Clark', a form of
the meadow cranesbill with light blue flowers translucently veined,
flowers earlier, at lupin time. Both grow to about one metre.

One of the most beautiful blues of the flowering year is that of *G.* ×
magnificum. It only does it once, in early summer, but the clusters of
blue flowers on 60cm stems positively glow. The tidy clumps of foliage
act as good fillers for the rest of the season. *G. sylvaticum* 'Amy
Doncaster', another early one, is also a gorgeous blue, but with a white
eye. *G. himalayense* and 'Johnson's Blue' are two more excellent low-
growing early blues. The problem with the latter is that it is often
muddled up with *G. wallichianum* 'Buxton's Variety' (wrongly called
Buxton's Blue). Many disappointed gardeners have been fobbed off
with 'Johnson's Blue' instead of the paragon of late summer blue-
flowered plants 'Buxton's Variety', whose virtues I never stop
mentioning.

Another on-going muddle is about *G. maderense*, the Madeiran
cranesbill and its fellow countryman, *G. palmatum*. To finally settle the
argument, here are the facts. The one that seeds about in most of our
gardens is *G. palmatum*. It's hardy in most Irish gardens. *G. maderense*
has much more deeply-fingered leaves, a fleshy-looking stem and is
undeniably frost-tender. Both make decorative wide leafy mounds and
have huge clusters of light magenta flowers.

Now for geraniums suitable for the throw-it-into-the-soil-and-
stamp-on-it school of gardening. The star plant for this course has to be
G. macrorrhizum. If you can't remember the name, just look for the
geranium with the very sticky, clammy, aromatic leaves – once sniffed,
never forgotten. (The leaves of this species provide oil of geranium.)
G. macrorrhizum is unspellable, unkillable and utterly charming.
Unbeatable for growing in nasty dry shady places, it'll be only too
pleased if you put it in your best bed. The mourning widow geranium,
G. phaeum, with gloomy, slatey purple reflexed flowers, is equally
submissive to poor treatment (search also for the lovely white form). *G.
endressii* also produces a valiant display under such conditions. If you
have a clump of this, pull it to bits now, and replant a generous patch
anywhere there's a gap.

Geranium renardii has become a cliché. It's a damn good plant with
'starry, open white flowers with white veins' (G S Thomas). The elitest

geranium of the moment is probably 'Philippe Vapelle', a *G. renardii* hybrid. This inherits the superb blue–grey felty foliage but has dusky blue dark-veined flowers. You can understand why *Geranium rectum* 'Album' was renamed (who wants a plant called white bottom?). Now romantically called *G. clarkei* 'Kashmir White', this lovely early-summer-flowering geranium has large blush-white flowers delicately etched in maroon. It can be obtained from Hosford's Geraniums, who send good quality plants by post (Cappa, Enniskeane, Co Cork).

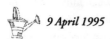 *9 April 1995*

Most Things are Going to Pot

The spring potting orgy is at its peak. I'm repotting every plant in sight – in outdoor containers, in the house and in the greenhouse. For the past six months, plants' roots have been reluctant to venture through constipated old soil. Repot too early – in March say – and the plants sit in sullen immobility; too late, and the spring surge of growth is wasted.

The commonest mistake beginners make is to choose too large a pot, either out of misplaced generosity to the plant, or laziness in not wishing to repot again during summer. Surplus soil becomes sour.

Handling plants is like handling puppies or babies. You must learn not to be frightened of them. To start with something simple, like a geranium (*Pelargonium*): turn the pot upside down and, giving it a sharp tap on a bench, catch the plant as it comes out. Wriggle your fingers around through the old soil, shaking off as much as you can. Trim the roots to encourage new ones to form. Prune back all lanky top growth.

Terracotta pots should preferably be soaked for 20 minutes before use – clay is porous and draws moisture away from the roots. Clay pots also need some drainage – broken flower-pot, small pieces of brick or stones – placed over the hole. Plastic pots need no such preparation.

Put some compost in the bottom of the pot. Holding the geranium in the pot, fill up with compost, giving the pot several taps to settle the soil round the roots – I often bang it down on the bench for the same reasons. The level of compost round the stems of the plant should be exactly the same as before. Don't overwater to begin with.

Containers should be stuffed full of plants and lavishly fed and watered. Here are a few notes to jog your memory.

For shady patios Try hydrangeas, aucuba, skimmias, privet (much maligned but super in a pot), ivies, busy lizzies, begonias, clipped box, francoas, ferns, hostas, fatsias, aspidistras, wandering Jew (*Chlorophytum*), periwinkles and nicotiana (tobacco plant). The enormous prickly umbrellas of *Gunnera manicata* add a splendid architectural note in shade provided the plant is kept well watered. *Fuchsia* 'Thalia' stands shade well and, unlike most fuchsias, flowers non-stop.

For the kitchen Pots of parsley, chives, mint, sage and rosemary grouped around a standard miniature apple tree.

If you can't be bothered to water There are only two possible plants for here – sempervivum and sedum.

For a Mediterranean look Lavender, santolina, clipped *Viburnum tinus*, bay and myrtle, plus a potted lemon tree (this must have winter protection).

Architectural plants for sun Melianthus, yucca, cordyline.

Fast-growers for a wall Golden hop, annual cup-and-saucer vine (*Cobaea*) and the white potato vine (*Solanum jasminoides* 'Album').

To tumble down the edge of a pot Ivies, *Campanula poscharskyana*, fuchsias and *Glechoma hederacea* 'Variegata'.

Wind-resistant trees and shrubs for balconies Cotoneaster, *Elaeagnus* 'Quicksilver' (silky grey leaves), pyracantha, *Brachyglottis* 'Sunshine', corokia, hebe and privet.

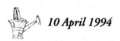 *10 April 1994*

The Gentleman Doth Protest Too Much

It has been a thorn in my side that I should suffer the indignity of being on the same page as Mr Aodghan Feeley NT.[2] How dare he describe us non-Catholics as 'quaint'? Does Mr Feeley not understand that the

---

2. Mr Feeley was a spoof columnist in *The Sunday Tribune*.

backbone of Irish horticulture consists of Protestants alone? Does Mr Feeley realise how our dedicated network of Protestant lady gardeners rigorously holds the fort at plant sales? Well I remember being offered my first Protestant biscuit at one such 'do'. For those of other persuasions, I should explain what these are: a simple butter-based shortbread biscuit with no frills – no fancy icing, and no question of superfluous cherry on top. An indication of acceptance in these circles is the rite of the offering of the biscuit.

Our splendid group in South Dublin of tweedy, doggy, no-nonsense ladies is responsible for the circulation (naturally among ourselves alone) of rare plants. Members of our group may be quickly recognised by our dress-code: *de rigueur* see-through plastic mackintosh, shopping basket for extra cardigan and emergency supply of egg sandwiches.

Fortunately Mr Feeley was not witness to the one occasion when our renowned Protestant manners gave way – the tug-of-war over the only specimen of *Fascicularia* or monkey's bottom plant – when a senior member became so agitated that she threw her sandwiches at our lady chairman. 'Protestant ideas are behind much of what ails our nation … is it any surprise considering that they are descended from either planters or morally degenerate stock,' says Mr Feeley. How dare he cast aspersions on the esteemed members of The Hardy Plant Society (always affectionately referred to as 'The Planters')? As for 'morally degenerate' – this surely applies to Mr Feeley himself? (Although I do not entirely believe the unsavoury story about my colleague, his mother and the sofa.)

Mr Feeley stoops to denigrate the Adelaide, a hospital dedicated to the training of Protestant nurses. Readers may remember my horror on being threatened with the Last Rites after my celebrated tumble through the greenhouse roof last year (after my unfortunate accident with the rake – when my co-gardener received the blame for giving me two black eyes). I was taken to the Adelaide. What a comfort it was, coming round after the anaesthetic, to know that there was no danger whatsoever of being sprinkled with holy water. My colleague is no doubt unaware of how Irish gardening society operates. Plant sales aside, there are two main social activities: the exclusive Gardening Lunch, and the Garden Visit. Both occasions offer boundless opportunity for inter-gardening gossip of the bitchy kind.

An esteemed gardener I once knew had his own personal way of separating others from ourselves: he insisted that under no circumstances would Catholics eat offal. He delighted in organising gardening lunches with *tripes à la mode de Caen* or *délices de rognons saignants* with a liver paté starter. As they staggered hungrily through the ensuing tour of the garden, he would chuckle happily at their discomfort.

On Garden Visits you may notice two elderly ladies, whose fragile appearance belies their true role. These two are none other than our Joint Operations Managers, in charge of new plant acquisitions for the group. One indicates the plant required, by inserting her umbrella into the soil beside it. Their wobbly tour of the garden continues. At the moment when it seems that they are just about to leave, one of them suddenly remembers the umbrella, and goes to fetch it. She conceals the plant in folds of the umbrella. Mission accomplished.

True Protestant grit such as this is going to be hard to replace, but we are in the process of training junior members. If this is what Mr Feeley is referring to as 'creeping Protestantism' long may it last. Lastly, I cannot forgive my colleague for presuming to attach the suffix 'NT' to his name. He thus gives great offence to one of our more sacred Protestant institutions, namely the National Trust, the saviour of all British gardens: Sissinghurst, Hidcote *et al.* It is an abomination that places of pilgrimage for Irish gardeners should be associated with Mr Feeley.

This week

Prick out seedlings under glass. Move daffodils after flowering. Deadhead all bulbs, only removing the faded flower – leave the stem to help build up the bulb for next year. Plan planting for summer containers. Take fuchsia and argyranthemum cuttings. Tie in clematis often. Watch out for slugs on emerging hostas.

 *16 April 1995*

Sowing a Few Seeds of Doubt

Never believe the blurb written on a seed packet – 'Sow in early March' and suchlike. Filthy weather can rot the toughest seeds. The time-honoured method of deciding whether the soil is warm enough for outdoor sowing is to sit down on the ground.

With regard to seed sown in pots, after years of cynical observation, I have the following to report. Of 50 different packets of seed, about 25 will germinate. Within a week, 10 lots of seedlings will ' damp off' – horticultural euphemism for dying – the seedlings topple over at soil level, never to recover. Although the congestion on the kitchen windowsill will be relieved, what to do with the remaining millions of tiny plants? Buy numerous seed trays. Laboriously prick out all the seedlings. With a forest of young plants on every windowsill, the house has now become a plant nursery, fragile domestic peace reaches snapping point, the bath can only be reached by negotiating an assault course of assorted seed trays.

The next stage is that of 'hardening off'. The seedlings are gradually introduced to the world outside by putting them out on warm days and taking them in at night. A few more trays succumb through being dropped or trodden on. Of the eight remaining trays of seedlings, two will turn out to be major weeds and five will be quite nice. But the last tray will contain a brilliant new plant, which warrants all the effort. Theoretically I now only grow plants from seed that are impossible to get by other means. But I defy you to resist some of the tempting offerings in the catalogue of Chiltern Seeds. You can muse about suggestive offerings such as the soursop, *Annona muricata* – 'a biting wild taste ... and a flavour of perfumed cream'. Wow!

I first sowed larkspur (*Delphinium consolida*) 15 years ago. It has self-sowed ever since. The slender spires of blue (occasionally pink or white) are marvellous gap-fillers, so this week I've been moving around the seedlings accordingly. Smart gardeners may sneer at nasturtiums (*Tropaeolum majus*), but they were good enough for Monet's garden at Giverny, where splendid trails of scarlet and orange tumble over the gravel walks. Here nasturtiums will be sowed to brighten a bed of mainly early-flowering bulbs under an umbrella of golden-leaved gleditsia.

The only way to be certain of virus-free lilies is to grow them from seed. *Lilium longiflorum* might even flower the first year, and certainly the second. *L. regale*, here renewed regularly from seed, is an essential and beautiful lily, with heavily fragrant white trumpets flushed with purple.

For a bit of easy fun, try *Paulownia tomentosa*. This is in fact a tree, with violet foxglove-like flowers. But, cut to soil level and reduced to one stem every March, it rapidly does a jack-and-the-beanstalk act to 10 feet, the huge, velvety leaves presenting a superb foliage effect. Children would enjoy paulownias, plus traditional childhood seeds – radishes, cornflowers, poppies, Virginian stock and pot marigold (*Calendula* – the true marigold, not *Tagetes*, the mop-headed African monster) and sunflowers.

I particularly liked Chiltern Seeds catalogue's comments on impossible-to-grow *Androsace helvetica*: 'Can, in late spring, be covered with small white flowers' (note the tense) and 'Not all that hard to grow'. Unusually honest for a seed catalogue.

 *17 April 1994*

Tales of a Dark Side

A friend told me how she was going to cope with what she described as a 'dank, sunless tunnel between two high walls, floored in concrete'. Her solution is impressively simple: have lots of pots filled with foliage plants of the highest order. Forget about flowers, concentrating instead on gathering together plants with exceptionally decorative foliage. Think of the colour of their leaves, yes, but more of their architectural shape and texture. Pots of plants with spiky leaves, polished round shiny leaves and rough bristly leaves can be juxtapositioned in a myriad of different combinations. The first plant she had chosen was a decorative rhubarb, *Rheum palmatum*. When its huge umbrella-like leaves unwrap in spring they are flushed in dark crimson. It is not hard to smile when the flowerbud expands, for it is quite the rudest-looking member of the plant world. Hostas were essential of course, and the larger the leaf the better for this sort of gardening – I would choose *Hosta sieboldiana* 'Elegans'. If you don't want to buy an expensive new hosta, with only one or two snouts to the pot, you can easily transplant an existing one from the garden.

A plant you may know well, without knowing its name, is *Peltiphyllum peltatum* (to aggravate the situation, its new name is *Darmera peltata*). You usually see it at the streamside in bog gardens, and it is such a lover of moisture that it quickly sulks in a dry garden. But by standing its pot in a large saucer of water for the summer its handsome larger orbicular leaves (a foot or more across – the sort cartoon frogs sit under) will stay fresh all summer.

Acanthus, rodgersia, the beautifully striped form of the yellow flag iris (*Iris pseudacorus* 'Variegata'), ferns in profusion, epimediums, heuchera, macleaya, *Arum italicum* (for winter), *Fuchsia magellanica* 'Versicolor', Solomon's seal and *Saxifraga fortunei* are other suggestions.

 *18 April 1993*

Clematis is Rooted in Class

The British class system is rooted firmly in the plant world. They say you can tell which flowers are to the fore at the London Show just by looking at the crowd – grey suits and Eton accents mean rhododendrons (pronounced 'rod-o-dendron', don't you know), whilst raincoats and Brummingham mean sweet peas.

The late nineteenth century produced a multitude of titled plants – from queens and princesses down to baronesses. Duchesses are scare (unless you include European duchesses from the *Almanac de Gotha*, who aren't quite the real thing). 'Duchess of Albany' is a clematis. Bred in 1890, when American heiresses were rushing to marry the English aristocracy, one of her parents was *C. texensis*, a famous American species, and her other parent was dashing, large-flowered purple 'Star of India'. Out of the same stable came 'Duchess of York'. Said to be charmingly modest, she's now extinct (no remarks about vulgar duchesses here).

Clematis texensis hybrids are quite different from other clematis – the flowers are small, pitcher-shaped with pursed lips and sticky-up. They require (as you'd expect from Texans), warm sheltered spots. Look out for 'Gravetye Beauty' (cherry red). The exception among Texans is 'Etoile Rose', which has pendant as opposed to erect flowers in silvery pink. Divine. All these used to be impossible to get, but are now comparatively easily found.

I'm on to my third *Clematis* 'Duchess of Edinburgh'. The first, magnificent in her day, was eventually overshadowed by a silver pear, and the second succumbed to overnight wilt. The beautiful Scottish duchess has creamy-white flowers like blowsy roses, with a greenish tinge. Not easy with her charms when young, she only produces single flowers on growth made this year. You must wait for the stems to mature for double flowers. My smallest duchess came from the cemetery in Richmond, Virginia. There she was, a lovely neat bush, a mass of double rose-pink flowers, a tea rose of 1857, namely the 'Duchesse de Brabant'. (It's no use having crises of conscience when taking cuttings in graveyards – this rose isn't in *The Plant Finder*, and all the better rescued for posterity.)

When I looked up my newly acquired duchess, I find she's synonymous with 'Comtesse de Labarthe' and 'Comtesse Ouwaroff'. (Typical suspect European title.) Perhaps she got married three times, improving her station the while? But rules of botanical nomenclature insist that the first name that a plant received is the correct one: hence the interminable muddle between clematis 'Marie Boisselot' and 'Madame le Coultre'. They are one and the same clematis, but the former name is correct because it represents the maiden name of the person that the clematis was called after.

Countesses are two a penny. *Clematis* 'Comtesse de Bouchaud', as you'd expect from any parvenu, is a blatant sort of pink, but a good doer, apparently immune to wilt. 'Countess of Lovelace' (her name sounds like that of an S & M heroine) is 'tricky to start but can be vigorous enough when established', according to Christopher Lloyd in *Clematis*. With me she was so tricky she never even got to the flowering stage.

Now on down the line to the ladies. Rose 'Lady Hillingdon' has soft apricot faintly tea-scented flowers. Like many an aristocrat, she doesn't

Item   1025286
Title: On gardening / Helen Dillon.

Author: Dillon, Helen.

Pickup   Wexford Bunclody

Hold note:

Pull date: **Mon 07 Feb 2022**

Abbrev Surname / First Initial

FLE   I A

Library Card   **9061115**
Number:

like to be cut, and pruning should be restricted to a light nip here and there. *Primula* 'Lady Greer', bred in the 1930s in County Leitrim, is pale and interesting in creamy-yellow. *Agapanthus* 'Lady Moore' is rather special, as you'd expect of a plant named for the wife of the director of the Botanic Gardens at Glasnevin earlier this century – a diminutive pure white.

Queens in the plant world are common enough. You may know the rose 'Queen Elizabeth'. Born in the USA in 1954, bursting with vigour, her manners are more those of Mrs Windsor. Although a superb rose for picking, with a long supply of sugar pink blooms, she doesn't know when to stop, and sends up ungainly stems in all directions. 'Queen Alexandra', on the other hand, is a beautifully behaved auricula-type primula in flower now. Apparently there's a clematis called 'Princess of Wales' (mauve, free-flowering and glamorous – the flowers six to eight inches in diameter) and, needless to say, a 'Prince Charles' (very like 'Perle d'Azur' but not quite so nice). There's also a clematis now called 'Princess Diana'.

Priority for the week

- Tie in clematis before they wrap themselves into knots – they're growing so fast you can almost see the stems move.

PS: My computer thoroughly disliked this piece. When checking grammar and spelling it complained eleven times that I'd used 'gender-specific' words. It didn't like 'Lady Hillingdon' or 'Lady Moore'. It suggested using 'person' or 'individual' instead. In future look out for rose 'Individual Hillingdon' and agapanthus 'Person Moore'. My name, incidentally, is Person Dillon – Helen is too gender-specific.

 *23 April 1995*

The Romance of Borders

We are in the middle of the era of the lavender bag. Unbleached linen clothes, natural soap, cotton prints, trugs, straw hats, Laura Ashley,

Body Shop and basil until it comes out of our ears. Nostalgia reaches its apotheosis with the herbaceous border. Herbaceous borders evoke languid Edwardian afternoons, when there was nothing better to do between lunch and tea except to stroll lazily beside the flowers, as an army of unseen gardeners made themselves scarce behind the hedge.

Gardening books abound with ravishing pictures of borders, each more delectable than the last – double borders framing vistas of eighteenth-century statues and backed by ancient yew hedges, one-colour borders immaculately shaded, regiments of delphiniums standing to attention, and an ever-ready gardener's boy ready to pounce should ground elder dare to raise a leaf.

Little does the beginner realise. For herbaceous borders are the most difficult form of gardening. Nothing so well combines the art of arranging colour, height and flowering season with the craft of growing good plants. And nothing is worse than a bad border. The latter may be recognised by a surfeit of daisies: those not yellow will be the dirty mauve Michaelmas one, which has remarkable powers of survival.

The armchair gardener may enjoy these pictures of borders (he has no intention whatsoever of actually planting one), but I find the pictures intensely irritating. Muttering 'how pretty', and turning over the page, I am annoyed because I don't know how to begin. But a new book *Best Borders* by Tony Lord (Frances Lincoln) gives detailed planting plans.

Every time I visit Sissinghurst I make notes of plants in the sumptuous purple border, but never remember exact groupings. This book shows exactly what's growing next to what. I've the greatest respect for Tony Lord: he's the editor of *The Plant Finder*, so there's no better man for getting the names of plants correct, he trained at Kew and was Gardens Advisor to the National Trust, one of the most senior positions in the world of horticulture. I didn't know he was also a brilliant photographer.

I have been fiddling around with my blue border for several years. It's never going to be right. But, should someone (with a disapproving wave of the colour wheel), attempt to explain, yet again, Jekyllian theory on matters of colour, I shall take no notice: I adore blue flowers; they are scarce enough at the best of times; my method is to mix all shades together, making a glorious muddle of different blues – never mind whether they are of turquoise, sapphire or lapis lazuli. Purists will say that you shouldn't mix pure blues with mauve or violet blues, but the loveliest effects can be made by breaking the rules. Indeed it is hard to see where the blue stops and the mauve begins, but on its better days my blue border gives an impression of a misty haze of blue, shading to mauve and violet in the shadows, here and there illuminated by some silvery mounds of artemisias.

Perhaps the most useful tip I can give you for improving a border is to remember the famous saying (with regard to choosing a site for a business) 'location, location and location'. In gardening terms it's 'repetition, repetition and repetition'. Now is the last minute for reshuffling your border. Force yourself to repeat groups of the same plant. My blue border contains (in order of flowering) groups of *Geranium pratense* 'Mrs Kendall Clark' and blue lupins; delphiniums; a profusion of larkspur, *Galega officinalis*; monkshoods and *Campanula lactiflora*; *Salvia patens*, *Aster* × *frikartii* 'Mönch', *A. thomsonii* 'Nanus'; many different agapanthus; *Salvia* 'Indigo Spires'; *Aster* 'Violet Queen'. Blue pansies, love-in-a-mist, penstemons, verbenas, stokesia, sea hollies and *Clematis* × *durandii* provide more essential blue. Any more suggestions?

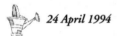 *24 April 1994*

Beware of Killing with Kindness

One of the most spectacular plants I ever killed was a peony, *Paeonia obovata* var. *alba*. How to murder such a lovely thing? Smother it with kindness. We are taught to give peonies lavish feeds – of well-rotted manure, garden compost, and, of course, nourishing concoctions of bonemeal and general fertiliser. Absolutely correct gardening lore. But if, in a fit of over-generosity, you cover the crowns (growth buds) of the peony in too thick a blanket of rich humusy pie, the crowns will rot: underground slugs will encamp therein, and all that remains will be the sad reminder of an empty patch of soil. So, be warned, never, ever plant the crown of a peony below the point at which it was originally growing.

Paeonia officinalis 'Rubra Plena', the favourite old double red, is the peony you are most likely to know. It is remarkably long-lived ('it loves peace and sunshine – as we all do' – Graham Thomas) and its huge, deep crimson satin flowers may be seen peering from the nettles in long-neglected gardens. Twenty or thirty years is nothing in the life of a peony, and it can remain *in situ* all that time. But if you have old clumps of peonies that are flowering sparsely, if at all, make a note to divide them in October. Prepare the ground well: handle the fleshy roots carefully and divide them into sections with two or three shoots each, using a sharp knife.

Most herbaceous peonies are derived in part from *Paeonia lactiflora*. Their sumptuous flowers are often so heavy petalled that the stems need some support. The most satisfactory method is to use semi-circular metal hoops, which may remain in position from year to year. Emerging peony foliage is often beautifully suffused with red, which looks divine interplanted with pink tulips. Herbaceous peonies may be single or double and their colour ranges from white through peach and salmon and pearly pink to many a shade of red. Perhaps the most entrancing peonies of all are the so-called imperial sorts – single flowers with glorious petaloid centres such as the aptly named 'Bowl of Beauty' – scented, pale fuchsia-pink, with a creamy centre.

Paeonia mlokosewitschii. Such an impossible name may account for the fact that this heavenly plant from the Caucasus, with rounded clear lemon fleeting blooms, is not in every garden. Its alternative name is Mollie the witch. Full sun and good drainage is essential, as it is for the rose pink *Paeonia cambessedesii* (from the cliffs of Majorca). Do not despair when nothing comes up the first year you sow peony seeds. Peonies germinate in two stages, first cautiously sending down a root and then waiting till the following spring before sending up a shoot. All the peonies mentioned today are herbaceous.

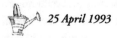 *25 April 1993*

Less Know-How, More Fun

A visit to a garden centre is one of the few occasions when one envies the beginner – for the less you know, the more fun you have. The plants all seem equally desirable, and as you have no idea how big they are going to get, and whether or not they would like your soil or conditions, you fill up the car with plants, rush home, dig holes in any available gaps, push in the plants, wave the watering can over their heads, and hope for the best. That's one approach, too, to planting trees and shrubs – buy everything you fancy, enjoy them for a few years until chaos sets in, and then have a grand thinning out programme.

One way round the problem is to think of plants in terms of first and second class. Decide which are going to be your important trees and shrubs, that no other plant is going to interfere with, and fill in the gaps with easy, short-term fillers – herbaceous plants, short-lived shrubs such as penstemons or cistus, or summer bedding plants.

There is even skill required when buying summer bedding plants. Many small shops are displaying enticing pots of annuals at the moment – begonias, busy lizzies, pelargoniums and petunias. Unless you can give them shelter at night, wait until the middle of May. One cold night could give these plants such a check in growth that they would take months to recover.

If you see *Argyranthemum* 'Jamaica Primrose' (*Chrysanthemum frutescens* 'Jamaica Primrose') a tender perennial grown as an annual, buy it straight away (in case you don't find it again) and protect it at night. A delightful plant, it will go into non-stop production of soft yellow daisies and ferny foliage right through to November.

Most gardeners plant far too many trees and shrubs to begin with, but if you include some that do not object to pruning, the inevitable muddle will be easier to control. It is not for nothing that yew, box and holly have been beloved for centuries by garden designers – regular assaults on their twigs and foliage leave them quite unconcerned. Fuchsias can be cut to the ground every year, *Buddleja davidii* cultivars have to be pruned or you will get a jack-and-the-beanstalk effect and you would not see the butterflies that so love the flowers, because they would be hovering way above. You can do what you like to a pyracantha, train it firmly to the wall to better display its creamy flowers and bright berries, or allow it to make a large evergreen buttress. Penstemons, artemisias, *Romneya coulteri*, *Ceanothus* × *delileanus* 'Gloire de Versailles' (but not other ceanothus) will all take hard pruning in spring.

However, you do have to know which shrubs you can take liberties with – to even approach a magnolia or daphne with the secateurs would be a sort of horticultural blasphemy.

One could not say enough good things on the subject of *Rosa glauca* (used to be known as *R. rubrifolia*): it has heavenly foliage, a sort of rosy-mauve with a bloom on it, with single delicate pink flowers, followed by clusters of scarlet hips. You can treat this rose entirely as a foliage plant by cutting it to within one foot of the ground in spring.

 *26 April 1992*

Crossing Plants with Silver

Silver foliage is a brilliant mixer. Adding something with silver leaves has a miraculous effect on an existing group of plants. It's like buying a tube of white paint for the paint box – suddenly you can make lots of new colours and paint highlights into the borders with little patches of silver.

Plants are grey or silver because the leaves have developed a layer of hairs as a protection from extremes of weather, be it cold, heat or excess wind. The hairs form a silvery veil over the leaf, catch the light and glisten in the sun. Some plants have silver leaves cuddly as a thermal vest, such as the great plate-sized leaves of *Salvia argentea*. Some have lacy leaves, cut out of grey plush, such as those of *Senecio cineraria* 'Silver Filigree'; and others have the leaves of Excalibur, such as *Astelia chatamica*.

Included in the genus *Artemisia* is a wide selection of useful greys. 'Powis Castle', a fast-growing shrub, making a soft mound of finely-cut leaves, would be my first choice for new gardens. Smaller-growing *Artemisia alba* 'Canescens' is a favourite, with leaves like crumpled silver netting. More upright *A. ludoviciana* is a rampager, running in and out of neighbouring plants. Dwarf *A. schmidtiana* is the choice for a rockery, or to tumble over wall edges. All prefer poor, dry soil, and all have indifferent flowers, particularly *A. absinthium* (wormwood or lad's love) – in flower like an old-fashioned grey floorcloth. The exception is the excellent *A. lactiflora,* with beautiful creamy plumes of late summer flowers. This prefers damp, peaty soil and has ordinary green leaves. The paragon among silvers for containers is *Helichrysum petiolare.* This entwines itself through all other plants, making your container look like a beautifully planned professional job, instead of a haphazard muddle. (Even if your plants survived the past mild winter, you'll get a better, quicker effect by putting out young plants in mid-May.)

Santolina chamaecyparissus, or cotton lavender, makes a soft aromatic hummock. Hard pruning in spring and a starvation diet makes for the whitest, neatest plants. Among lavenders themselves, search for *Lavandula lanata,* with exceedingly woolly white leaves (but inconspicuous flowers), which requires shelter and full sun. *Anthemis punctata* subsp. *cupaniana* is such a useful, no-trouble, instant effect plant it deserves many mentions. It has feathery, silky white leaves and a long-lasting display of white daisies. Gardeners sometimes mistake it for *Leucanthemum hosmariense* (now listed as *Rhodanthemum hosmariense),* which also has feathery silver leaves and white daisies, but is an altogether fussier plant from Morocco, requiring the hottest available position.

The classic example of a silver tree is the weeping silver pear, *Pyrus salicifolia* 'Pendula'. I pruned mine last month, and further pruning takes place in late summer; any awkward branches heading off in the wrong direction are cut off, and the bottom tips of the branches are trimmed round like the hem of a ballerina's skirt.

Cytisus battandieri is a remarkable broom. The laburnum-like leaves of this small tree are covered with silky, silvery down. The flowers are deep yellow and fragrant of pineapple. I used to grow this against a wall, where it reached to 20 feet, but it had to be pruned hard after flowering to reduce the weight of the branches, as they are susceptible to wind damage. Do you know heavenly *Convolvulus cneorum?* This (first cousin of our monster weed with the white trumpets), is a tender little shrub with leaves of lustrous platinum that fingers itch to stroke and beautiful creamy-white flowers, pale pink on the outside.

 *30 April 1995*

May

Lean Cuisine for Some, Pile on the Riches for Others

There was the plant in the garden centre, fat as a Strasbourg goose, its overlush leaves bursting over the sides of the pot. You cannot blame the nurserymen for wanting to produce the largest possible plant in the shortest possible time, so plants are often grown in peat compost over-stuffed with nutrients. On arrival in the garden, though, you can imagine the plant saying to itself 'Oh my God, you can't expect me to grow in this!' The sudden change, to the comparative wasteland of a garden environment, may prove too much of a shock. Plants raised on caviar may refuse to adapt to porridge. I suspect many unexplained deaths of new plants are due to their roots' reluctance to sample an alien soil. This is one of the reasons why I'm forever bullying on about adding buckets of compost, manure or peat, to make the garden soil invitingly loose and crumbly, and similar to the soil in the pot. Conversely, plants from nurseries where they are grown 'hard', on a lean cuisine of gritty soil-based compost, will be charmed at the easy living to be had in the garden, and quickly settle into new conditions.

I think it was Margery Fish, the much-loved gardening writer who died in 1969, who remarked that women usually overfeed plants. The nurturing instinct promotes an overindulgent hand. The temptation to offer a little extra helping of compost cannot be resisted. But some plants can be killed with kindness, the perennial wallflower (*Erysimum* 'Bowles' Mauve'), for example, will become so gross and cabbagey that the roots cannot cope with the extra weight and the plant topples in a gale. Too much nitrogen results in a mass of leafage and few flowers. Liquid tomato fertiliser is full of potash, which encourages flowers and fruit – I use this regularly for bulbs, alpines and greenhouse plants.

Starvation corner in this garden is in the gravel drive, where the miserable soil beneath the pebbles promotes sturdy growth – a trowelful of better soil is all plants get to start with. This is the end of the line for certain plants, to curb their invasive tendencies. *Rubus illecebrosus* is such a one, an amusing plant on account of its juicy-looking, large red enticing fruits, a mixture between a strawberry and a raspberry – their lack of taste disappoints even blackbirds. Other plants happy in this area include sedums, nerines, *Geranium palmatum*, and the sea-holly known as Miss Willmott's ghost, *Eryngium giganteum*. (The gravel must be in full sun for these modest feeders.)

My pot plants get liquid feed from March to September. I can never decide which product is the best, and in any case it's good to vary them. Breda Roseingrave of Mackey's Garden Centre Ltd, Sandycove, Co Dublin, tells me that Phostrogen is top of the sales charts, it's very economical and suits every purpose, followed by Miracle-Gro and Bio Plant Food. I find it irritating that as soon as a packet of Miracle-Gro is opened, the fertiliser seems to absorb moisture from the air, so some is inevitably wasted. Breda also mentioned that Osmocote (a granular general fertiliser formerly only available to the trade) is now marketed for home gardeners. This is an excellent, long-lasting addition to your potting mixture.

This week the hardiest plants under glass (azaleas, agaves, lilies) are being moved outside to make more room for young stuff. Cuttings are being taken of penstemons, fuchsias, argyranthemums, pelargoniums. Auriculas are being divided and repotted.

Herbaceous lobelias, looking as sick as ever with the post-winter blues, must wait until early May before being divided, when they should make a rapid recovery. Divided too early they simply sulk to death.

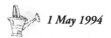 *1 May 1994*

Bridging the Gap before Summer

The reluctant gardener is just coming out of hibernation. He may be seen on the road heading for the garden centre, chequebook to the ready. The reason that he has been goaded into activity is the imminent collapse of the last of the tulips. Irish springs are deliciously slow – as a succession of different flowering plants present themselves, it seems the display will never end. Until some time around now, when suddenly there's very little in bloom: the May Gap has arrived.

Columbines, aquilegias or granny's bonnets. It doesn't matter what you call them, they are one of the stars of the season. Even if you start off with the sophisticated modern hybrids, with elegant long spurs and vivid colours, their self-sown seedlings will gradually revert to the old-fashioned sorts, the 'Pink and purple Columbine' of Spenser, with frilled and very double centres. The Clematiflora hybrids from *Aquilegia vulgaris* var. *stellata*, with no middles at all, are suitably named – their flowers are indeed similar to those of the clematis (to which they are related, both being members of the Ranunculaceae, or buttercup family). With the exception of the rather unpleasant variegated forms, columbines are one of the mainstays of early summer.

The next plant on your list for filling the gap should be the perennial honesty, *Lunaria rediviva*, a most suitable plant for the reluctant gardener, as opposed to honesty itself (a self-seeding biennial) for which you should struggle out of the deck chair in late summer to thin out the seedlings. But you never have to give another thought to perennial honesty, except to mutter gratefully 'What a nice plant,' each May. It will do in shady places and indifferent soil.

The fresh green of Solomon's seal (*Polygonatum*) seems the epitome of May. Its graceful, arching stems and pendant waxy flowers are good enough to pick and put in a vase all on their own. There are many different species of *Polygonatum*, including the diminutive *P. hookeri* (one inch tall, pale pink, Himalayan) and *P. verticillatum* (a striking plant for foliage contrast). A shady spot is preferred and most will flourish in the poorest positions.

The last tulip of all is yet to flower, *Tulipa sprengeri*, a connoisseur's bulb from northern Turkey. Its little bright scarlet flowers have none of the brash 'look at me' air of the large modern cultivars. It is easy from seed, but you will have to search specialist society seed lists for it, such as that of the Alpine Garden Society. (Do not be intimidated by the word 'Alpine' – most true plantsmen join this society, even if they don't grow rock plants.) It is worth making notes now, while spring is still in mind, of where tulips would look good next year.

Lest the reluctant gardener in a fit of enthusiasm starts buying tender plants (such as petunias and begonias), it is far too early to put them out. One cold night will set them back considerably, and may even kill them. In sheltered gardens you might risk putting out argyranthemums and verbenas but wise old gardeners will wait a while.

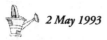 *2 May 1993*

Collapsing Clematis

Have you ever had a clematis that collapsed and died overnight? Anybody who has tried growing clematis usually has, though they may not admit to it. The scenario is as follows: the plant appears in exuberant health and is covered in fat buds just about to burst into flower; the next morning, the stems have collapsed and the buds are drooping pathetically; full of guilt, you rush for the watering can, but to no avail – a typical case of clematis wilt, a distressing fungal disease.

The large-flowered clematis hybrids seem specifically prone to this, but some of the prettiest clematis (though small-flowered) such as spring flowering *Clematis alpina* and *C. macropetala* and late-summer flowering *C. viticella* and its hybrids seem immune. *C. viticella* 'Purpurea Plena Elegans' deserves a special mention. It has wonderful rosettes of dusky purple double flowers in great profusion, just when you are looking forward to something new in late summer. Like all its *C. viticella* relations, you prune it to within three feet of the ground in late autumn, so you do not have to look at a bird's nest of dead twigs for the winter. *C. macropetala* 'Maidwell Hall', blooming at the moment, with lovely double flowers in pale indigo-blue with white petticoats, should never be pruned. (Never lose the label when you buy a clematis, so you can look it up and find out how to prune it.)

There are some clematis so lovely they are worth countless efforts to grow such as 'Perle d'Azur' (large, light blue), 'Duchess of Edinburgh' (a double that masquerades as a frilly white rose), or *Clematis texensis* 'Etoile Rose' (little pink bells with silvery margins). This latter is still scarce but can be hunted down in specialist nurseries.

Whoever first thought up the romantic idea of planting clematis up trees has a lot to answer for. Occasionally it works to divine effect, but often yet another clematis label joins the sad little pile in the potting shed. What you want is a small tree that is not too greedy – a young apple or pear tree would be ideal – and an exceedingly well-prepared planting hole for the clematis. The hole should be dug a few feet away from the trunk of the tree, and the clematis guided into the tree by a firm stake.

First mark out an area three feet square, take out the topsoil to the depth of a foot, and place it to one side. Unless your garden soil is very good, dig out the next 18 inches of soil and get rid of it. Mix up the topsoil (collect more from somewhere else in the garden if you haven't got enough) with at least two large buckets of well-rotted farmyard manure or garden compost, two large buckets of moist peat and three large handfuls of bonemeal, and fill up the hole.

From the moment of purchase a clematis in its pot is an unstable and worrying object; the cane to which it is still attached is heavy compared to the pot and the whole thing is likely to topple over in the slightest breeze, which means that the cane falls out, usually breaking fragile stems. The best thing to do, before taking the plant out of its pot, is to prune it to within six inches of the base, and remove the cane before it does any damage. (Don't worry about all this – all clematis without exception, should be pruned this way at planting time, to encourage strong basal growth. Deep planting also helps the plant to regenerate from below soil level, if attacked by wilt.) The roots will be tightly encircling each other, so gently tease them apart. Work two handfuls of general fertiliser into the planting hole, put the clematis in a few inches deeper than soil level, water well and keep watering (two gallons three times a week) till the end of the summer.

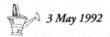 *3 May 1992*

Ideas by the Container Load

Each May I'm dying to plant my containers. Each May I'm running around like a headless chicken, dithering about what to plant where. Half of me wants to repeat the most successful of last year's efforts, the other half is planning wildly original arrangements, using plants never before restricted to containers. Sometimes I use a wonderful jumble of colourful plants, cottage style. But this year I'm endeavouring to practise 'less is more' (the remark of a landscape architect friend who is desperately trying to control my collector's instinct). Thus I've planted two large pots with divisions of the *same* hosta, and *nothing* else. It looks rather good. Try it. If you've got a large hosta, chop it into sections – hostas can be divided whenever you like. The simple use of lots of the same plant is specially effective if the container itself is decorative.

The secret of mixed containers is to think of planting in layers: a tall plant in the middle greatly adds to the dramatic effect – a young cordyline, phormium or standard fuchsia for example. Next fill in with medium plants – argyranthemums, geraniums, petunias, verbenas, busy lizzies. Then you need plants to tumble over the edge – trailing lobelias, ivy-leaved geraniums, ivies, pendulous fuchsias or *Bidens aurea*. Finally, the masterstroke, plant a weaver such as *Helichrysum petiolare* or its smaller sister, *Plecostachys serpyllifolia*, to run through everything else and unite the whole. For containers in shade there are tobacco plants or *Nicotiana*. I love their murky colours, the way they droop on sunny days, the way their fragrance carries in the cool of the night.

But the plant breeders have been interfering with nicotianas, turning them into travesties of their natural selves. Breeders decided that the public preferred flowers that didn't droop to protect themselves in sun, flowers that stood upright and stared at you in the heat of the day, in dull red and yellow. The faded blossoms of the yellow hang grubbily on. Beware the Nikki hybrids, unless you want rows of uniform dwarves. Look out instead for *Nicotiana langsdorffii*, a species that hasn't been tampered with. The small tubular flowers, elegantly poised on two-foot stems, are bright lime green with navy blue stamens. *N. sylvestris*, the tobacco plant of the woods, is quite another matter, a giant with a stout stem growing to five feet. One of the best bits of gardening I saw last year was in a tiny garden, consisting mainly of a small lawn and a large old apple tree. I laughed at the friend who owned it when he bought a quantity of *Nicotiana sylvestris*. 'Ridiculous,' I said. 'Far too big.' But late last summer I went there to an evening party. A stately avenue of the nicotiana led up the lawn, the white flowers, heavily fragrant, gleaming luminous in the dark. Rows of candles made flickering shadows. An ordinary Dublin back garden had been transformed into something magical.

Now to a brainstorming session of container ideas: a spring-flowering clematis, such as blue *Clematis macropetala* or *C. alpina* tumbling out of an Ali Baba jar; copy Miss Jekyll and try francoas or bridal wreath in pots; white datura, underplanted with variegated, scented-leaved pelargoniums; arum lilies (*Zantedeschia aethiopica*), underplanted with trailing *Glechoma hederacea* 'Variegata'; *Abutilon* 'Canary Bird' underplanted with *Bidens aurea* and *Helichrysum* 'Limelight'; *Melianthus major,* all on its own, stylish and unbelievably beautiful; one of the imported oriental jars made watertight for a miniature waterlily, such as *Nymphaea* 'Pygmaea Helvola'; flattish, saucer-shaped containers filled with sempervivums or houseleeks; *Pelargonium* 'Frank Headley' (salmon, variegated leaf) with salmon-pink alonsoa, white argyranthemums and white petunias.

The list is endless, try anything – your favourite rose, shrubs, Japanese acers (in sheltered places), herbs, a collection of ferns in shade – just remember the rules of good container planting: (1) Stuff in as many plants as possible and then add a few more. (2) Water regularly (up to twice a day in hot weather) and feed once a week. (3) Renew the potting compost at least once a year (except for permanent planting such as camellias or bay trees, in which case pots should be top-dressed annually).

Last year I went to Tuscany, to the village where small factories have been making and exporting terracotta pots for hundreds of years. But they had nothing better than the traditionally designed pots made by Kiltrea Bridge in Enniscorthy, Co Wexford. Furthermore, Kiltrea Bridge pots are guaranteed frost-proof. Give yourself a treat – go there and pot up.

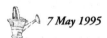 *7 May 1995*

The War of the Worms

Last year, on my way to an airport in New Zealand, I stuffed a potted plant into my handbag. At Los Angeles airport (an unusually boring place, where transit passengers are locked into a sort of concrete pen with nothing to do) I went to the Ladies as a diversion and unwrapped the pot. To my horror, the soil started to wriggle. I flung the pot, plant and all, down the loo. Somewhere, in the sewers beneath Los Angeles, New Zealand flatworms are making merry. The New Zealand flatworm, no doubt in some irresponsible person's handbag, arrived in Northern Ireland several years ago, and from there has spread south. Its existence has been confirmed in several counties.

We have many different earthworms in Ireland which feed at different soil levels. The New Zealand flatworm, a predator of surface-feeding earthworms, secretes digestive juices through its body wall. These liquids dissolve the earthworm, as was alarmingly illustrated on *Gardeners' World* on the BBC. This creature, liver-coloured with a paler sole, is *Artioposthia triangulata*. It can be 10–12cm long.

To confuse matters, it appears there is another flatworm here in Ireland, *Geoplana sanguinea*, reputed also to be a predator of earthworms. I saw one the other day. The nurseryman who squidged one – under my nose and far too close for me to enjoy the next few dinners – said he thought *Geoplana* was common in nurseries and gardens. *Geoplana* looks like a pale, pinky–orange, flattened slug with a slithery surface, considerably smaller than *Artioposthia*. You find it in permanently damp spots, such as underneath flowerpots.

Once you remember the classic situation of any predator, flatworms should be no cause for alarm. At first the flatworm will increase as it reduces the earthworm population. But at a certain stage the predator has less to eat, its population in turn is reduced, and the earthworms start to recover. There is thus continual reciprocal behaviour in the population of both.

What can you do to control flatworms? If you haven't already got them, be extra cautious with any new plants, whatever their origin. I now scrupulously wash off all soil in a bucket of water, rinsing the roots clean. The egg capsules of the New Zealand flatworm are apparently shiny black and visible to the naked eye. To help delicate plants re-establish quickly when repotted, I dip the wet roots in a mixture of peat and sand. If there's still such a thing as a garden free of vine weevil, the root-washing regime would be vital.

Priority for this week: weeding. The more you do the easier the summer will be. Self-sown seedlings of foxgloves and poppies, much as

I love them, must be watched, as just one of their leaves could smother a small plant.

 *8 May 1994*

Two-Toned Guidelines

Why do smart gardeners insist on despising variegated plants? Their argument is that variegated leaves are a travesty of nature, which would not survive long in the wild. Under a low Irish light, however, especially on a dull day, variegated leaves can illuminate a dark corner like a patch of sunshine.

There was a time when I bought anything variegated, no matter what. But you need to differentiate between those plants with clean and handsome variegation and those plants with leaves so odiously mottled that virus immediately springs to mind (which indeed is often the cause of variegation). Take, for example, the unspeakable *Persicaria virginiana* 'Painter's Palette' (formerly *Tovara virginiana*). Imagine a dizzy combination of green and ivory-yellow, with streakings and splashings of dried blood randomly scattered on top. Or perhaps worse, *Houttuynia cordata* 'Chameleon'. Even in early days I found this plant totally resistible. Sometimes variegation is so intense that it causes the leaves to pucker, further adding to the deformed look.

Just about to bloom is one of the best variegated plants, *Iris pallida* 'Argentea Variegata', a form of the Dalmatian iris, with typical lavender blue flowers. Its leaves, evenly striped with pale green and cream, will grace the garden right through till late October, unlike other bearded irises which dissolve into a tattered mess in late summer.

I must tell you about an excellent variegated grass, *Molinia caerulea* 'Variegata'. Its neatly striped cream and green leaves have just appeared. The purple-leaved Labrador violet, *Viola riviniana* 'Purpurea', has seeded around it. The grass remains tidy all summer but it is in autumn when there is not much fresh, light-coloured foliage around that you will most appreciate its little grassy fountains.

There is a rare variegated agapanthus, a variegated strawberry which can become a raging nuisance and a yellow-spotted nightmare in the variegated daisy. The long list includes a variegated nettle (just as attractive to butterflies), and a rather pleasant variegated sage. Some variegation can be most attractive, such as in *Lamium maculatum* 'Beacon Silver'. This makes a lovely silvery carpet. By a fortunate coincidence I planted a group on top of some pink tulips. It worked so well I'm trying it again next year. By midsummer it will have turned into an untidy, greenfly-infested rug. If you chop it back hard and give it a thorough soak of water it will quickly renew itself with fresh foliage.

Top of the list must come three different dogwoods, namely *Cornus controversa* 'Variegata', *Cornus alternifolia* 'Argentea' and the cornelian cherry *Cornus mas* 'Variegata'. Any of these large shrubs or small trees light up the garden to magic effect. The last of the three is probably easiest to grow and, what is more, it will stand considerable pruning. Its fruits are the same colour as the red pebbles you find on the beach.

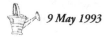 *9 May 1993*

Built-in Maintenance Clause

The truly hopeless gardener never reads beyond the first sentence of a gardening column. Every few weeks he mows the lawn with deep reluctance, skidding up and down the grass with the mower, slicing off the dandelions and daisies and skating over the lumpy bits and leaving them bald of grass. Hoping nobody notices the tattered lawn edges, he packs the grass cuttings into a bag (compost heaps haven't yet entered his head) and sends it off with the bin-men.

What he needs is plants that will do the gardening for him – the sort of plant that will survive total neglect and come up smiling, usually in the oddest places – a self-propagating plant, with a built-in maintenance clause. Unlike the myth of a self-cleaning oven, these plants do actually exist, albeit not in the average garden centre. They may be found in muddy yoghurt pots at plant sales, they peer from the nettles in many a run-down garden, and now and again they jump over the garden wall and you will see them happily blooming away in a hedge – such dedication to survival should be exploited.

Viola riviniana 'Purpurea' has rosy-lilac flowers delicately veined inside, and dark green kidney-shaped leaves beautifully flushed with purple. If you saw it at its party best, dressed up in a smart pot at a flower show, you might think it was a choice and difficult plant. But unlike some pampered violas, that have to be grown each year from cuttings, such as 'Irish Molly' (strange greenish brown flower) or 'Jackanapes' (a two-toner joker in maroon and canary yellow) you only have to buy *Viola riviniana* 'Purpurea' once. Plant it, forget all about it, and it will potter around the garden, seeding itself into odd empty patches and filling in the gaps.

Another of the great survivors, the white musk mallow (*Malva moschata* f. *alba*) is a native of Europe and an ardent coloniser. It is sweeping through Canada at this minute. But in the garden it seems to know where to stop and there always seems to be just the right amount of it. A thoroughly useful and delightfully easy plant, it grows to about three feet, does not require staking, spraying, feeding or watering, and has a long succession of saucer-shaped white flowers over fresh green ferny leaves from mid-summer on.

Neither of these plants needs much elbow-room, and what the hopeless gardener wants is a few of the real takeover merchants, such as *Geranium procurrens*. The first year it will sit and look at you, as sweet as could be. But you might have deduced from its name (*procurrens* – running or spreading out below ground) that this is a plant that means business. Its pinkish–purple flowers with dusky black centres appear from July to November, over long, trailing leafy stems that make new plantlets at each leaf node. It will soon be in total occupation of any hitherto weedy corner – don't let it anywhere near your best beds.

Lastly, a little eulogy in praise of *Alchemilla mollis*, or lady's mantle. If you already own this plant you will consider it a fearsome but beautiful weed (another plant you need only buy once). Sprays of lime-green fluffy flowers hover over clumps of velvety leaves with scalloped edges. So beguiling is this plant that when you first acquire it you will allow its flowers to linger on and drop their seed. The hopeless gardener could do no worse than let it have its way, until finally the garden becomes a foaming sea of pale green, as it masks the weeds and finally squeezes them out (except, of course, arch-weeds like convolvulus, ground elder and scutch). Once you have decided enough is enough, chop it back,

leaves and all, before the seeds ripen, and it will rapidly bedeck itself
with new young growth.

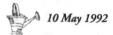 *10 May 1992*

The Darling Buds of May

I used to have a So-Called-Friend. She considered that plants in my
garden would be all the better for a move to hers. Luckily, she wasn't
observant. If I stood in front of a plant, tried to look even fatter than
usual and distracted her attention to something else, she usually missed
it. But May was the problem month. There was virtually nothing in
flower. Except for the camassias. Waving their spires of glorious blue
amid a sea of green, you couldn't fail to see them. Wary of a visit from
So-Called-Friend, terrified of being bullied into digging them up, my
only recourse was to pretend to be away in May.

Camassias are bulbous plants of the lily family, the name coming
from the native American name quamash. The roots formed a large part
of the diet (together with dried salmon) of Indians in northwest
America. In autumn 1805, when the expedition of Clark and Lewis
(the genus *Lewisia* is named after the latter) was in Idaho, they were
presented with roots of *Camassia quamash*. That night Clark and Lewis
ate a 'Supper of roots boiled, which swelled us in such a manner that we
were Scercely (*sic*) able to breathe for several hours.' Lewis wrote that
'Camassia root disagrees with me in every shape I ever used it.' Despite
his aversion, he was much impressed by a field of the flowers in bloom
'It resembles lakes of fine clear water – I could have swoarn (*sic*) it was
water.'

Camassias prefer deep, humus-rich, moisture-retentive soil. *C.
leichtlinii* is the finest garden-worthy species, with beautiful deep blue
star-like flowers arranged on slender spires, but 'Electra' is the most
thrilling, and lives up to the name. When you look at the flowers
sideways, the blue shimmers with flashes of turquoise. 'Electra' caused
trouble in May last year, when an English nursery person came to stay.
'Electra' looked gorgeous. Its beauty was endlessly remarked on. The

weekend was cluttered with multiple hints for me to dig some up. I resisted. Weeks later, after wheedling telephone calls, I gave in. (Assertiveness course required.) The good part of the story is that the remaining bulbs were planted in such a rich mixture they have now increased.

Since the early days of my erstwhile friend, I've always made an effort to find more May-flowering plants. (Naturally those who garden on acid soil needn't worry, being spoilt for choice with rhododendrons and azaleas.) Of course there are peonies and lilacs, honesty and sweet rocket. There are choice woodland plants such as trilliums, uvularias and podophyllums. And you can never have too many columbines. Parrots and *Tulipa sprengeri* are the last of the tulips to bloom. Dwarf bearded irises are front-of-the-border delights, with less obtrusive foliage than the tall varieties; 'Green Spot', 'Cherry Garden', 'Zoe Blue' (frilly, ice-blue) and 'Austrian Skies' are favourites. A frothy pink cloud of tiny flowers hovers above London pride, an excellent shade-tolerant carpeter.

I can't think why I was so slow to acquire the rose 'Canary Bird'. It flowers in May, has pretty neat ferny leaves, and each stem is covered from tip to base in single yellow roses. Charming. It makes a good standard. Pink 'Madame Grégoire Staechelin', a vigorous climber, comes into flower late in the month, a full two weeks before the main flush of roses.

May is the month for lily-of-the-valley. Long-loved in gardens, this is a plant with a mind of its own. Well may you prepare what you think is a suitable spot for your lily-of-the-valley – in shade, not too dry, rich in humus. Well may it choose not to flourish. Conversely, let a bit into the rose bed, and it'll make a nuisance of itself. There is a pink form available, *Convallaria majalis* 'Rosea'; a nice double, slow to increase, 'Prolificans'; variegated, expensive, desirable 'Albostriata'.

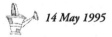 *14 May 1995*

Mollie the Witch to Joseph Rock

The first mistake I made with a peony was due to shaky geography. *Paeonia cambessedesii* comes from the Balearic Islands, to which I'd never been. Assuming that these islands consisted mostly of sea and sand, the compost prepared consisted largely of gravel. The plant never flowered. Lesson number one: all peonies like rich living.

This provoked the second mistake: in a subsequent fit of generosity to a Chinese peony, *P. obovata* var. *alba*, I covered the crown with a deep crumbly mulch of topsoil, compost and manure, so deep that the plant was smothered to death. Lesson number two: the crown of a peony should not be covered with more than one inch of soil.

Paeonia cambessedesii has metallic, sea-green leaves. The flower stalks and the backs of the leaves are washed in crimson. The fugitive, single, rose-pink flowers appear in early May but the foliage of this wondrous plant provides a long season of beauty. No more than 15 inches tall, it is suitable for a sunny raised bed and also good in a terracotta pot. *Paeonia obovata* var. *alba* has single, pure white, equally short-lived flowers; the petals glisten in the sun – it is so beautiful that I wouldn't care if it only flowered for a day.

One of the lesser-known peonies is *Paeonia mascula* subsp. *russii*. My specimen was grown from seed collected by a friend in Sardinia. Purple-tinged young leaves and glowing deep rose single flowers with pale yellow stamens are an opulent sight in April. A warm, well-drained position is required.

Paeonia mlokosewitschii, sometimes know as Mollie the witch, is inexplicably difficult to find. The emerging shoots – downy, dusky purple – look succulent enough to eat (steamed, perhaps, with an hollandaise sauce – but don't be tempted, peonies are poisonous).

Paeonia tenuifolia from the Caucasus is instantly recognised by its finely dissected leaves. Under 18 inches tall, this nice, tidy little peony, is very scarce. The flowers are deep crimson and the stamens yellow. I don't understand why *P. tenuifolia* should be so rare, as it increases rather well at the root. The double form is a recent acquisition, and the pink 'Rosea' on the wanted list. *P. veitchii* var. *woodwardii* from China has pale pink flowers and, unlike most herbaceous peonies, whose foliage becomes messy by late summer, its leaves remain in good condition. Easy to grow and easy from seed, which is variable. Unlike all the peonies mentioned above, this does nicely in light shade.

The most wanton, extravagant beauty of the garden is *P. suffruticosa* subsp. *rockii* (formerly 'Joseph Rock'). The single flowers are enormous.

Frilled creamy-white petals, satiny to touch, splodged with liquid crimson–purple at the base, surround quivering golden stamens.

Early autumn is the correct time for transplanting peonies, but I'm in the middle of a new project, which involves laying a path. A plant of the old double crimson peony (*Paeonia officinalis,* in cultivation since 1548) had to be moved on 28 April. Carefully lifted and watered every day, it has never looked back. If you have trouble with peony wilt (mildewy leaves and collapsed stems) spray regularly with fungicide.

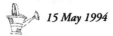 *15 May 1994*

Starting Things from Scratch

Today, back to square one. Or probably rectangle one. I mean the empty new back garden, just vacated by the builders. The builders themselves have gone, but their paraphernalia will remain – heaps of half-buried miscellaneous rubble with a scattering of old lunch packets.

A couple of Sunday afternoons will deal with this lot, but what is going on below ground is another matter. Weeds are a good sign – if they will grow so will the plants. But if the ground is empty and looks like a dried-up river bed, or else is covered in puddles which don't drain quickly away, this means the soil is compacted, due to being repeatedly run over by heavy machinery.

By all means hire a rotavator to get you started. But whereas a rotavator churns up the top layer of soil well, it further compacts the next layer down. For the best possible results, double digging, working in humus (decayed vegetable matter) as you go, is the answer. If you can only get fresh manure, store before use for about three months under a sheet of polythene, to prevent rain from leaching the goodness away. However much you long to start planting, this thorough preparation will pay immense dividends in years to come. (You can often tell the lawns of new houses by the yellowish look – a typical sign that the soil has not been properly prepared.) You may have to use weedkiller on serious weeds (docks, ground elder, convolvulus etc), but with other weeds the important thing is to stop them seeding this year. So keep busy with the hoe, specially on hot days, so they quickly shrivel in the sun.

You are now looking at an empty canvas in the course of preparation. This will give you time to have a good long think: decide on the sunniest place for positioning the patio; decide where you are going to put the washing line (many is the good garden I've seen ruined by an obtrusive line of washing); decide where the main paths are going (try and avoid little wiggly paths, but think of graceful curves); decide where, and what shape, the lawn is going to be. Are you going to divide the garden, by trelliswork, or with planting? This is often a good idea, even in the smallest gardens, for it creates an illusion of more space. Try out different shapes for paths and beds by laying a row of stones, bricks or a garden hose.

Consider the plan for a few days, then adjust to taste. Unless your soil is in good condition, satisfy the craving for flowers by using annuals this year, rather than risking expensive trees and shrubs. Possibly the most difficult decision to make, if you've only room for one tree, is which to choose. An apple tree, a weeping silver pear (*Pyrus salicifolia* 'Pendula'), a birch (*Betula*), *Amelanchier lamarckii*, a mountain ash (*Sorbus*), or a crab apple (*Malus*) are all good, though standard, suggestions that shouldn't let you down. In a very small garden, if I had to choose, I'd probably go for an apple or a pear tree. You have blossom in the spring and fruit in the autumn. They lend themselves to pruning to size or shape and, most important of all, they are not particularly greedy, so many plants will grow happily in the soil beneath them.

 *16 May 1993*

Glorious Vulgarities in a Tub

You can be as daring as you like when planting containers – this is the place to grow exotic-looking tropical plants like daturas, cannas, and such gorgeous vulgarities as the large-flowered tuberous begonias – plants that would seem quite out of place in the garden proper. A glorious array of tender annuals and perennials, only visiting for the summer, are at our disposal. By using containers, you can afford to make glaring mistakes, invent dashing colour schemes and grow plants that don't like your garden soil.

Lime-hating camellias and rhododendrons will live for years in a large tub and if you yearn for brilliant blue hydrangea, this too can be yours. Hydrangeas are invariably pink on lime, but on acid soil will be miraculously transformed. The aim when planting up tubs and pots is to give an impression of a cornucopia of plenty, a tumbling mass of flowers and foliage, so when deciding how many plants you need, think of a number, double it, and add on a few more.

To keep up this great exuberance of growth, and summer-long flower production, water generously (once or twice a day in hot weather) feed extravagantly (twice a week with liquid feed) and deadhead every time you pass by – the life-cycle of these plants is geared to producing seed as quickly as possible and then dying – to thwart their plans, remove their fading flowers before they set seed.

One of the keys to success is to forget about flowers and think about foliage. *Helichrysum petiolare* has leaves and trailing stems in palest grey. It does the most wonderful weaving act in and out of other plants, uniting the dottiest of colour schemes. The tiny grey leaves of *Plecostachys serpyllifolia* do the same on a smaller scale. A pot full of marigolds in vivid orange (one can hear the sniff of the discerning gardener) achieves new elegance when mellowed by one of these helichrysums, *Melianthus major*, with huge, slightly frilly, blue-grey leaves, making striking contrast to other bedding plants that have, on the whole, different foliage. By nature it is a large frost-tender shrub but can be treated as herbaceous by cutting down the stems in spring.

Long-flowering verbenas are an excellent choice, but rather than planting a mixed batch, for a more restrained composition use only one or two of the named cultivars, such as 'Pink Bouquet'. The lemon-scented verbena (*Aloysia triphylla*) is an essential; its flowers are deeply insignificant in wishy-washy lilac, but the leaves when crushed are perfumed like expensive soap – the sort that looks like lemons and comes in wooden boxes.

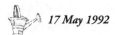 *17 May 1992*

Time to Plant up the Pots Again

Making a garden often seems unbearably slow, but the big treat of the year is planting up pots of summer colour, when you can magically change the view in a moment or so. Containers can be used to make instant focal points, to disguise man-hole covers, to cheer up gloomy corners and are specially good at the edge of steps.

Pots of summer bedding should be planted with extravagance: stuff in as many plants as possible and then try and squeeze in a few more. As regards what compost to use, I mix up my own of six parts of fresh topsoil, three parts damp peat and two parts horticultural sand with added general fertiliser according to the directions on the packaging.[3]

The need for regular watering cannot be too strongly stressed: for, say, a large container, you need a whole can of water per day in hot weather, sometimes two, with added liquid fertiliser at least once a week. The only plants which will stand neglect are sempervivums, echeverias, agaves and some sedums. Always place plenty of drainage material, in the bottom of the pot: ideally start off with some pieces of broken clay pot, placed in a convex position over the drainage hole. Then fill up with stones or gravel for a further three to four inches (more for larger pots), before topping up with compost.

Invaluable tender, evergreen shrubs for summer bedding are marguerites (*Argyranthemum*), sometimes known as Paris daisies. 'Jamaica Primrose' (soft yellow), 'Vancouver' (pink), *A. maderense* (nice bluish leaves, pale yellow daisies) and a new double white are all recommended. If you like a wild enthusiasm of bright yellow daisies, redeemed by lacy foliage, try *Bidens aurea*.

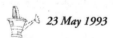 *23 May 1993*

No Shrinking Violets

I've just returned from Long Island, New York, where I was giving a talk to the Garden Club of America. This is a club for ladies who garden.

---

3. For up-to-date potting mixture, see page 6 (True Grit).

Like their counterparts, the ladies who lunch, eating and gardening are secondary. What really matters is what you wear doing it. Before I left Ireland, I asked a friend what Long Island society was wearing for spring. 'Lovely little Chanel type suits,' she replied. 'You know the sort, unbelievably expensive soft tweed, in pink or primrose with gold braiding and shiny buttons.'

The gold coast of Long Island was the scene of fabulous parties in the 1920s. This is the land of the Great Gatsby, and the discreet perfume of old money still hovers over secluded mansions, cosseted from intruding eyes by extensive woodlands. Flowering dogwoods, breathtakingly beautiful in their tiers of pink or white, blossoming cherries and red buds, and a thousand magnolias guard the portals of the last refuge of great wealth. Women of the Garden Club of America have to go through what's known as the 'process' before joining the club. This may take a year, and involves knowing five members of the board, and having a proposer and two seconders. Neither money nor religion nor family is mentioned at any stage, although all are the chief influences on the final decision.

Any ideas I had about garden clubs consisting of whiskery old men growing giant leeks or home-made jam competitions at country flower shows disappeared the moment I arrived at the auditorium. The clothes. And the jewellery. Each piece seemed to speak of 1930s weddings, grandmothers' dowries, coming-out balls, fortunes made on Wall Street or newspaper heiresses of long ago. It was too late for regrets about wearing the old navy dress again.

American audiences are amazingly appreciative. I don't think they approve of my exhortations about digging in lots of manure, but they do sit quietly for precisely 50 minutes before I detect the first clank of a charm bracelet, and subsequent fidgeting signifies the desire to stop.

Driving through a less exclusive part of Long Island I came across an enormous garden centre, almost a city of gardening. It could be described as hamburger gardening, as all the elements of a successful McDonald's could be noticed. As with hamburgers, uniformity is important. Perfectly matched plants stretched in unending rows and everything comes with a promise of instant gratification – even herbaceous plants were either in flower or just about to. Prices were high, with large-flowered clematis at $89.

Americans love turning plants into standards. I saw a superb pair of standard white wisterias in pots, a pair of standard pelargonium 'Mabel Grey', standard rosemarys, myrtles and leptospermums. May is a good time to start making a standard. Fuchsias are perhaps the easiest to begin with. What you need is a juicy, just-rooted cutting. Train it to a stake, leaving the leading shoot. Pinch out side-shoots as they form, but leave the leaves to feed the stem. When the main stem reaches two-thirds of the desired height of the finished standard, allow five or six of the side shoots to develop. Pinch out the growing tip of these at every two to three pairs of leaves until the head of the standard is formed. To encourage fast growth, pot on frequently and liquid feed regularly.

Throughout America, but especially in Long Island, I met nothing but great kindness and hospitality.

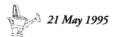 *21 May 1995*

The Bully in the Garden

Lawnmowers should bear a government health warning. The most maddening machines, in order of increasing aggravation, are hoovers, word-processors and lawnmowers. Ensuing rage when the first two refuse to start is nothing compared with that caused by a recalcitrant lawnmower. The more you try and start it, the more the engine will flood with petrol, and the less likely it is to start. Your only recourse (giving the mower a parting kick), is to wander off, pretending you don't care whether it starts or not.

With its constant demands for mowing, edging, feeding, watering and weeding, the lawn is the bully of the garden. Forget it one weekend, you have an instant hayfield. Forget to feed, it turns sickly yellow. Decide either to have a good lawn, thus committing yourself to a summer of slavery, or announce that from now on you're having a flowery mead, so you can doze in the sun, lying on the daisies with a bottle of wine, clover, blue speedwell and creeping thyme.

I think it's those lawns half-way between the two which are unsatisfactory – the ones with the raggedy edges, the baldy bits and the patches of weed grass (annual meadow grass and scutch). The slavery method, as adopted here, is as follows:

- The lawn is mowed twice a week with a rotary mower, with the blades set fairly high – the closer you mow the more the faults will show. The finest lawns are mown with a cylinder mower, but mistakes in the form of a scalping job on the turf are more likely to happen with these. Manual mowers require little maintenance while electric mowers are not for the clumsy.

- The grass is fed every three to four weeks with Fisons Evergreen. Prior to feeding, the weather forecast is anxiously studied, for the grass should be dry when the fertiliser is applied, whilst a deluge is required immediately afterwards to wash it in. Otherwise we find the grass gets burnt. We invariably end up watering it in.

- In autumn or spring the lawn is scarified. Scarifying removes what's known as the thatch – a build-up of decaying grass and roots. Too much thatch prevents water reaching the roots. By removing it, young grass is encouraged. You can rent scarifying machines by the day.

- Weeding. This is done by hand, using a nice little tool called a daisy grubber. When the weed situation was worse, we used spot weedkiller, made specially for lawns. My least favourite gardening question is the one about moss on lawns. Moss-killer does indeed get rid of moss. But if the problem is due to bad drainage, the moss will recur.

This week I saw some absolutely beautiful turf – velvety, silky-smooth, best-quality Wilton stuff. You can order it this minute from Emerald Lawns, Campsie, Co Derry. Ask for their luxury grade, which is ryegrass-free. No job is too small; they deliver throughout the year. Don't order until you have the ground well prepared, as if for sowing grass seed. At this time of year the rolls of turf keep for about four days; in the winter they'll keep for a week. Emerald Lawns will also lay the turf for you, for a charge depending on the area to be covered.

 *22 May 1994*

A Flamboyant Touch to Early Summer

The huge, flamboyant flowers of oriental poppies, with glistening petals of crumpled silk, lend dazzle and excitement to the early summer garden. For years the only one I grew was 'May Queen'. Its double flowers in piercing vermilion was a colour too hard to take, so I decided it had to go. I dug it up, or so I thought, as next year back it came, regenerating from the roots, its floppy flowers fizzing with the chemical colour of an orange drink.

This gives a useful clue to the management of oriental poppies. After they have flowered, their bristly leaves rapidly yellow and sprawl around in a messy heap, spoiling the look of the mid-summer garden. But they are one of the few (if not the only) herbaceous plants that don't mind their foliage being pulled off as soon as it starts to fade. You can fill in the gap with summer bedding plants or try planting them near *Clematis* × *durandii*, a semi-herbaceous clematis with dark blue flowers that will drape itself prettily over the empty space.

If you like your colours hot and strong 'Goliath' is your man. It is a fine upstanding poppy four feet tall with whopping flowers in glowing scarlet with dark maroon blotches at the base of the petals (plenty of cool green foliage is essential nearby). 'Cedric's Pink' is an alluring dusty-pink, a shade usually reserved for ladies' underclothes. For those with even more refined taste, there are 'Perry's White' and 'Black and White', an uninspired but descriptive name for a beautiful poppy. Unlike peonies (the other sumptuous flower of early summer) poppies are not particularly greedy, and will flower without fail every year provided they have plenty of sun.

May is the season for meconopsis, or Himalayan blue poppies. The blue of their petals is almost unbelievable – a shimmering brilliant turquoise. Whereas oriental poppies come from the hot dusty plains of Turkey, and thus revel in the sun, meconopsis need cool, moist conditions, the nearest you can get to a Himalayan mist, where the plants are prematurely saturated in droplets of water. Happy in areas of high rainfall, in dry Dublin gardens a bed with added peat, leafmould, garden compost or old manure is essential, plus regular watering and division every three years.

Despite the fact that to grow them is technically illegal, annual opium poppies (*Papaver somniferum*) are permanent residents in most gardens. At the moment they are making fast expanding rosettes of blue–green leaves. You have to watch them at this time of year, because they are growing at such a rate they can smother one of your best plants to death overnight. If you go out in the early morning you will see them unwrap their buds – the tightly packed mass of petals swells with inner force and pushes the bud casing off. The new petals are all crinkled up at first but quickly smooth themselves out and the minute they are fully expanded, bees will rush to bury themselves in the centre of the flowers. A brief morning's buzzing, and by noon the flower is pollinated.

For the next few weeks you have the further decoration of sea-green pepper-pot seedheads, until the stems start toppling over and suddenly you've had enough of poppies and pull them all but one – left to drop its seed for next year. The most usual colour is pale mauve, but they can be cherry red, pink or purple. It is too late to sow annual poppies this year but make a note to order frilly double ones next spring (Chiltern Seeds) and also the prettiest, most ethereal poppies of the lot, *Papaver rhoeas* 'Fairy Wings' in delicate shades of grey, mauve and smoky white, some with picotee edges (Thompson and Morgan, distributed here by Mr Middleton, South Anne Street, Dublin 2).

 *24 May 1992*

Waging War in the Battle of Nature versus Nurture

Today I met somebody who had just inherited a natural Dublin garden in Clanbrassil Street. Brambles, butterfly bushes, nettles and sycamore saplings are the key plants, but the undergrowth reveals skip-loads of old prams, supermarket trolleys, VP sherry bottles, lager cans, single trainers, odd socks and various unmentionables.

Nothing makes me crosser than people wittering on about Natural Gardening. It seems that the louder they proclaim its joys, the less they know about it. You can always tell when somebody is about to broach the subject. Suddenly the dreamy look in their eyes changes into a challenging stare, and they launch into Meadow Gardening, Wild Flower Gardening, giving Nature her head, and have I heard about growing peonies in rough grass? The high moral tone doesn't let up, as they romanticise on about wandering around, fresh as a reborn Druid, scattering packets of wild flower seed.

Gardens were originally created as havens from the wilderness outside. A garden is an intensely cultivated area, in which man, with great arrogance, attempts to discipline nature. Plants from all corners of the world, gathered from wildly differing habitats, are all expected to grow in the same patch. Here they may be drenched with sprays, or fed with chemical fertilisers; even the greenest of gardeners practises thinning out, staking, watering in drought, top-dressing, winter protection and general fussing to make plants grow. Unending war, even if it's organic, is conducted against slugs, snails, weevils, aphids and the newest horror, the flatworm. Natural?

If you examine one square metre of a field in Connemara, there may be up to 20 different species growing in it, including purple orchids, blue milkwort, vetches, clover, and a little yellow flower I've always known as scrambled eggs. The proportion of each plant to the group as a whole varies little from year to year. Nature has it all miraculously organised, the vigour of each species is in perfect balance to the others. Levels of soil nutrients, prevailing weather conditions and degrees of sheep or rabbit grazing, all have precise influence on the tapestry of flowers underfoot.

My argument goes as follows: by all means have a go at Natural Gardening, but only if you are going to play God. It is the most difficult gardening of the lot. To imitate nature's balancing act, by keeping control of the bully plants, but allowing one or two for special effect, while at the same time encouraging more fragile species, requires a rare dedication. However, a few great gardeners have done it, such as Christopher Lloyd at Great Dixter in Sussex, in the meadow started by his mother earlier this century. 'Remember that most grassland plants like full exposure to sunlight and poor soil. The poorer the soil, the more varied its contents.' says Christopher in his book *Christopher Lloyd's Flower Garden* (Dorling Kindersley). The grass is mown as late as December, to provide close-mown turf for early bulbs. The tapestry starts with snowdrops and crocuses, followed by old-fashioned small-flowered polyanthus and primroses, wild daffodils, dog's tooth violets and fritillaries. May brings orchids, moon daisies, yellow hawkbit and red clover. Blue meadow cranesbill starts in June, followed by English irises at the turn of June and July, and tufted vetch (*Vicia cracca*). The grass is cut several times between July and December, thus reducing turf vigour and further encouraging flowers. In August there are yellow daisies, and for early autumn there are colchicums and real autumn crocuses.

Many plants naturalise themselves under garden conditions. To me gardening is about controlling the chaos, up to a point, and then waiting for the infinite surprises that nature provides with self-sown seedlings. Admittedly you get a million weeds – but foxgloves, campanulas, love-in-a-mist, larkspur, honesty, columbines, linarias and a million poppies will turn up – as if by magic. Of this kind of Natural Gardening I approve.

 *28 May 1995*

Flowers: to Pick or Not to Pick

Gardeners are divided into two sorts: those who like picking flowers for the house, and those who hate it. Myself, I would rather part with a pint of blood than pick certain flowers. I'll never forget the woman who insisted on having my best yellow lilies for her daughter's wedding. The worst part was that she hovered around while I picked them – I couldn't get away by only giving her the small ones.

I should have known. I'm suspicious of anyone who reads the *Daily Telegraph*. I'm also wary of drivers who have little dangly things stuck to the back windows of their car. My beautiful lilies left, wrapped in that newspaper, lying on the back seat of the car, beneath a veritable toyshop of fluffy objects with eyes that lit up. I felt ill.

The unenthusiastic picker should grow plenty of good foliage plants (hostas, *Euphorbia amygdaloides* var. *robbiae*, *Pittosporum* 'Silver Queen', eucalyptus, heucheras, *Arum italicum* subsp. *italicum*, bergenias, euonymus, *Elaeagnus* 'Quicksilver'), which will form the background to the arrangement.

I find that the most useful plants for picking must be easy to grow and flower for a long season. Above all, they must be the sort you don't mind picking, pretty little nonsenses such as *Alchemilla mollis* and *Tanacetum parthenium* (formerly *Chrysanthemum*) 'White Bonnet'. Poppy seed-heads are brilliant. Such plants will seed around in unimportant places and a snip here and there won't matter. If you buy a cheap bunch of flowers, or can bring yourself to pick one or two peonies, roses or lilies, these little fillers-in will make something special.

What prompted this discourse was that I met some ladies from an altar society yesterday. I was amazed to find that they had never heard of astrantias, the best possible flowers for picking. If you multiply the number of churches in Ireland by an average rota of flower-arranging ladies, it must indicate that there are thousands of ladies out there who need to know about astrantias. So here goes: *Astrantia major* 'Rubra' (formerly listed as *A. carniolica* 'Rubra'), or greater masterwort, is an herbaceous perennial, easily grown in sun or part shade, and all the better if the soil is rich. The flowers are a very interesting and beautiful shape, each an individual posy of tiny florets, arranged in a dome, with a collar of bracts, on stems about two feet high. Try and acquire the cultivar 'Shaggy' sometimes known as 'Margery Fish', in which the bracts are larger and tinged with green. The leaves of 'Sunningdale Variegated', a crisp combination of cream and green, will illuminate a patch of shade.

Astrantia maxima is madly pretty. The flowers are rose pink. It flowers for a long season and likes a position that is not too dry. *Astrantia minor* is an obscure little plant, which you wouldn't notice in a crowd. The flowers are delicate fairy pincushions on slender, foot-high stems – a collector's item.

Astrantia carniolica 'Rubra' is quite special, the flowers a mixture of crimson and green. But the sensation among astrantias is the new cultivar *A. major* 'Ruby Wedding'. This is a dream of a plant, a form of the greater masterwort with glowing deep red flowers. Keep an eye out for it.

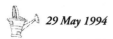 *29 May 1994*

Uniquely English

Cotton frocks and straw hats, champagne lunches, strawberries and cream and a regimental band playing in the shade of the chestnut trees – you cannot imagine an occasion more uniquely English than the Chelsea Flower Show. The sun beat down on the great marquee (over 3 acres in size), a wave of heat greeted you at the entrance, the perfume of flowers mingled with the more human scent of the 35,000 visitors a day, who were swept past great banks of flowers in a never-ending stream, to admire or sneer, according to their taste.

A bevy of Sloanes hurried past the begonias, their noses wrinkling; one felt almost sorry for the flowers – each begonia was looking its party best, each a horticultural triumph. Exclamations of delight in Bradford accents could be heard round the sweet pea stands, while the rhododendron displays attracted those in pin-striped suits or pearls.

Despite the one-way traffic system in the aisles to control the crowds, it always breaks down at the clematis stands. The jostling and shoving round Valley Clematis Nursery lasts all day. 'Excuse me,' people announce, as they stand on your foot – presumably these two words give them a right to trample, an English custom new to me.

Nostalgia for the past is high fashion in gardening. Perhaps the greatest use of modern gardening illusions is that of Cottage Gardening an idea that most appeals to those marooned in London flats without a garden. Wistful types could be seen round the stand of Hardy's Cottage Plants. Their nicely unpretentious stand had many charming, ordinary plants, such as sweet rocket (*Hesperis matronalis*) and very double aquilegias or granny's bonnets – always good for a wallow.

In the scientific section, one stand honoured by a Silver Gilt Medal shone from the rest: it was that of the Irish Garden Plant Society sponsored by Bord Fáilte, with a theme of distinguished natives and honoured guests: there were many unusual plants including rare Irish wild plants. In spite of the heat wave, and the journey over the Irish sea, the plants and the hard-working stand organisers all did us proud on the day.

Eventually I was swept out with the crowd to the mid-day sun, and bewildering alleys of outdoor stands. Accompanied by announcements on the tannoy about where to go if you got lost, the river of people dispersed into different streams – some heading for the ice-cream and cold drink stands, some to picnic beneath the trees and rest their poor, hot feet, some to browse among the stands of garden furniture and ornaments.

Here you could buy anything from a giggling terracotta pig to a Coadstone figure of what I thought was Flora, but I was contemptuously informed by the salesgirl that it was Ceres.

Of the show gardens 'A Paradise Garden' sponsored by the *Daily Telegraph* was particularly exciting. Designed to evoke the eroticism of Persia, it was divided by narrow channels of water crossing at a central fountain. There were several gazebos, one disguised as a flamboyant Turkish tent, and cascading vines and roses. The colour scheme was soft colours, punctuated with lots of purple alliums (decorative onions) that look like starry, purple balls on sticks (*Allium hollandicum*, formerly *A. aflatunense*).

Chelsea Flower Show is a great occasion for which you have to apply for a ticket well in advance from the Royal Horticultural Society, Vincent Square, London SW1P 2PE, England. Travel as light as possible, but take into account that the weather is likely to do anything and bring something to eat and drink to save queuing.

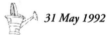 *31 May 1992*

June

Footloose and Fancy Free

Rose 'Madame Caroline Testout' arrived here 20 years ago, strapped to a car's roof rack. Her roots trailed over the car boot, desiccating in a hot wind, and her poor buds drooped over the windscreen. She was 10 years old and 10 feet tall at the time, a present from a friend who was moving house. It was May.

I didn't have the mercy to trim her torn roots before planting. Greedy for the buds to open, I didn't even prune the stems. I simply shoved the tattered roots into the soil at the base of an arch, draped the stems up and over it, tied them to it so they couldn't collapse, and stood back to admire. After a week's fainting and many protests of limp leaves, she rallied. Today her huge pale pink blossoms flaunt themselves from the top of the arch.

I don't think there's a rose in this garden that hasn't been moved at least once. 'Mrs Oakley Fisher' was moved one August. 'Souvenir de Saint Anne's' was moved last September. I woke up last night thinking 'Charles de Mills' could do with some Miracle-Gro, to compensate for his recent move. (I must admit that his buds are somewhat slow in developing.) 'Hermosa' has been shifted twice. Whereas late autumn or winter would be a better time to transplant roses, sometimes necessity dictates the moment. Major changes in garden design, imminent arrival of builders, moving house – whatever the reason – plants may have to be moved at the wrong time of year.

Don't copy my horrible treatment of poor Madame Caroline – water well before moving, lovingly prepare the planting hole with compost and other goodies, trim damaged roots neatly, prune the stems hard, water and sprinkle the leaves often until recovery begins. My friend up the road, who has a magical garden (although she protests she doesn't do much in it), has just moved *Viburnum plicatum* 'Mariesii' (the lovely one that grows in tiers with creamy, lacy flowers). The builders were in to extend the balcony and the viburnum was now blocking the way through to the garden. I remember Rose Mary buying it many years ago when we were young. Now fully 12 feet in diameter, it was copiously watered before the move. The leaves were just about to unfurl. Two men (large) with builders' shovels heaved it out of the ground with as big a root ball as possible. After planting, the viburnum went back a bit, the leaves undecided about whether to continue unfurling, but suddenly in the last few days they have opened fully. The plant now looks indescribably lovely, the pearly flower buds also just about to bloom. My friend reckons that repeated sprinklings of the foliage with water have contributed much to the success of the operation.

'I could almost be called CIE, I move things so much,' she remarked. An eight-foot white lilac was moved in late spring, and has never looked back. 'I move anything, at any time of year.' A colony of agapanthus have just been moved out to a sunny gravel path. Two 15-year old box balls came from next door. All the yuccas have been shunted several times. 'I'm always moving that sun-loving fern (*Blechnum tabulare*) – it's always in the wrong place and has to be moved on.'

 *4 June 1995*

Getting the Best out of Clematis

For me clematis hold a fatal attraction. Fatal, that is, for the clematis. I've killed more of these irresistible climbers than anyone else, so I feel quite entitled to pontificate on their cultivation or lack of it. Books will tell you that clematis prefer their feet in the shade and their heads in the sun. Herein snag number one: the sort of shade they mean is cool, humid gloom that never dries out. The vital thing to remember about clematis is that they are greedy to the nth degree and require an immense amount of water. The just-purchased clematis is in a very dangerous condition. The thoughtful nurseryman has bound its stems tightly to a cane, so that when you remove it from the pot in order to plant it, the cane will most likely topple over, snapping the stem as it goes. So before even taking the clematis out of the car, prune it to within one foot of soil level and remove the cane. This initial pruning is the only way to encourage more stems from the base, giving more protection against wilt.

I also think that some clematis, specially the large-flowered doubles such as 'Duchess of Edinburgh' (white buds tinged with mint green),

'Vyvyan Pennell' (violet blue) and 'Countess of Lovelace' (lilac blue) have a limited life span. I have killed them all.

But there is a French countess with whom I've never had any bother – 'Comtesse de Bouchaud'. Described in the *RHS Dictionary* as 'satin pink, flushed lilac, abundant, stamens cream.' I would more describe her as 'a vulgar pink, but a damn good doer.' No sniff of wilt has ever sullied her leaves or stems, and she's been flowering and growing with graceful enthusiasm for 15 years or so.

 *6 June 1993*

Avoiding the Plastic Bag Trap

'Grow it in a large plastic bag of peat,' said the garden centre, as I was looking longingly at a rhododendron in full flower. What rubbish. The results of his recommendations – dead rhododendrons in plastic bags – are seen in many new gardens where their unsuspecting owners have fallen into the plastic bag trap.

Growing lime-hating plants in large plastic bags, sunk into the soil of a limey garden, doesn't work – the roots are trapped in their individual deserts and the plant is destined to a slow death. But by building a special bed for peat-loving plants, you will immediately have the right conditions for camellias, azaleas, heathers and choice members of the heather family (Ericaceae), such as menziesia, gaultheria and zenobia. Such plants enjoy cool conditions, and constant watering in summer is vital.

The useful thing about ericaceous plants is that they have shallow roots so the peat bed doesn't need to be deep. The bed is better raised, or you risk lime filtering through from the surrounding soil. The walls of the bed (made of brick, stone or logs), only need to be about 18 inches high. It should be situated in dappled shade with plenty of light – in the rain-shadow of next door's overgrown hedge won't do. I use a mixture of 75% peat and 25% lime-free soil.

Raised beds situated in sun, not lime-free but filled with your ordinary garden soil plus extra drainage, in the form of about 30% grit or small washed pebbles, are an excellent addition to small gardens, even if you're not an alpine enthusiast. This is the place for choice little things – pinks, small campanulas, saxifrages, helianthemums, erodiums, origanums, daphnes, thymes and pulsatillas. As your centrepiece, choose the only true dwarf conifer, *Juniperus communis* 'Compressa'.

Raised beds of alpines look good when mulched with washed pebbles, about two to three inches deep. This will assist drainage around the plants in winter, help conserve moisture in summer and deter weeds. And I imagine slugs dislike scratching their bodies on sharp stones. As good grit has always been hard to get, I've always pinched gravel from the drive. But now Bord na Móna are marketing 25kg bags of natural decorative small stones, in three colours – Amber Gold, Barleycorn and Rustic Red.

A special tree – *Acer griseum, Betula utilis* var. *jacquemontii* or even an apple tree – in its own raised bed could make a desirable feature. A good way of dealing with the shady area around an existing deciduous tree, is to have a slightly sunken paved area beneath, and then build a small raised bed around the trunk of the tree. Be very careful not to change the soil level round the base of the trunk. With regard to the filling of raised beds, remember Dillon's Law – it takes twice the amount of soil that you thought was needed.

Plant of the week is the most decorative of all the onions, *Allium hollandicum* 'Purple Sensation'. In effect, it's a deep purple ball of flowers on a 3-foot stick and, for once, it's aptly named. It is sensational. Make a note to get it.

 *6 June 1994*

Climbing the Walls with this Clematis

The large-flowered clematis are as fickle as they come. Most of these beautiful climbers, with flowers that seem impossibly large for their slender stems, are guaranteed to break your heart. Some, such as 'The President', have collapsed with wilt so frequently here that I've given them up.

'The President' was first planted with 'Mrs Cholmondeley' on the potting shed wall. He wilted away in her arms. Next, he was ensconced in what (I thought) was a prime position against a shady wall. Before even producing any buds, he vanished. Finally, thinking how good his large purple flowers would look entwined with pale pink rose 'New Dawn', I planted them both together. Same story. I now adopt a 'don't care' attitude to these clematis: love them, and if they wish to leave, too bad. Get another one.

'Lasurstern' has huge, deep blue flowers and creamy stamens. I can see the first flowers out of the corner of my eye. Growing in a large container, regularly fed and watered, 'Lasurstern' has managed to wander over nearby ground-cover plants and clamber up a yew tree. But lovely as this looks, it wouldn't work if the clematis was actually planted at the base of the yew, for such a position would be too dry. My theory on wilt is that any of the large-flowered clematis may succumb, but they are more likely to resist the disease if they are never subject to stress, i.e. are never short of food or water, particularly now, when the weather is warm and growth is rapid. A further point is that clematis are too often recommended for growing near walls: such a position is more than likely to be dry. They have a better chance if grown in the open garden, supported by trellis-work, an arch or growing through some non-greedy shrub.

'Comtesse de Bouchaud' is a tough old bird. I've had her growing on an arch for years. Described by Christopher Lloyd in his excellent book *Clematis* as 'Nothing subtle about 'Comtesse de Bouchaud', one has to agree when you see her great masses of crude, pinky-mauve. Still, such tenacity must be admired. 'Beauty of Worcester', a heavenly double blue, grows nearby. Double large-flowered clematis such as this, 'Duchess of Edinburgh' and 'Vyvyan Pennell' should not be pruned, because they flower on old wood, produced last year. If you've recently bought young plants of these, don't be surprised if all you get is single flowers in late summer.

The large-flowered clematis are indeed wonderful plants, even if their built-in death-wish necessitates a changeful collection. I have no less than four different plants of divine, sky blue 'Perle d'Azur', growing through a silver pear tree, over a small myrtle, as a background to a mostly yellow border and on a wrought-iron arch.

If you've never seen a herbaceous, non-climbing clematis before, *Clematis integrifolia* is intriguing. Blue–violet bells on two-foot stems appear for several months. *C. integrifolia* crossed with *C. viticella* produces an excellent hybrid, *C. × eriostemon*, a sprawling, semi-woody (and to date non-wilting) shrub. Now in bud is *C. addisonii*, a must for clematis fanciers. This is also herbaceous, to about three feet, with little upside-down pitcher-shaped, deep violet flowers. Clematis are members of the buttercup family, the Ranunculaceae. My opinion of this family is that they are a greedy lot. To thrive, they should be spoilt rotten with compost, manure, bonemeal, general fertiliser, liquid fertiliser and loving admiration.

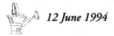 *12 June 1994*

Cutting Clematis Down to Size

I think it was Vita Sackville-West who remarked that clematis hate the touch of the human hand. But touched they must be, for I swear clematis can grow a foot per day in wet weather. Their stems seem intent on tying themselves into an impenetrable knot, wrapping their tendrils tightly around expanding flowerbuds, preventing them from opening. They must be gingerly unravelled and tied to their support. One of the best ways of supporting clematis is to use chicken-wire (the sort with quite large holes).

The rules for clematis pruning can be said in one line: spring-flowering – none, early summer-flowering – a little, late summer-flowering – a lot. So there. For example, spring clematis (such as *C. alpina, C. montana, C. macropetala, C. armandii* and so on) do not need to be pruned at all. Early summer large-flowered cultivars, 'Nelly Moser', 'Lausurstern', 'Vyvyan Pennell', 'Duchess of Edinburgh', 'Beauty of Worcester' etc just need a careful trim in late winter down to the first pair of healthy buds. Late-summer flowering clematis (such as *C. × jackmanii*, 'Perle d'Azur', 'Comtesse de Bouchaud' 'Rouge Cardinal' and all *C. viticella* cultivars) should be given a major hack, down to two to three feet, in winter.

Do not make the same mistakes as I did with *Clematis armandii*. Planted at the base of the south wall of the house, it promptly shot straight up to 20 feet in the first year. Amazing growth, yes, but it makes an ugly picture since the lower half of the plant is entirely naked of leaves. As soon as the fledgling blackbirds have left their nest at the top, the clematis is going to be chopped right down to within three feet of soil level. Have you tried growing clematis on the flat? *Clematis × durandii* has long been successful grown this way. It is growing in a sunny border near a pale blue geranium, 'Mrs Kendall Clarke', and the oriental poppy 'Perry's White', both in bloom at the moment. The clematis is already in bud, and its stems will drape themselves nicely over nearby plants. It produces its indigo-blue flowers until early autumn. One of its parents is the herbaceous *C. integrifolia* and the other well-known deep purple *C. × jackmanii*. It can be pruned hard back in winter.

I disagree with the idea that there is no such thing as an ugly clematis. 'Ville de Lyon' (in the Dublin area anyway) always seems to have yellowish foliage, making an unfortunate clash with the carmine flowers. But this one excepted, clematis are quite wonderful plants. I'm specially fond of all the *Clematis viticella* kinds: 'Purpurea Plena Elegans' (dusky purple double flowers), 'Madame Julia Correvon' (rosy red, very easy), 'Etoile Violette' (deep purple, creamy stamens), 'Alba Luxurians' (white, green-tipped sepals), 'Minuet' (white, mauve, veins), 'Royal Velours' (velvet purple) and 'Venosa Violacea' (purple-edged sepals fading in the centre to white, veined mauve). *Clematis viticella* cultivars admittedly have smaller flowers than most, but I've never known them to get the dreaded clematis wilt and they flower later in summer, when it is good to have something to look forward to.

 *13 June 1993*

Old Roses in their Own League

It is easy to be put off roses by the sort you see sold as cut flowers in cellophane packets – born in the glasshouses of Holland, programmed to flower at any time of year and tightly swaddled to prevent them fully opening before you get them home. By being bred for the mass flower markets, all their charm has been taken away. With neither soul nor scent these are the battery roses of factory gardening. They never seem to reach the beautiful full-blown stage of a fading rose – they just slowly shrivel.

Red is one of the most dangerous shades in the garden, not least because the word brings images of wildly differing colours to mind. With regard to roses, it can mean anything from the eye-hurting vermilion of the rose 'Alexander' (albeit redeemed by good copper-tinted foliage) to 'Guinée', a climbing rose with petals of darkest crimson velvet. The colours most beloved of modern rose breeders veer more towards ferocious scarlets and salmons, with more than a hint of orange. These shades disturb and aggravate, and are far from the soothing, mellow tones of the old roses.

I was far too long in obtaining 'Charles de Mills', an old and very beautiful rose of unknown parentage. Every year I made a note to get it, and then decided against it as it only blooms once. But what a blooming! It is a wonderfully voluptuous rose, the flowers so full of petals that they are furled around each other in a delightful quartered pattern; the colour is a divine mixture of purple and deep red, and it has a scent filled with all the romance of an old rose. Furthermore it has a robust constitution – it is no fragile, antique beauty, that demands constant fussing with sprayer and watering can.

The petals of 'Souvenir du Docteur Jamain' (*c* 1865) are sumptuous ruby red, and the innermost recesses of the flower shade to inky-black. Who was Dr Jamain, one wonders, and why was this rose named for him? Perhaps he faithfully visited the consumptive wife of the rose breeder (Lacharme, in France) or perhaps he was just a notable personage of the town who needed flattering. His rose is repeat-flowering, although it is subject to blackspot, not very vigorous, and highly liable to burn if planted in full sun. But still, a rose of such quality, with a colour and perfume to die for, is a pearl beyond price when you can still find a bloom in late October.

With all the rage for old roses, it is the middle-aged roses that are disappearing into obscurity – those roses bred in the middle of this century such as 'Josephine Bruce' (UK 1949). Agreed, she has poor deportment and a gawky habit, with branches sticking out all over the place, but the rest of her is a lovely bosomy creature, her flowers the epitome of a red rose, large and lustrous dusky crimson with a heavenly scent.

Modern roses should mostly return to where they belong – on the lids of chocolate boxes, or covers of greeting cards – but there is no denying that they do have a value in the garden, which is their propensity for non-stop flowering (just like the poor battery chicken, who lives on the egg-laying treadmill). This can be very useful when you are making a garden picture. I do entertain the rose 'Marlena', and although I don't like her very much she is quite a nice deep blood-red, has good clean foliage and is remarkably generous with her flowers. (It is the shape of these latter that irritates – they seem slightly malformed, with a rather lop-sided air, and as for fragrance, not a sniff of it – she's modern isn't she?) Still 'Marlena' presents a comely sight with the rich bronze-red foliage of *Heuchera micrantha* 'Palace Purple' at her feet, both complemented by a scattering of vivid scarlet *Verbena* 'Lawrence Johnston'.

If you are wondering where to get these roses try ordering them as soon as possible for next year from Carewswood Garden Centre, Castlemartyr or Hosford Geraniums and Garden Centre, Cappa, Enniskeane (both in Cork) or from Murphy and Wood, Cabinteely, Co Dublin.

 *14 June 1992*

It's Bursting Out All Over

The garden is a hive of activity at the moment. The explosion of the greenfly population is almost under control. They had a dose of Roseclear a week ago and of Multirose yesterday. The sprayer now has malathion at the ready for any plants suddenly needing treatment. Specially liable to infestation are roses, penstemons, pinks, violas, berberis, lilies and wall plants in general. Delphiniums are looking good. This year the emerging shoots were thinned by half in March, and the plants sprayed fortnightly with Roseclear, in an effort to prevent mildew, to which the rare old double 'Alice Artindale' is very prone. The thinning of surplus shoots allows air to reach the centre of the plant.

Germination in the seed department has been less embarrassing than usual. Young seedlings are being thinned out and misted over with a hand sprayer several times a day. Cuttings have been taken of fuchsias, penstemons, an alpine phlox called 'McDaniel's Cushion' (I reckon the parent plant is on its way out) plus several recent arrivals – *Alyogyne huegelii* and an exciting new salvia, *Salvia* × *jamensis* 'La Luna'.

The remains of bulb foliage have been cleared away and I've made a note, before all ideas of spring goes out of my head, of good tulips I want more of: 'Burgundy Lace', 'Angelique' and 'Shirley' and parrot tulips for their wonderfully decadent May flowers. Aquilegias, from the deep purple, double granny's bonnet type to the exquisite lemon *Aquilegia longissima*, have come before the selection committee.

Greed is the problem of the moment. I adore poppies and foxgloves, linarias and white mallows – I cannot get enough of them. But some must be pulled up now, before their all-enveloping, rapidly developing leaves smother small neighbours. Laziness is another problem: I didn't bother to order fresh seed of runner beans, and germination of three-year-old seed was so poor that the bean frame has been planted with nasturtiums – a double pale orange – and the perennial *Tropaeolum tuberosum*, a nice thing with blue-green leaves and orange scarlet flowers over a long season. The few plants of scarlet runner beans should tone nicely with these at least.

Bald patches on gravel paths and raised beds are being topped up. Trays of nicotiana are being bought and the plants potted individually, to be used for filling gaps in the border next month. Serious watering is commencing every day for pots under glass and containers outside, every two days for recently planted bedding plants. Staking is on-going – at this time of year I hide stakes and ties in various spots around the garden, to save fetching them from the shed. My co-gardener, annoyingly, insists on tidying them away again. If you haven't already got metal supports – a semi-circle of metal with long legs that you push into the ground – they are brilliantly useful. The ones with shorter legs are good for gentle support for bulging, front-of-the-border stuff; the stronger ones can stay put around shrub roses and peonies. Weeding is now beyond the stage where you systematically work your way through a bed. It is more a case of wandering round with a bucket, hunting underneath leaves and in the crowns of herbaceous plants. Each weed in the bucket means less work later.

This is high season for the reluctant gardener. Herds of them may be spotted, scrabbling among the trays of petunias and geranium pots outside the hardware shops and small supermarkets. Beware buying bedding plants that have been too long in their trays, with starvation signs of yellowing leaves and puny, premature flowers. (When plants think death is imminent, they make rushed attempts to flower and seed.) Buying geraniums at the last minute means a limited selection. Why not telephone Hosford's Geraniums, Enniskeane, Co Cork (023–39159) and ask them to send you some? I saw wonderful plants in their nursery – 200 different varieties. They have twenty different kinds with scented leaves. The clusters of insignificant lilac flowers of 'Attar of Roses' are nothing special, but the crushed leaves are deliciously fragrant. If you haven't got a greenhouse, scented geraniums (*Pelargonium*) will survive winter on a bright windowsill.

 *19 June 1994*

Middle-Aged Roses

Spare a thought for the middle-aged rose. Old-fashioned roses, heavenly as they are, have all the publicity these days, whilst some of the roses bred this century are all but forgotten. 'Mrs Oakley Fisher' (bred in the UK 1921) has soft apricot single blooms, the shape of a Tudor rose. Said to be highly fragrant (I can only detect a faint perfume), she has splendid healthy leaves, lightly flushed with red. There is nothing brash about 'Mrs Oakley Fisher'. One can imagine her namesake drifting round 1920s tea dances or vicarage garden parties, never to be seen without her hat or gloves.

'Frensham' I found particularly hard to come by. It dates from 1946, and, typical of roses bred at that time, has gradually dropped out of fashion. A lovely, real red, clean without being too strident, a highlight of the red border at Tintinhull (a famous National Trust garden in Somerset), I wanted it to replace the odious 'Alexander' (Harkness 1972, eye-hurting, luminous, vermilion).

Incidentally, remember Specific Replant Disease, and never plant a rose in the same spot from which you have just removed another one.

'Nathalie Nypels' is a bit of a fraud. Bred in Holland in 1919, she has managed to masquerade as an old rose, exquisite as she is with her silky, pink flowers with a hint of salmon and obliging modern ways of repeat-flowering; you could do worse than do a mass planting of 'Nathalie Nypels' with an edging of lavender or catmint.

'Madame Grégoire Staechelin' comes in the same category. A superb sugar-pink cabbage rose of Spanish origin (1927), this is a vigorous climber which only flowers once, but at a most useful time, a good two to three weeks before the main flush of roses – all the more valuable when you haven't seen a rose for a year.

Apparently 'La France' was the first hybrid tea ever, bred in 1865, with silver pink flowers and a sweet, old-fashioned scent and a delicate constitution, as befits a grand old lady of the rose world. I finally had to give up growing this fastidious, antique rose, lovely as she was in her rare moments in bloom. Alas, she was a martyr to blackspot, rust and greenfly, all at the same time. (By the way it is too early to congratulate yourself that there is no blackspot this year, for it doesn't usually appear until later in the summer. Spray, at regular intervals from now on, with Roseclear.)

'William Lobb', a true old rose dating from 1855, is in wonderful, mossy bud, each one covered in velvety green chenille. The fragrant, semi-double frilly flowers are a divine blend of soft purple, grey, pink and magenta – no wonder it is the great designer Sybil Connolly's favourite rose. Although it is only in flower for a month or so, it has such good leaves of a bluish hue that it well deserves the space it occupies. You can either let it form a large bush, up to seven feet tall, or else prune it hard to three feet and keep it more compact.

 *20 June 1992*

Placement of Strong Colours is the Key

One day somebody will write a complicated thesis on the subject of why women dislike strong colours in the garden. Most take exception to red, strong yellow and orange in particular, and prefer to drift around in a haze of pastel good taste, choosing flowers in sweet pea colours and foliage in silver grey. And as for white gardens, they have remained supremely fashionable for nigh on half a century, with a seal of approval from Vita Sackville-West, the arch-duchess of twentieth-century gardening.

To miss out on the vivid colour range of scarlet, vermilion, orange and strong yellow is to deny oneself the chance to experiment with the most exciting shades. Like difficult guests at a dinner-party, they simply need some thought as to their placement. Not to invite such plants as the Maltese cross (*Lychnis chalcedonica*), because it insists on wearing startling red and is likely to argue with its neighbours, is too cowardly an approach. Plant it next to *Dahlia* 'Bishop of Llandaff' (the best of all dahlias, with rich purple foliage throughout the season and single flowers of dazzling red) and watch the sparks fly. To further stimulate the company, plant *Crocosmia* 'Lucifer' nearby, a super vigorous montbretia. True, the flowers are an uncompromising shade of red, but the spiky leaves are so fresh a green that the total effect is almost soothing. The dashing red *Verbena* 'Lawrence Johnston' would make a pool of scarlet flowers round their skirts.

The key to using strong reds is to combine them with purple foliage. *Cotinus coggygria* (used to be a rhus) is a highly obliging plant, prepared to adapt itself indefinitely to the gardener's whim: you may do what you like to it, prune it to any size you choose, and plant it in any soil or position.

The almost metallic, shining, plum-purple leaves of *Heuchera micrantha* 'Palace Purple' is a perfect peace-maker to separate the fighting colours from the rest of the party. A plant comparatively new to commerce is *Euphorbia dulcis* 'Chameleon': a must for euphorbia fanciers, it has dusky purple leaves and bracts surrounding tiny lime-green flowers. It is a plant with wonderful wet-day appeal – a delightful sight as the raindrops tremble on the leaves like drops of mercury.

Not all reds are frightening. What about the soft red plush, like the seats in old cinemas, of *Lobelia tupa* for example? If you have never seen this plant, it is as unlike the normal blue bedding lobelia as you could imagine. For a start it is about six feet tall when doing well, has large pale green leaves that are soft to touch, and intriguing velvety flowers. It requires a sheltered sunny position and rich soil; once established, do not disturb.

Orange is admittedly more difficult to control than red. *Lilium* 'Enchantment' is a vicious, strident orange – most unsuited to a lily. But *Lilium henryi*, introduced from China by Augustine Henry in the late 1880s, veering more towards dark apricot, is far more acceptable. The flowers are shaped like turk's-caps and are nicely spotted inside. I am not committing myself as to the exact shade of the spots – Dr E Charles Nelson (known to be a reliable source) describes them in his excellent book *An Irish Flower Garden* as 'green', whereas the new Royal Horticultural Society's *Dictionary of Gardening* (Macmillan) says they are 'black'. (I will let you know when it flowers in August.) *Lilium henryi* is an exceptionally easy, long-lived lily. It does not mind lime, gives a good account of itself on dry, Dublin soil and will flourish for years without division.

 *21 June 1992*

Light-Fingered Green Fingers

A lady remarked the other day that a friend of hers thought 'propagation' meant taking cuttings from other people's gardens. I think she must have paid me a visit recently, for how else to explain a detached piece of *Geranium maculatum* f. *albiflorum* fainting on the ground beside the parent plant? And what on earth could have happened to *Salvia microphylla*? Its young shoots, half-torn from the stems, were waving limply in the morning air. It could not have been a bird, even pigeons – most idiotic of birds – would not be silly enough to try and land on such fragile twigs.

Apart from the tell-tale signs that you have had a visit from this sort of would-be propagator, you can sometimes recognise them in advance by their behaviour. Why, for example when the remainder of the party are continuing around the garden in a clockwise fashion, do they suddenly need to go into reverse? And their progress is punctuated with pauses – to fumble in their handbags for who knows what – sandwiches or extra cardigans or, in the worst cases, a polythene bag (serious propagators never travel without one). They will hover over a plant for ages, fingering the flowers, and the moment you are looking the other way, the shoot is in the bag and the person is gazing blankly into space.

A nice story of horticultural detective work involved a valuable seedhead of a *Meconopsis*, or Himalayan blue poppy, at a National Trust garden in Perth, Scotland. The director of the garden had anxiously watched the single seedhead on the plant slowly ripen. He was just about to collect the seed, but when he went to do so it had vanished. There were only two visitors in the garden, a man and his wife, and the only clue was a footprint in the soil near the plant from a shoe with a distinctive pattern. The director approached the couple, and politely remarked to the woman, 'I think you've got something stuck to your shoe.' As soon as she lifted her foot to investigate, the pattern on the sole was revealed. Finally, after a heated argument, the seedhead was returned.

Incidentally, the euphemism 'light-fingered' sounds quite charming, almost as if the fingers are doing a little ballet dancing, or playing a pretty tune. But let us be quite clear about it, taking cuttings in somebody else's garden is stealing.

The trouble with would-be propagators of this kind is that their fingers are usually as green as they are light – if they took a cutting of a telegraph pole it would probably take root. They would also know that now is the high season for taking summer cuttings – old fashioned roses for example root quite easily just as the flowers start to fade from the first flush of bloom. Pretend you are picking a rose for the house, with a stem about six inches in length, preferably with a little 'heel' of older wood. Trim off the faded flower, and cut off neatly the tail end of the heel. Take off one or two pairs of lower leaves. Make a mixture of two parts of damp peat, and one of horticultural sand. Take a small pot (say three inches in diameter), fill up with the mixture and make firm. Insert the cuttings round the edge of the pot, making quite sure that each cutting is firmly in position. Water, using a can with a fine rose. Firm gently again. The idea is to keep the leaves of the cutting fresh and plump with moisture, without drowning them, until they get the idea of sending out roots. How you organise this depends on your general gardening arrangements. Put the cuttings in a propagator (the sort with a clear plastic lid, not the light-fingered sort) or under an old-fashioned glass bell-jar. Keep them shaded in hot weather, and regularly mist over the leaves with water from a hand-sprayer. In a month to six weeks they should have rooted and you can gradually admit more air. Pot them off individually when you see plenty of new growth.

 *28 June 1992*

July

When Some Plants are More Equal than Others

The garden is an undemocratic place. There is no doubt that some plants are more equal than others. They insist on the garden equivalent of a stately home – rich soil, a sunny aspect, and water supplied on demand. Delphiniums, for example, are not worth growing, unless you're prepared to stand over them with a silver salver of bonemeal – plus stakes, string, slug-stuff, water, compost, and an anxious eye on the weather.

At the other end of the class spectrum are the common or garden plants. 'Why haven't you got alchemilla?' remarked a visitor. 'You're always going on about it.' Indeed I do have it. Very fond of it I am. But not for a moment is it allowed to grow in the best positions. *Alchemilla mollis* (lady's mantle) produces its flowery froth of lime-green just as well under a bush. This is the sort of plant that will grow in a dustbin corner, the draughty alley running between two houses, or in dry shade – the garden equivalent of the Bronx.

Dustbin corners require some thought. The smartest dustbins I know are surrounded by wooden trellis-work painted dark green, entwined with white clematis 'Marie Boisselot'. Very *House and Garden*. The problem with dustbins is that they usually sit on concrete, not a substance noted for being garden-friendly. But the smart dustbins mentioned above were situated on soil, so it was possible to grow large-flowered clematis. The only clematis tough enough to grow in a hole in concrete would be *Clematis montana*. This clematis would be suitable for planting in the passageway between two houses, where with a lot of encouragement it could be persuaded to transform a windy alley into a magic tunnel. By the way, large-gauge wire netting is a cheap and unobtrusive clematis support – it weathers fast and is easily put up.

Now to the Bronx – the dry shady area with which we all have to contend. (I'm not talking about the no-go area beneath a coniferous hedge, where almost nothing will grow, although I do know a thriving colony of autumn cyclamen under a massive elderly yew.) The three premier plants for dry shade are *Geranium macrorrhizum* and its hybrids, *Euphorbia amygdaloides* var. *robbiae* (lime-green flowers, year-round rosettes of healthy dark green leaves on a three-foot clump) and the inestimable Japanese anemones. Go round your garden today. Note plants occupying premier positions that would do perfectly well in any old corner. Note plants which could benefit by a move upmarket.

 *3 July 1994*

Keep Your Eyes Down

The chief problem of gardening is one of application. How often does one set off with the firm intention, say, of watering the beans, only to be so distracted *en route* that you never get there? Well, there was the rose that needed deadheading, so you had to go back for the secateurs. Going to fetch the secateurs, you spot some seedlings crying out for water. Returning with the watering-can you pass petunias, in even more urgent need of water. Now you may as well deadhead them whilst you are about it. Now back in the deadheading mode, off again for the secateurs. But on the way to the shed you notice a hairy bittercress, loathsome weed, its seedheads just about to burst. Imagining all the valuable time it will save you to remove it then and there, straight away your mind is on weeds alone, all ideas of deadheading immediately vanishing. Beyond the bittercress is a miniature forest of meadow grass, so much of it that you need a bucket to collect it in. Off again to the shed for the bucket.

As usual, all the buckets have migrated to the compost heap area. Typical. Something at last achieved, you collect a bucket. But on the way back to the meadow grass, horror of horrors, a delphinium is leaning over and just about to snap. Focusing forthwith on staking alone, you make a temporary prop for the delphinium with the bucket, and rush off for a stake and some string. Usually at this point the telephone rings, and everything gets forgotten.

Gardening and pottering are synonymous. Amazing how long you can spend doing nothing whatsoever. But although the nicest part of gardening is wandering round in a daze, wondering at the flowers and scents and colours, what you need to run a garden is plenty of work ethic. The only way to get some simple task (such as watering the beans) done, is to head for the beans with a can of water, looking neither to the right nor to the left. Look down at all times, and try not to notice any weeds in the path.

The lazier you are the more diligently you should weed. For every weed you remove before it seeds, you are giving yourself an extra few minutes lazing time. The enemy of the moment is a sneaky little epilobium. Earlier in the year it was a small rosette of bright green (very fooling to those new to gardening as it looks more like a choice alpine plant). The epithet 'weedy' could have been invented for the epilobium, for its mean and grubby pink flowers. Adept at concealment, it is often already in seed before you spot it.

But there is one excuse for not weeding too carefully, and that is self-sown seedlings of plants you want to keep. Watch out now for seedling foxgloves. If you haven't room to grow them in a spare patch of ground, plant the seedlings in seed trays and fatten them up for planting out in autumn. One can never have enough foxgloves for their miraculous midsummer spires. If you only want white ones, examine the seedlings carefully: ones that are going to be white have no trace of pink on the backs of the leaves.

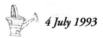 *4 July 1993*

Plants 'Lost' to Drought

'I lost it,' is a remark you will often hear, referring to a plant that has died, just as if it was a handbag. Correctly translated, in the world of gardening, it means 'I killed it.' If you have been losing a lot of plants recently, the most probable reason is that you forgot all about them. The garden in summer is so laden with flowery distractions and intoxicating scents that you may have spent too much time walking round in a haze of admiration. Established plants are forming leafy umbrellas, beneath which a small plant can quickly thirst to death.

Even if you did water immediately after planting, what exactly did you do? If you only lightly sprinkled the leaves with drops of water, it may well have looked very pretty, but would have done no good at all unless the roots were thoroughly soaked. For a herbaceous plant you should apply at least half a large can of water and for a young tree or shrub, two large watering-cans. Newly planted plants should be soaked at least twice a week, unless there has been heavy persistent rain.

To qualify 'rain' for a moment: although heavy rain will reach open areas of the garden, trees and shrubs form a rain canopy, below which smaller plants can remain dry. Take special care to water plants growing near walls – north walls in particular deflect rain and the soil beneath them can be very dry.

One way to conserve water is to mulch the plants. A mulch is a layer, four to six inches deep, of bulky organic material – partly decayed manure, garden compost, shredded bark or spent mushroom compost. Make sure the soil is clear of perennial weeds – dock, ground elder, convolvulus etc. Thoroughly soak the soil before applying the mulch (two cans per square yard). Don't allow the mulching material to actually touch the stems of the plant, as it could cause them to rot. Mulching prevents evaporation of water from the soil, greatly reduces germination of annual weeds and eventually rots down and adds humus to the soil. But beware of mulching all plants indiscriminately. Small sun-loving herbaceous plants, alpines in general and pinks (*Dianthus*) in particular do not like a thick layer of organic matter tucked round their necks. A layer of washed pebbles or pea-gravel is ideal for these plants, and not only keeps down weeds and conserves moisture but also assists drainage round the collars of the plants in winter.

It is not until you have 'lost' a great many plants that you will deserve the attribute 'green fingers'.

 *5 July 1992*

In an English Country Garden

Last weekend I went to stay with my brother in Berkshire. Arguments began the moment I arrived about the design of a rectangular section of the garden to the side of the house. We paced the site back and forth, sticking stakes in the lawn to mark the position of the proposed surrounding hedge. As soon as I moved the markers two feet one way, he moved them five feet the other. Should the hedge be beech or hornbeam or yew? Should there be a wall instead? The argument subsided briefly when we sat down to eat, but raged once more when anointed by bottles of wine and sunshine.

He refused to understand that the hedge should continue the whole way round, ie on three sides of the plot (with the house on the fourth). It was no use pointing out that what he wanted was like having a picture with one side of the frame missing. In desperation, I dragged him along to visit Hidcote, a garden in the Cotswolds designed by Lawrence Johnston early this century, a must-visit place for all aspiring gardeners. Johnston, one of the fathers of twentieth-century gardening, started the whole idea of making garden 'rooms' – formal compartments surrounded by hedges or walls. A garden divided up this way allows different themes to be developed in isolation.

On a hot hayfeverish Monday afternoon we arrived in the car park at Hidcote, now owned by the National Trust. Never let it be forgotten that the Trust is a huge business. The fact that the properties are owned by its members doesn't stop one feeling on arrival like a pig ready to be processed through the sausage system. Irritated by the suspicious attitude of the cashiers as she inspected my £20 note, unimpressed by the exceedingly good taste green-painted wooden gothicky litter bins at the entrance, we began the tour. Gardens are meant to be places for quiet contemplation, for gazing at flowers, for restoration of spirit. But a visit to a famous English garden at the height of the tourist season is more like a battle. Ladies in cotton frocks attached to reluctant husbands panted on shady seats. Batteries of cameras queued up to snap the famous Red Borders. Flowers wilted in hot windless corners. Unseemly shoving took place on narrow paths.

Manners were strained to breaking point, despite cries of pardon, excuse me and sorry. Flowery scents hung on the air intensified by the warmth. Tickets had been bought and regardless of the flow of the crowd the throng of garden lovers struggled on, determined to enjoy.

I noticed a clever bit of planting – I think it was in the Pillar Garden. By that time I'd pointed out so many hedges to my brother and said sorry so many times on narrow pathways that I'm not certain which room we were in. You could see rows of herbaceous peonies and one or two tree peonies – all heavenly in late spring, but now finished. I then spotted the follow-on plants for late summer – there were masses of strap-shaped agapanthus leaves, emerging lilies and fuchsias tucked among the peonies.

But in the little garden near the large old cedar, which is underplanted with a cottagey mixture of flowers in pastel colours and silver foliage, was a prominent patch of bare earth. Hidcote can have upwards of a thousand visitors per day (at £5 per head). With such an income there's no excuse for less than perfect standards. What about Canterbury bells? What about sweet williams? So what if plants in this area must be laboriously changed three times a year?

From a congestion of lavishly planted compartments, you look through restrained grassy vistas to the countryside beyond. On such a rolling sweep of lawn, I met a largish lady in a wheelchair. Thinking that, I for one, was going to behave in a civilised manner, I asked her if we could help her down some steps. Not a bit of it. She climbed out, man-handled the chair down the steps, clambered in and trundled off. Suspiciously muscular arms protruded out from what was definitely a frock as opposed to a dress. When we reached the area of the old French roses, there she was, having obviously got there before us. But it was only when we joined the ice-cream queue, after being nearly asphyxiated by the smell of chemical pot-pourri in the Trust's shop, that I understood. There she was, fit as could be, ordering a large cone, her chair parked in a prime spot in the shade.

The following morning my brother announced his decision on the hedge. It was to enclose the garden on all sides – all his idea of course.

 *9 July 1995*

The Splendour of Opium Poppies

For a few weeks I adore opium poppies. Their vibrant colours introduce fresh sparkle to the borders. And every year I marvel at the design brilliance of their pearly, grey-green seedheads, and wish I was a silversmith making elegant cruets of silver seedhead peppers and salts reclining on silvered leaves. Then suddenly I've had enough of opium poppies, as their fading stems start toppling over, and I crossly yank them out, all except those wanted for seed.

Your own seed strain of opium poppies is remarkably simple to organise. I inherited washy lilac poppies only, but by marking any slight variants – lighter, darker or faintly pink – with a cane, and letting only these drop their seed, I now have cherry red, rich purple and rose-pink.

The most ethereal annual poppies were given to me as Cedric Morris's fairy poppies (now marketed by Thompson and Morgan as 'Fairy Wings' or 'Mother of Pearl'). Their flowers are composed of petals gossamer-fine, in muted hues of peach, dusty pink, and smokey greys and mauves, some with a picotee edge, some traced with lines of infinite delicacy, others with petals like shot-silk – the colour changing with the angle from which you view the flower. (Note: the first year you grow poppies from seed you'll probably only get disappointingly spindly plants, but when they become established self-seeders you'll get proper results.)

Now for some poppy relations. *Meconopsis quintuplinervia*, Reginald Farrer's 'myriad dancing lavender butterflies', comes from Tibet and China. Tuffets of basal leaves are clothed in stiff, russety hairs. The solitary, nodding, four-petalled flowers are borne on 15-inch stems. I am honoured that this heavenly poppy graces my garden. The plant spreads slowly by underground runners, easily detached for propagation. The sort of plant you can never rely on, I regularly transplant a spare piece to a different spot.

I once rashly grew some Welsh poppies, *Meconopsis cambrica*, from seed. There's no controlling these Celts, they seed precisely where they fancy, usually into the centre of your choicest specimen. But their yellow flowers vividly illuminate a dull corner in dry shade by the yard gate, dotted through the green fronds of the male fern, *Dryopteris filix-mas,* the most forgiving fern for such a position.

Double Welsh poppies (*M. cambrica* 'Flore Pleno') are considerably more sober in their habits. They seed themselves mildly, roughly 70% double. Singles must be taken out the instant they reveal themselves. Their vivid colours positively glow from the centre of my new orange, yellow, blue and white bed. Oriental poppies are just going over and their bristly leaves are looking a mess. Three plants will grow up to disguise them: gypsophila, *Clematis* × *durandii* and perennial sweet pea (*Lathyrus latifolius*), this last often suggested by Miss Jekyll for that purpose.

 *10 July 1994*

Underneath the Arches

Are you bored with your garden? Does it seem to lack something no matter how many bedding plants you stuff in? Are you itching to make some instant and dramatic change? It could be that it needs some height. A tree you think. But the trouble with trees is that they are often unpredictable. They do not necessarily grow to the height required and then, conveniently, stop. What you need is a man-made height. An archway, bedecked in climbers, spanning a path, invites you to investigate further. Or a series of arches, forming a tunnel, will give an illusion of length in a small garden.

Arches can be bought ready made so you can change the look of the garden by lunchtime. Or you could have sophisticated metal arches made to you own design. (Harry Page of Structural Welders, 67 Leeson Close, Dublin 2 is full of good ideas: their arches, rustproofed and painted matt black, should last a lifetime.) In a country garden a rustic effect of an arch made of larch poles would be more appropriate.

Another satisfactory way of creating controllable height is by planting an ivy and training it up a pole, seven feet or so in height. This adds a touch of formality, giving the same effect as an Italian cypress (*Cupressus sempervirens,* a tree not reliably hardy in colder parts of the country). Such a strong upright feature acts as a full-stop at the end of a vista or flower border, drawing the eyes onwards and upwards, adding a pleasing and evergreen note of sobriety in a border of mixed flowers and bulging shrubs. The pole should be bedded in cement. It should preferably be metal, but you could use a stout wooden pole treated with a wood preservative safe to plants (creosote gives off injurious fumes and should not be used). Wrap the pole in several layers of chicken wire. This will give something handy to tie the ivy to at the beginning. The best way of deciding where to place your instant height is to invite some tall friends to a gardening lunch and make them stand round the garden afterwards pretending they are columns of ivy. More romantic friends might like to act like columns of clematis or honeysuckle. Keep going back to the main viewpoint of the garden and adjust the friends accordingly.

Runner beans trained to climb up a frame are another excuse for some instant height. Harry Page (mentioned above) has just made me a wrought-iron wigwam of six uprights, reinforced by two circles, one about a foot from soil level and another higher up. With curlicues on top surrounding a decorative metal knob, it is nice to look at throughout the year.

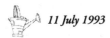 *11 July 1993*

Silver Brings a Little Order

You may have a flowerbed that never seems quite right. It is a higgledy-piggledy conglomeration of plants, a confusing mixture of shape, form and colour, and however much you shuffle the plants around it never presents a pleasing picture. One simple answer that often works is to add some plants with silver foliage. Most of them grow relatively quickly, and even if you plant them now, they should be making their mark by autumn.

Artemisia 'Powis Castle' may well be a common plant, but it is a wonderful rectifier of planting mistakes, be it of colour scheme or plant association. For a start, it has a nice, comforting, rounded, cushiony shape – a soothing hummock of foliage, to contrast, with spiky-leaved plants, or bold large-leaved plants like hostas or bergenias. But it is also a great diluter – of other colours, I mean. Glaring clashes will melt away when modified and softened by the finely-cut, feathery, silver leaves, which will have formed a gleaming mound of platinum by autumn. It looks well near any colour, particularly so near lavender-blue flowers.

You could never say that *Artemisia ludoviciana* (the western mugwort from the USA and Mexico) is well-behaved. It runs about all over the place, and you will even spot it waving cheerily from the middle of a clump of your best herbaceous plant. But it too is wonderful for bringing the whole flower border together. 'Such an artistic arrangement,' remark passers-by, little realising that it has nothing whatsoever to do with you – as its running two-foot stems, wreathed in frosted silver leaves, rapidly colonise the border, winding their silvery route through everything they meet, to delightful effect. It likes a sunny place, and when it gets too much of a good thing, you cut the stems off for the house – I am told that it is one of the best grey foliage plants for flower arranging.

Now to a plant which is admittedly hard to come by, *Senecio candidans*. Its leaves are quite remarkable. Large, oval and shining silver, the reverse of the leaves is almost white, and their undulating edges catch the light. It is only when it flowers that it betrays its origins, for it is merely a groundsel in disguise. It has miserable, squinny, ugly yellow flowers of a groundselly persuasion. It grows on the beaches of the Falkland Islands, in cool, wet conditions, thus it dislikes hot sun and too dry a position.

Gardening lore has it that all grey and silver-leaved plants come from dry areas such as the *maquis* (dry scrub close to Mediterranean shores). The reason their leaves appear silver is that they are closely covered in fine hairs to protect the plant from losing too much moisture from drying wind and sun.

But there are exceptions to this rule (as with the paragon above, *Senecio candidans*), and also with *Anaphalis triplinervis*. (You probably do know this plant but never knew its name. It is the silvery-grey plant that flowers in autumn, with little starry papery-white everlasting flowers, found in most old gardens.) Very easy to grow, in early spring it makes tidy rosettes of pleasant grey foliage at ground level and remains neat all summer, before a long autumn flowering season. As it comes from damp meadows and light woodland high in the Himalayas, it is one of the few grey-leaved plants that will take part shade and damper conditions. Use it to provide cool patches of grey in your shadier borders. Do not be fobbed off with *Anaphalis margaritacea* var. *yedoensis*, an altogether more straggly customer.

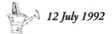 *12 July 1992*

How to Bear with the Bores

Gardeners who are content to take pleasure from their own gardens alone lead impoverished lives. Good gardeners are passionate garden visitors. Gardens, rather than words about gardens, are the best teachers of the art and craft of growing things. There is something to learn in any garden, be it an unfamiliar plant or the imaginative use of an ordinary plant. Every garden has its unique personality, where you go to 'consult the genius of the place'. I adore visiting gardens, and get a fair number of visitors myself, most of whom are delightful – say 99 per cent. One per cent came last Tuesday.

She arrived unannounced at the door. She had beetle-shiny eyes and a cotton hat set at rather too jaunty an angle. I showed her out to the garden and hurried back to the word-processor. Hidden by a curtain of *Clematis armandii* and abutilon I spotted her through the window thoughtfully fingering a geranium. Whereupon (thoughtful fingering is invariably a danger signal) I immediately forgot work. I'll have to mind this one, thought I.

Standing beside my regale lilies – neither their beauty nor their scent was remarked on – she launched into a monologue about her garden back in Sydney, dropped a few names of southern hemisphere gardeners I'd never heard of, and finished with some handy advice on lily growing for me. Of all bores, the Gardening Bore is perhaps the worst. As a guide to garden visiting, I've compiled a list of rules:

1. Weeds. Pretend you don't see them, and on no account think you are doing a favour by pulling them out.

2. Don't go into the flowerbeds to look at some plant. Squashed plants may never recover. You can always assume it is safe to walk on grass, unless a sign says not to.

3. Ask permission before you take photographs. It will usually be given, but it is a courtesy to ask. Tripods can easily damage plants.

4. If the plant has a label, don't pull it out, wave it around to show your friends, and stick it back either through the crown of the poor plant or in the wrong spot causing much mystery to come. Instead ask what the plant is – you'll probably learn how to grow it too.

5. Hovering furtively over plants causes anxiety to the owner and it goes without saying that taking cuttings, seeds or little pieces around a big plant and stuffing them in your pocket is forbidden. If you have unbearable lust for a plant, ask which nurseries stock it.

6. Don't ask the Latin name for a plant without listening to the answer. Don't giggle foolishly and say 'How d'you expect me to remember that?' A notebook and pencil waved around will show the owner you're serious and you'll be able to buy the exact plant you've seen, instead of the 'frilly pink thing with green leaves'.

And there are two rules for garden owners: Never say 'Pity you weren't here last week – the garden was so much better,' which implies a failing on the visitor's part. And never agree, however modestly, that the garden looks nice.

Good Gardens Guide (Ebury Press) lists over 1000 of the best gardens in the British Isles and Europe and includes a good section on Irish gardens.

Work this week

Reading about a cross old lady who 'took it out on the flowers by cutting their heads off' has nearly put me off deadheading. However, deadheading is vital to the look of the garden for the remainder of summer. Foxgloves and poppies, except those wanted for seed, are off to the compost heap. Roses, violas, campanulas are checked over almost daily. Early herbaceous plants such as lupins, irises, peonies, polemoniums, doronicums and columbines have old flowering stems removed unless seed is wanted. Twiggy, just-flowered wood of deutzias, weigelas and philadelphus should be cut off to allow space for young stems to develop. Bedding plants – argyranthemums, verbenas, petunias, pelargoniums and even marigolds – will flower for longer and look better if regularly deadheaded. Newly-planted shrubs and trees, suffering from recent drought, should be well watered (two cans minimum per plant) and heavily mulched (4–6 inches deep) with well-rotted manure or compost.

 *16 July 1995*

The Art of Containing Plants in Pots

Mrs Esther Merton is famous for her containers. Last week I went to see them for myself. Mrs Merton's garden (The Old Rectory, Burghfield, Reading, Berkshire) is only open some Wednesdays, so there was quite a crowd when I arrived. The sun beamed down. Cars were queuing to park in a buttercuppy field.

Little parties of three or four went round the garden discussing every plant. Each member of the group seemed duty-bound to report on how the plant in question was doing in their own garden. Their strident voices carried over the double borders, disturbing the serenity of the old roses, and echoing from the lily pool below.

I hate the word 'container'. It reminds me of something that holds margarine or washing powder. Mrs Merton's plants were growing in something far more elegant – extremely large, undecorated, terracotta pots. These were arranged, majestically, in a straight line on the terrace, against the mellow crumbly brick of the Old Rectory. So surrounded were they by enthusiasts that I had to wait to catch a glimpse between the straw hats and whirling notebooks.

The pots were absolutely brilliant. The most pertinent thing about them was that each had an important, very large plant in the middle, four or so feet high, such as a cordyline, phormium, abutilon or datura. Thus (including the height of the pot itself) each pot was a tumbling mass of colour, six feet or more in height, full to bursting with closely planted flowers and foliage. My containers are wimps compared to hers. When planting next year's display I'm determined to copy Mrs Merton by putting a giant plant in the middle.

Perhaps the most dazzling was a pot planted with different shades of red, centred on a fine purple-leaved cordyline. (Cordylines, like puppies, are invariably sweet when young, it's only when they get a bedraggled underskirt of old leaves that they lose their charm.) *Fuchsia* 'Thalia', the one with the deep bronzed leaves and pendulous, tubular scarlet flowers, featured prominently. There was a tall, velvety red salvia (probably *Salvia coccinea*) and rich deep red *Mimulus glutinosus* propping up its neighbours and also leaning gracefully over the edge of the pot. There were several plants of a red (I think it was a double) ivy-leaved pelargonium. A variegated form of *Helichrysum petiolare*, with soft grey and cream leaves, wove its way through everything else, adding essential contrast to the mostly dusky foliage.

Another of Mrs Merton's splendid creations was in softer tones: the spiky leaves of a purple-leaved phormium in the middle of the pot provided strong architectural contrast with a pretty little variegated fuchsia, 'Sharpitor', which has flowers of palest pink. (For some reason this fuchsia, unlike all others, is a brute to propagate.) *Verbena* 'Sissinghurst' in shocking pink, pale pink double zonal pelargoniums, a standard *Fuchsia microphylla* and a pink francoa completed the picture. Mrs Merton's garden is very special. If you get a chance do go there.

Later on that day I went to Green Farm Plants, John Coke's nursery near Farnham. This nursery is full of wildly exciting plants. They don't post. You have to go there. (You'll need a furniture van and an overdraft extension.) I managed to get a plant there that I saw once, nine years ago, and made a note 'must have', namely *Prostanthera walteri*, one of the Australian mints that makes me go wobbly at the knees: the colour of the flowers is extraordinary – greeny–grey finely etched with maroon, reminding me of dragon-flies' wings. Even if the plant recovers from being squeezed in its newspaper sausage, by a

throng of returning World Cup fans at Heathrow, I suspect it will have
to be cosseted under glass.

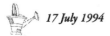 *17 July 1994*

When Blue is the Colour

'What on earth did you mean, a blue gypsophila?' said I to a friend who
badly wanted one. Weeks later I have realised what she means. Of
course – *Limonium platyphyllum* or sea lavender, its flowers an airy
cloud of lavender-blue, which hover like minuscule butterflies over
shiny green leathery leaves. A plant that takes a few years to show what
it can really do, since to begin with it does little but attract slugs. From
there on, it's a dream. Well-adapted to dry soils, it insists on sun and
good drainage to remind it of its native home on the wind-swept
steppes of Russia. One illustration in *The Gardens of Russell Page* would
convince you. (By the way this book, by Marina Schinz and Gabrielle
van Zuylen, (Stewart, Tabori & Chang, Inc, 1991) is an education for
gardeners at every level.) Here you see limonium interplanted with
santolina and lavender, all within formal box-edged beds, to heavenly
effect, as if the garden is covered in a haze of blue mist.

Greed will out when it comes to limonium – one immediately wants
more of it. Gardening books will announce that it can be divided. Last
year, I tried this, to near-disastrous results. The foliage fainted leaf by
leaf, there were few flowers, and the plants dwindled before my eyes. But
this year all is well, and I can hardly wait for them to bloom. Obviously,
whether just planted or newly divided, limonium takes time to get its
roots down and going. Blue, in many different shades, is a colour to
crave as summer progresses, to counteract the plethora of yellow daisy
flowers to come – coreopsis, rudbeckias, heleniums and so on.

On a constant search for something blue to take over after the
delphiniums, I'm trying *Galega officinalis*, an old-fashioned plant that
people seem to have forgotten about, not exactly blue, but you can get a
nice pale lavender. Individual florets are like miniature sweet peas, and
the unopened buds form a charming shape like a pointy hat at the top

of the flower spike. Around four feet in height, it forms a satisfying, long-lasting clump of hazy mauve. Very easy to grow, you can divide it every year to make further groups.

One of the taller bellflowers, *Campanula lactiflora*, is an indispensable plant for the July border. To be had in various shades of milky blue, all desirable, its flowerheads form a great mass of little bells. (The pink one, 'Loddon Anna', is a somewhat grubby pink, and needs careful placing, perhaps near purple foliage.) Cupid's dart, or *Catananche caerulea*, has been flowering for weeks and will go on for many more. It is only about 18 inches tall, and a frontal position in full sun is an absolute must. If you cannot find plants in the garden centre, it is easily grown from seed, and should flower in its first year. Papery silver buds open to lavender-blue cornflowers with dark eyes.

Pure bright blue is rare at any time of year and is specially desirable in late summer. *Salvia patens* is a blue to dazzle with, whilst its paler form, 'Cambridge Blue', is self-descriptive. Two feet tall at most, it requires sun and well-drained soil, where it will make a good perennial, although usually considered half-hardy. Easy from seed if you cannot buy plants.

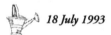 *18 July 1993*

Soothing Scented Geraniums

My first recollections of scented-leaved geraniums (strictly speaking pelargoniums) were from visits to my godmother in Edinburgh. An austere person, equally devoted to the church and pedigree border terriers of the yapping kind, she ate her porridge standing up (with salt rather than sugar, of course) in proper Highland fashion – to avoid being surprised by the enemy while having breakfast.

Her house, Georgian Edinburgh at its most forbidding, was a triumph of Scottish cleanliness. The only relief from the atmosphere of wax polish and gloomy piety were the scented-leaved geraniums, which crowded in their terracotta pots on every windowsill, their leaves pressing to the windowpanes, reaching towards the light, each leaf inclined towards what little sun managed to filter down between the tall buildings. The adaptability of plants never ceases to amaze – for these plants, native of South Africa, grew and flowered with abandon, despite the fact that most of their windowsills overlooked the sort of basement areas where 'damp souls of housemaids . . . sprout(ing) despondently'. Although gaunt and woody with age, the leaves of the plants, when pinched or crushed, exuded rich and varied fragrances – of peppermint, rose, apple and nutmeg – and to sample their different scents was one of the few diversions from the daily round of church and dog-walking.

Constance Spry gives a recipe for geranium-flavoured apple jelly and the leaves can be used to flavour sponge cakes (one leaf in the bottom of the tin), custards and in bags of herbs to scent linen. The rose geranium *Pelargonium* 'Graveolens', is widely used for the production of geranium oil. Three to look out for are *Pelargonium crispum* 'Variegatum' (tightly frilled variegated leaves), 'Lady Plymouth' (a good form of the rose geranium, with leaves prettily margined in cream) and *Pelargonium quercifolium* (the oak-leaved geranium, strongly scented of balsam). They all make superb, long-lived house plants, unlike many other plants recommended for use in the house which after a few months turn into the sort of poor, sad creatures you see in badly run zoos. They are easily grown from cuttings and if you cannot find them in garden centres, try visiting godmothers or elderly aunts.

Mrs Beeton recommended that a scented geranium leaf should be floated on the water on each finger bowl at dinner. You might consider that finger bowls are an unnecessary affectation these days, or people wouldn't know what to do with one – indeed a friend of mine once drank the water from one by mistake – but it is still nice to know what is the appropriate item to float thereon. Mrs Beeton also suggests using a leaf of the lemon-scented verbena, *Aloysia triphylla* (formerly known as *Lippia citriodora*). If you haven't got this plant, put it on the list immediately. The crushed leaves have a delicious, sharp lemony smell, remarkably soothing for headaches in general and bad temper in particular. It will live for years in a pot (brought under cover in winter) or planted at the foot of a sunny wall outside.

Lavender leaves and flowers have more crushability than any other plant – their fragrance is so reviving, they are a must for any garden. All lavenders are good, but one more so than all the rest. It is irresponsible of me to recommend a plant that is hard to find, but still the charms of *Lavandula* × *intermedia* 'Hidcote Giant' deserve to be widely trumpeted. (Do not confuse it with the very well-known *Lavandula angustifolia* 'Hidcote', a much smaller but still good plant, with a comparatively short flowering season.) 'Hidcote Giant' is three feet tall, is highly aromatic and flowers for months and months, producing a constant succession of fresh flowering spikes, which is just as well if you pick another one every time you go by. If you want to dry lavender, pick the flowers when they are at their best – the temptation is to leave them on the plant too long. Tie them in bunches and hang them upside down in an airy place. Lavenders must have sun and good drainage and should be clipped over after flowering to keep the bushes tidy. After five to seven years the plants will have become straggly, and full of dead wood. They will need replacing – try to anticipate this by taking cuttings – they root very easily at this time of year.

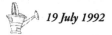 *19 July 1992*

Spanish Non Secateurs

I'm sitting under a bougainvillea tree in Deia, Majorca. The mistral blows in warm enervating gusts, swirling magenta petals along the terrace. Parasols clatter, metal on metal. A fat man huffs and sploshes in the pool. Cypresses sway in the wind. Blue plumbago tosses in the air and bashes down on the walls. Sun filters through a haze of heat. Runnels of moisture drip from my glass through wooden table slats. Am now feeling guilty about doing nothing.

Yesterday I climbed a hot and dusty little road up to the church. Little gardens were shaded by figs, grapevines, ancient olives twisted with age, and oleander hedges in white, pale pink and crimson. Curtains of ivy-leaved geraniums draped walls, intermingled with orange campsis. Huge succulent rosettes of spiny agaves guarded expensive villas. The agave is commonly known as the century plant, which refers erroneously to the great age that some species attain before flowering – even the very large take only 30-40 years. The houses were silent, siesta quiet, the only sound was of the crow of a cockerel and the distant rev of a motorbike. Behind the church a little cemetery commands a view of encircling mountains, unequalled in the area. My feet scrunching over dried pine needles, I picked my way past family vaults, the outline of bricked-in coffins disturbingly close to the sunny world outside.

A narrow path bordered in irises led to the plot of Robert Graves, his headstone surrounded with lavender, white alyssum, petunias, gazanias, santolina and artemisia. I set off down hill towards my hotel, examining the flowers *en route*, wary of eyes staring through closed shutters. I, of course, would never dream of taking cuttings on holidays. As for taking polythene bags with me, heaven forbid. For those unable to resist temptation, here's some advice.

Pelargoniums are well worth taking cuttings of – indeed they root better if the ends of the stem have dried off in transit. Also you may find old cultivars on holiday that produce more flowers than modern ones. Beautiful as they are, I don't think it's worth taking cuttings of oleander (*Nerium oleander*) – there's not enough sunshine here to induce proper flowering, and furthermore the leaves are extremely poisonous. Likewise, *Lantana* or shrub verbena, is unsatisfactory in Ireland. The trumpet creeper, or *Campsis radicans*, a rampaging twiner, with exotic clusters of large flowers in orange reds and apricot, will certainly grow, but rarely flowers unless grown in the hottest of positions. Bougainvilleas make good pot plants, flowering well with confined root-runs, but may need a heated propagator to root.

Plumbago auriculata (formerly *P. capensis*), the climber with heavenly clusters of pale blue flowers, roots easily and makes a good short-term pot plant. Free-range plumbagos grown in the greenhouse border are slower to flower. The terrace at my hotel was decorated with large shrubs of *Datura*, or thorn apple. Pollinated by nocturnal moths, it has a fabulous heady evening fragrance and huge dangling trumpet flowers. The delicious almost evil smell seems to warn you that all parts of the plant – particularly the flowers and fruit – are toxic. *Datura* was used as sacred hallucinogen by the Aztecs – never sleep under a flowering datura, or you may never wake up. Their leaves are prey to every sort of fly, and a martyr to red spider. Young plants are easier to cope with –

even these need a large pot – and are best brought outside for summer, where they are marginally more resistant to red spider.

This week

Deadhead from morning till night. Gather foxglove seedlings and grow them on in rows for planting out in autumn. Sow newly-ripe hellebore and columbine seeds (these are both members of the Ranunculaceae or buttercup family, of which the seed must be sown fresh).

Trim rock plants and propagate by division or seed any deteriorating with age. Trim just-flowered shoots (about a foot) off carpenterias. Feed pot plants regularly as their containers fill with roots. Clip box hedges and ivies on walls. Cut out weak wood from old-fashioned roses, trying to leave the centre of the bush open to the air.

 **23 July 1995**

Short Back and Sides for Summer

What your garden looks like for the remainder of summer very much depends on what you do now. You can get away with it in May. You may get away with it in June. But July is quite another matter. The major deadhead of the year has just been done. It took a week, and the garden is all the better for it. In many cases the dividing line between deadheading and pruning disappears: old-fashioned roses which only flower once – 'Charles de Mills', 'Céleste' and 'Madame Hardy' and suchlike – have had weak and old growth removed and sappy young shoots cut back by about a third.

Weigelas, deutzias and philadelphus, beautiful in flower but undistinguished in shape, have had old flowered stems cut back. Established wisterias should have all the young, willowy growth cut back to five or six buds (two to three inches) from the old wood – or so say the gardening books. In reality I find that with the rapid growth of wet summers you need to snip a wisteria practically every time you pass it. The same goes for *Chaenomeles* (japonica or Japanese quince).

Fading delphinium stems are being cut to the ground and the plants given a few handfuls of general fertiliser, three cans of water, and two buckets of manure to encourage further flowers in September. *Campanula persicifolia*, and violas are being deadheaded daily. Petunias are done twice a week. Make sure you nip off the faded flower *behind* the fattening seed-head: the whole point is to stop the plant setting seed. Coarse, messy oriental poppy foliage can soon be cut to ground level, without detriment to the plant, but all other herbaceous plants must be allowed their stems and leaves to nourish the roots.

Box hedges and topiary have just received their annual trim. I once asked a novelist exactly what a 'certain age' was – he having written a book about a woman thus described. I've now discovered the definition for myself. 'A certain age' applies to those women who dislike box: they grew up during the anti-box period, when box hedges were being torn out by the mile, accused of being labour-intensive and harbourers of slugs and weeds. Yesterday a garden visitor remarked on the amount of box in this garden, and commented on all the work required. Nothing would convince her that you only have to trim box once a year.

Now the answers to a few recent queries. Somebody moving house next spring wanted to know about taking some peonies with them. I do agree about peonies – older varieties are difficult to find, and they're such long-lived plants they may have sentimental value. Peonies move best in early autumn. I'd recommend dividing and potting up the plants in October ready for the move. Another query involved some perennials grown from seed. Should they remain in their pots? I think not. They grow so fast they would begin to starve and would be much happier planted out until the day of the house move.

 *24 July 1994*

Stressed Out Among the Greenfly

I was told by good authority the other day (admittedly the same type of authority as myself, who believes implicitly in planting on a rising moon and suchlike) that an ailing plant emits a sound which can only be heard by greenfly, who immediately rush to the attack. Which could explain why a sick plant is always covered in greenfly – a typical chicken-and-egg argument that could go on for ever.

The modern complaint of stress is not only suffered by bored housewives and currency dealers, but plants too become stressed out. If greenfly move in, to add their excrement (euphemistically known as honeydew) to the leaves, this sticky substance will in turn provide ideal growing conditions for sooty mould, a fungus which clogs the pores of the leaves, preventing proper functioning, and further aggravates the plant. (The leaves can be gently cleaned with a damp cloth.)

The answer is to prevent stress in the first place. Lack of water is the commonest cause. First the leaves assume a lacklustre look, which is rapidly followed by wilting. (I always feel the past participle of 'wilt' should be 'wult'. This would much better describe the poor sad object before you.)

One of the most fooling thing about potted plants grown in peat-based composts is that the surface of the potting mixture looks nicely dark and moist. It is only by picking up the pot and testing the weight that you can decide whether it needs watering or not. If it is suspiciously light, rush the patient to the water barrel or bucket of water and submerge the whole thing for an hour or more. Peat composts shrink away from the sides of the pot and if you only trickle some water on the top of the pot, it will all wash down the sides.

Lack of food – plant nutrients – is the next obvious cause of stress. One sign of a starving plant is that it makes a stupendous effort to produce flowers and set seed, in a mad last fling to reproduce itself. Leaves become pale and wan, and the plant seems to stop growing. This is probably caused mainly by deficiency of nitrogen. (Lawn feed consists mainly of nitrogen, which is why an application turns the grass green almost immediately.)

Signs of iron deficiency are usually seen on lime-hating, ericaceous plants – camellias, rhododendrons and heathers (except for *Erica carnea*, which tolerates lime). The leaves go yellow *starting at the leaf margins*. Often confused with shortage of iron is magnesium deficiency, in which the yellowing starts between the leaf veins. Many plants – trees, shrubs, perennials (my delphiniums had it this year) roses and chrysanthemums – are often affected by the latter.

The results of stress can be slow to show. Tender shrubs which have undergone a series of frosty nights might take several months to die. A slow death is unbearable to watch, and with a plant easily rooted from cuttings, take several and, as soon as they're rooted, dump the parent.

Now it is time to go round the garden to decide which plants need replacing, while the weather is warm enough for cuttings to root. The recent heavy rainfall has explained why certain shrubs have constantly ailed – tell-tale puddles around the plants showed that the water-table was so high roots were not growing but drowning. Flooding has also killed many gypsophilas and other plants which must have well-drained soil.

Anyway, at the first sign of a yellowing leaf, *do something* – there's no excuse not to, there are so many good liquid fertilisers available. Lashing around the Miracle-Gro or Phostrogen is a soothing occupation for the stressed-out gardener and will certainly benefit the plant.

 *25 July 1993*

Bearding the Irises

Bearded irises are the very last plants you want to think about at the moment, what with the first dahlias just opening, Michaelmas daisies starting to flower and autumn cyclamen already in bloom. Most gardens have a few irises stuck in an odd corner – you know that clump of spiky pale green leaves, that hasn't produced a flower for years? Even if an odd flower does appear in June, and you resolve to look after them properly, there are so many other flowery distractions by now (the ideal time for division) that irises have gone completely out of your head.

Dividing bearded irises is the sort of job you could put off forever, but remember that if you do force yourself to get on with it, the ugly knobbly surface roots known as rhizomes, if correctly dealt with now, are capable of producing sumptuous flowers for next summer, with colours ranging from deep velvety black (as in 'Interpol') through cherry red, salmon and ice blue to white. Their glistening petals are sometimes wonderfully frilled at the edges.

The method is as follows. Lift the plant with a fork and you will see that the outer, younger rhizomes have started to form fat, new white roots. Cut off and discard the old central rhizome (with tatty, dying, brownish roots) and replant the outer bits in soil enriched with well-rotted garden compost (one bucket per square yard) and bonemeal (a handful per plant), placing them on the surface, and firming the soil around the roots. The more the rhizomes are ripened by the sun, the better the flower.

Cut the top of the leaves off by at least half, otherwise they will act as a sail and the wind will rock the plant out of the ground. Keep them nice and moist for the next few weeks. Irises prefer limey soil, and it must be very well-drained. On heavier soils, plant them on top of a slight mound of soil to assist drainage.

Apart from demanding one of the best positions in the garden – open to all the sunshine going, by late summer they are looking decidedly messy, with blotchy leaves going brown at the tips. But there is one magic bearded iris you must hear about. This is _Iris pallida_ subsp. _pallida_ (more familiar as _I. pallida_ subsp. _dalmatica_). It has all the natural grace of a species, being identical to those found growing in the wild in what used to be Yugoslavia. Wild plants are invariably a perfect balance of flowers to foliage – as plant-breeders interfere in an effort to produce larger flowers in startling shades, they remove all natural elegance (rather like reproductions of antique furniture always seem out of proportion).

Once with a non-gardening party of people near Dubrovnik, who hadn't the least desire to look for plants, I ended up taking a stretch black Mercedes taxi into the interior to look for plants and, much to the bewilderment of the taxi-driver, ended up with colchicum, two euphorbias and a few rhizomes of this delightful iris.

 _26 July 1992_

Canna Keep a Good Plant Down

Until recently, you only had to say dahlia to clear the dinner table, and canna was a dirty word. But plants are subject to fashion just like anything else: cannas are rapidly rising in the charts, after years in the slough of naffdom. And just to whisper the Bishop will establish your position among gardening cognoscenti. (Note pronunciation of *Dahlia* 'Bishop of Llandaff': the Llandaff bit should be pronounced in the Welsh way – Clandaff.) By the way, the height of gardening chic is *Dahlia* 'Bednall Beauty'– similar to the Bishop, deep bronze-red leaves, glowing red flowers, only two feet tall. NB: Have now gone off 'Bednall Beauty' – it doesn't produce enough flowers.

Cannas were popular in Victorian times as an important element of tropical bedding, the perfect opportunity for rich merchants of the industrial revolution to show off. Plant hunters were exploring the jungles of the world, bringing back fantastic new species. Tender plants were all the rage, requiring regiments of gardeners to move their heavy pots out of sheltering hothouses for the summer. Exotic species with spectacular foliage were arranged in circular beds. Often the soil in the middle of these beds was mounded into a ridiculous hillock, better to show off the central palm or cordyline, like a giant plum pudding. This was the heyday of the canna, a tropical plant of the ginger order. Cannas have silky, orchid-like flowers. Their super large leaves make excellent contrast to the insignificant leaves of most bedding plants – the purple-leaved and variegated foliage varieties are worth growing for their foliage alone, as are the handsome sword-shaped blue–green leaves of *Canna glauca*. *C. iridiflora* is one of the tallest, with beautiful rosy-pink pendulous flowers. You can grow cannas without a greenhouse or conservatory, by lifting the roots in autumn, keeping the rhizomes nearly dry in a shed for winter, and repotting in a rich compost in spring. Plant out in late May in full sun. Easily propagated by division – leave a fat snout on each portion.

The steeple bellflower, chimney bellflower or *Campanula pyramidalis* is mysteriously unfashionable, probably because it is best grown as a biennial. You have to remember to sow it in spring, then it takes a full 18 months to bloom late the following summer. You see it depicted on embroidered pictures, beside thatched cottages and hollyhocks done in knot-stitch. The stems at flowering times are fully six feet tall, bedecked with hundreds of bellflowers in blue or white. My theory is that it isn't called the chimney bellflower because of its height, but because unless you grow it in pots which can be brought into the house and put beside the chimney to decorate the hearth for the summer, it isn't worth growing. Bees will kill to get at the flowers, which crumple the moment they're pollinated. In a bee-free sitting room the chimney bellflower provides marvellous decoration for nearly a month, a great six-foot pillar of blossom. More flowers come out each day, and stay in bloom for weeks, ever hopeful for a visiting bee. I've just repotted this year's seedlings, and they'll need repotting again before being put in a rich well-drained mix in their final flowering pots next spring.

Even last century William Robinson in *The English Flower Garden* was rather sniffy about the old pot marigold or *Calendula officinalis*. This commonplace and easy plant is just as beautiful as any pampered rarity. Sow the seeds now for late autumn flowering – in sheltered spots it will flower until Christmas. Pot marigolds are ideal plants for children's gardens, window boxes and for quickly filling late summer gaps. The daisy flowers range from cream to deepest orange, but I like best the ordinary yellow and orange ones, some with brown eyes. If you can only get a modern seed strain, let the plants self-seed back to the original, near-wild types. I've a patch of marigolds surrounded with blue-leaved hostas, silver artemisia and *Brunnera macrophylla* 'Langtrees', which looks rather good.

The Romans used the juice of calendula as a cure for warts and by the Doctrine of Signatures it was used for treating jaundice. Gertrude Jekyll gave over large areas of her garden at Munstead Wood to calendula to send to the field hospitals in France during World War 1, where it was used as a haemostatic (to stop bleeding). The petals may be used as garnish for salads, in meat and fish soups and summer drinks, and also as a colouring in cheese, butter, rice dishes and cakes. I just ate a mouthful of petals – I can't say they tasted of anything particular.

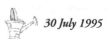 *30 July 1995*

The Magical Appeal of the Secret Garden

I must tell you about a superb piece of planting. Imagine a north-facing corner between high walls, the deeply-shaded narrow beds beneath the walls dust-dry. Gloomsville personified, or so it was, until transformed by John Bourke of Fairfield Lodge into a magical courtyard, sparkling with light and bright colour, complete with quietly trickling water into an oval basin. How did he do it?

First John painted the two concrete walls pale terracotta, the sort of shade that makes you think of Tuscany and ancient sun-baked bricks. He then attached wooden trellis to the walls to form arched niches, painted the trellis matt dark green, and built the raised oval basin of water in the middle. Apart from supporting climbers, the arches in the trelliswork prettily frame the planting. A lawn would be impossible to manage in such a position, so the remainder of the area is paved.

When you enter this little enclosed garden you're almost dazzled by light, for the planting is entirely on the theme of yellow, from bright gold to palest primrose and chartreuse. No other colour intrudes. The basic, evergreen structural planting consists of a pair of variegated hollies, *Ilex* × *altaclerensis* 'Golden King', standing sentinel at either side of the pool, a good aucuba, its dark green leaves broadly splashed with yellow, ivy 'Goldheart', *Choisya ternata* 'Sundance' and a large golden privet, clipped into the shape of an obelisk. The golden hop, *Humulus lupulus* 'Aureus' romps gaily along one side, reaching annually to 20 feet, entwining itself with everything else, a golden philadelphus and berberis at its feet. (An important note about many golden-leaved plants, these three in particular: in full sun their foliage is inclined to burn to a harsh yellow, but in shade the leaves are luminous lime – very nice.) The Spanish broom, *Sparteum junceum*, still splendid in middle-age, sends showers of golden-yellow pea-flowers from 15 feet above. Gaunt in habit, the appearance of this shrub much depends on judicious annual pruning. An endless supply of yellow blossom is provided by *Abutilon* 'Canary Bird' and *Euryops pectinatus*, a bulging shrub with delicate ferny leaves and cheerful yellow daisies. (These last two are both tender and should only be tried outside in mild gardens.)

Annual frivolity is provided by the climbing canary creeper, with blue–green leaves and lemon flowers, plus a dashing array of golden nasturtiums. Two standard yellow roses, 'Chinatown', in white-painted square wooden tubs, mark the entrance to the conservatory opposite. Coping with deep shade at the foot of a wall and consequent dryness (walls absorb moisture like a sponge) has been dealt with by using a special hose with many little perforations, through which water seeps. The hose remains *in situ* throughout the year.

The large umbrella leaves of *Astilboides tabularis* were in the pink of condition, due to the presence of the hose. A known moisture-lover, this is one of the finest foliage plants you can get (it used to be known as *Rodgersia tabularis*). It was beautifully complemented by its neighbours, the golden-leaved raspberry, the golden form of *Tanacetum parthenium*, yellow Welsh poppy and various ferns.

One of the cleverest things in this small garden is the unusual use of a common plant, namely *Euonymus* 'Emerald 'n' Gold'. (The name alone is tiresome enough, what with its two extra apostrophes.) This euonymus often suffers the indignity of being planted on roundabouts or, worse, being used as a focal point in heather gardens. But here, clipped into squares, it was occupying no less than five square wooden tubs. I like John's idea of having foliage colour that he can move around, giving patches of sunlight wherever he wants.

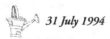 *31 July 1994*

August

The African Violet

The African violet or *Saintpaulia* is the perfect plant for those who like peeping through a lace curtain at passersby, for whereas it enjoys the bright light of a windowsill, it likes to be screened from strong sunshine by a muslin curtain. I have never been much good at growing these plants, but last week I met somebody so modest he professed to be hopeless at horticulture in general, but finally admitted that the one thing he wasn't bad at was African violets.

With the benefit of a lifetime of precise thinking, this retired accountant waters them exactly once per week, by standing them in a saucer of water. Watering should unfailingly be done this way, he said, for overhead watering may cause the plants to rot. The temperature of the water should be tepid. Every two years, no doubt on the same date, the collection is repotted, using a peat-based compost, Levingtons's to be precise. 'Be absolutely certain,' said the accountant, 'not to use too large a pot.'

African violets come from tropical east Africa and they range in colour through white, various pinks, rosy red and different blues to dark purple. Basically, they like the same temperature that we prefer, 17–25°C (63–77°F). Best of all they like kitchens, I was told, for they love the humidity, so if you are growing them in the dry atmosphere of, say, a sittingroom, stand the pots on wet pebbles in a tray. The evaporating water apparently creates a gently moist microclimate, and reminds them of their jungle homes.

My one and only African violet has had a horrible time since it arrived; it has spent the last eight months on the kitchen draining board, being splashed on occasion with washing up water, and acting as a general dust attracter. Still, it has put on a bit of weight in the form of extra leaves and has been making such an effort, under adverse conditions, that yesterday I took pity on it and repotted it according to the accountant's directions. Its poor leaves were so dusty that I washed them with a small brush and the requisite tepid water.

 *2 August 1992*

160

Border Patrols Stepped Up

There was I, minding my own business, deadheading a bulbinella under a bush, when the umpteenth argument of the day began. As you know, August is the season for garden arguments. I and my co-gardener have the row about the missing secateurs daily, the one about me hiding life-threatening thorny bits in the compost heap weekly, whilst the tug-of-war with the hose over whether it's on the lawn or the borders continues long into the night. The language of these discussions is not pretty.

The dead heads of the bulbinella (an early-flowering herbaceous plant, somewhat like a kniphofia) were destined for the compost heap. In this garden, the compost heap reigns supreme. Like a monster animal, in its wooden-slatted cage in the yard, its great mouth lies open, ever ready for a snack. My co-gardener, unreasonably fussy about its diet, was uncertain about the suitability of bulbinella heads. (If he had his way, it would be fed on a soufflé of grass cuttings and freshly minced weeds – I would simply chuck in everything regardless.)

The garden, like an ageing beauty, is subject to rapid collapse in August. Finished herbaceous plants are leaning on their neighbours, exhausted from the effort of flowering. Sagging stems must be propped up, and the garden relentlessly patrolled – tweaking and tidying, snipping off dead heads, removing yellowed leaves, and stirring up sun-baked soil. Mildewed phlox, struggling with drought, may revive when cans of water are sloshed on their roots. If water is in short supply, forget lawn, annuals and early herbaceous stuff, and save it for young trees and shrubs. Roses are remarkably resilient – even if they drop their leaves through stress, they'll recover and flower again in autumn. I was chatting to my friend the reluctant gardener the other day. He returned from his holidays to find the lawn burnt brown, his sweet peas gone to seed, his house plants pathetically drooping, and his pond emerald with algae. Lovingly watered seeds, from Monet's garden at Giverny, turned out to be only weeds. He'd nearly stung himself to death by grabbing at the bindweed that was strangling the nettles.

But he'd had the odd spectacular success: a forgotten packet of morning glory seeds sown in the spare bedroom had come up and entwined themselves into such an impossible tangle that he had planted the whole tray out in one piece. Now, to his enormous delight, trumpets of glorious blue were appearing daily. He'd also succeeded in growing white petunias to flowering stage *without* a greenhouse. Some feat. Post-holiday house plants in a distressed condition may recover if cut back and soaked in a bucket of water for an hour – peat-based compost once dried out is impossible to re-wet otherwise. We discussed foolproof plants that look good in August. *Lavatera* 'Barnsley' is one such – sun-loving, drought-resistant, long-flowering with pretty light pink flowers with a red eye. It is a brittle short-lived shrub. The wand-like stems need shortening in late autumn to make them sturdy in winter winds and they may need a further trim in spring.

Among bedding plants, cosmos are excellent drought-resisters. Mine are still looking good in rock-hard, cement-block, unwatered soil. Yuccas, lavenders, pineapple broom (*Cytisus battandieri*) smile through the hottest drought.

Plant of the Month has to be Russian sage or *Perovskia atriplicifolia* 'Blue Spire'. The effect of a single specimen is a ravishing soft misty blue, with grey aromatic foliage. Every time I see this plant I wonder why I didn't plant a hundred. The species itself is a native of Afghanistan, growing in rocky, open places, so plant it in full sun. (I'm a great one for these instructions, if only I could follow them – last year I planted three, in what I thought was a prime sunny spot, beside white gypsophila. This year the gypsophila lost control of itself, as did a nearby blue anchusa. Typical.)

Lastly, if you're looking for an unusual large (15-foot) evergreen shrub, try *Itea ilicifolia*. This has glossy dark green leaves and small holly-like prickles. Slender racemes of tiny lime-green flowers, up to one foot long and fragrant of honey, appear in August – looking cool and beautiful in an otherwise dusty month.

 *6 August 1995*

Happily Growing Beside the Seaside

I've just come back from the seaside. The real seaside I mean, the bucket and spade sort, where entertainment is a turn on the giant waltzer or a ride on the beach ponies. In the small fishing town of Elie, on the east coast of Scotland, the downtown area is deserted by 11 at night, despite festoons of beckoning lights.

Matrons were heading for the bakery in search of their morning rolls as I set forth to study the gardens. I wanted to see which plants would grow within a few feet of the sea, where even grass must bow to the relentless, salt-laden wind.

In one little garden, instead of a grass lawn there was a thrift lawn (sea pink or *Armeria maritima*), formed of stiff little tuffets of linear leaves covered in pale pink flowers. No plant better withstands being constantly washed by sea water. The occasional gap between plants was filled with pebbles and sand.

I was hoping for some brilliant enlightenment on the subject of seaside trees. I have to report that the common sycamore rules OK, but I did see some gnarled laburnums (with no sign of wind damage to their leaves), within a few feet of the sea wall. The roses were absolutely brilliant, the healthiest I've ever seen. As always by the sea, privet was doing splendidly – even if damaged by winter wind the leaves are always quickly renewed. Griselinia and olearia, the ugly New Zealand couple, are often seen at the seaside. Griselinia makes me think of little men in a leaf factory stamping griselinia leaves out of sheets of pale green plastic.

Now to the flowers. All of the jolliest, commonest sort, they were revelling in the sunlit seaside air. Marigolds glowed, nasturtiums gleamed, and the colours of petunias and geraniums seemed extraordinarily vivid. Exuberant pinks were second only to the roses in vigour. Montbretias were behaving predictably, as were fuchsias, pretending they were natives, just as they do in the west of Ireland. Campanula and valerian were seeding into the walls. Alyssum romped everywhere. Lavateras, short-lived shrubs of the mallow family, were providing non-stop flowers, each with attendant bumblebee. Scabious, thyme, catmint, lavender and santolina – just the plants you'd expect in seaside gardens – tumbled over each other in their enthusiasm to grow.

Leaning over the garden wall of a house forbidding as only a Scottish house can be, I spotted an echinops, one of the globe thistles, a genus of which I'm especially fond. The flowers were iridescent light blue. Very desirable. I debated with myself whether I dared approach the front door and engage in discussion, with the owner, of the weather and the price of fish, until conversation could be steered towards globe thistles, and the infinite reasons why this particular cultivar should be tried in Irish gardens. Suddenly a sheep dog, with the wild look a sheep dog has when chasing cars, the whites of his eyes rolling, leapt out at me. Neither 'Wally' nor 'Spot' nor even 'Rover' said in soothing tones had any effect on his humour.

The front door opened and a person appeared. I wouldn't call it a lady, more a Boadicea, in full armour of belted mackintosh, hairnet not entirely hidden by a scarf, and shopping bag to the ready. Being Scottish myself, and knowing there are certain types not to be trifled with, I fled.

 *7 August 1994*

New Perspective with Plants on the Move

Many plants in this garden are suffering from nerves. As well they might, for they are likely to spend most of the summer in the wheelbarrow, being trundled up and down the garden, in a final attempt to plant them for once in the right place. Occasionally, with a flash of inspiration, a decision is made straight away where to move them to, but more often than not they go back in the barrow and remain in limbo for weeks.

'We can't have this,' I thought as I noticed that a large clump of toad lilies was smothering *Thalictrum diffusiflorum.* Just the sort of treasure that is easily lost if you don't mind it properly, this meadow rue from Tibet is as tricky to grow as it is divine.

Life in Ireland is tenuous enough without being sat on by hefty neighbours. So the toad lilies were moved *en bloc*, with much heaving and muttering (on the part of the movers, not the toad lilies), and their roots flooded in with copious cans of water. (If you are going on holiday, don't attempt such drastic summer transplanting until you get back, when you can carry on the watering regime until mid-autumn.)

Plants must sometimes be moved for aesthetic reasons: a filipendula, for example, of an especially dangerous shade of pink, which annually waves its feathery plumes next door to a scarlet rose. And what about the pink phlox growing near *Crocosmia* 'Lucifer'? Something has got to be done.

Make notes of clashing disasters while the plants are in flower, and then shuffle them about in early autumn. But I sometimes find, as with the filipendula, that the exact shade of pink is impossible to remember, so I shall move it when the last of its flowers is just going over (fading). Then there are the host of plants which must be transplanted because they are not growing as well as they should – their position may be too dry, too crowded or too shady.

Last week I transplanted several miniature rhododendrons. They (and related plants, other members of the Ericaceae) all transplant easily as they have a neat ball of fibrous roots. When you dig up a fibrous-rooted plant, you will find that the roots are wound together in a tight mass, so the plant is barely disturbed during transplanting.

I also moved (for the third time) a nine-year-old, six-foot camellia, which has the same, easily-moved type of fibrous root system. Plants with roots shaped like a carrot (such as eryngium or sea holly) are nigh impossible to move without severing their roots, and take long to recover, if at all.

Another reason for moving plants is that you cannot see them properly when they are in full bloom. In drenching early July I transplanted several epimediums; their remarkably pretty flowers deserve close examination in spring, and they are now within easy reach of the path. Note I am saying 'transplant' which is quite another thing to 'divide'. I wouldn't attempt division for epimediums at the moment. However, some easy early-flowering perennials such as geraniums, heucherellas, primulas, brunneras, trollius, bergenias and lamiums could be divided now to make larger groups – this will save time in the autumn, when a million and one plants will need attention.

To consider again the poor plants languishing in the barrow. Well, there's the three kniphofias for a start – an orange, an apricot and a bright yellow. They were originally planted next to the rose 'Madame Isaac Pereire' (light magenta), forming an eye-hurting combination. So they are being moved up to be planted near blue-leaved hostas, seakale, blue agapanthus and *Aster amellus* 'King George'. So far, so good. But I forgot to mention that *Geranium psilostemon* (magenta, black eye) already grows in this new area, which now, in turn, will suffer the indignity of being put in the barrow.

Whilst the geranium would look good near the rose 'Charles de Mills' (velvety purple) up the other end of the garden, any space there is already full of plants. Unless, of course, they too join the throng in the barrow. But I suppose life in the barrow, however uncertain, is preferable to instant death in the compost heap.

 *8 August 1993*

Willmott's Prickly Ghost

The first sea holly I met, growing in the sand dunes near Dog's Bay in Connemara, was the native Irish *Eryngium maritimum*. 'Eryngo' means the candied root of the sea holly and for centuries this plant was considered an aphrodisiac, it was used to flavour jellies and conserves, and the candied roots were used as kissing-comfits (a perfumed sweetmeat for sweetening the breath). It has beautiful grey–blue jaggedy leaves and pale blue thistly flowers. Like all its family, it needs well-drained sandy soil and full exposure to sun: despite trying it three times in the garden (nursery-bought plants, take note, not plants dug up in the wild), it did not take kindly to captivity. But other members of its genus are spectacular, easy garden plants, mostly flowering in July.

The jewel in the crown of the sea hollies has to be *Eryngium alpinum*, about three feet tall, an incredibly fine, lacey, electric-blue ruff (quite soft to touch) surrounds the central cone of flower, and the effect of the plant in bloom is one of shimmering, silvery blue. It comes from the high meadows in the European Alps, and thus requires an open, sunny site (and perhaps the distant sound of cow-bells). Admittedly it is not easy to get, but such a sensational plant is worth hunting for. Also up in the top bracket is *Eryngium × oliverianum* – free-flowering and a good blue, but without the beguiling lace-like frill.

Eryngium bourgatii, in its cultivar 'Oxford Blue', is the star turn among the smaller eryngiums. Its leaves alone, conspicuously patterned in silver, are attractive from spring onwards and the colours of this plant when in bloom are unbelievable – the flowers open pale silver, gradually suffuse with deep blue, whilst the stems seem washed in violet ink.

A highly prickly reminder of the famous gardener Ellen Willmott (1858–1934) is *Eryngium giganteum* or Miss Willmott's ghost. By all accounts she was not the most likeable person, very rich and notoriously bossy. Her garden at its peak was said to require 104 gardeners, all in uniform. Never short of an opinion when garden visiting, if she considered some plant was lacking from the garden in question she would surreptitiously scatter some seed, as she did with this eryngium. A biennial, the first year all you have is a strange new seedling, but the following summer this develops into a striking greenish blue spiny flowerhead. It gradually pales to a ghostly grey white. Lovely as it is, luminous in the twilight, its brittle seedheads can still give you a vicious jab – a fitting memento of this unpopular, but highly talented lady gardener. (One can imagine the relish with which her contemporaries, tongue in cheek, christened this plant.) Like all eryngiums, it has a root like a carrot, easily snapped during transplanting, so does not move well; but once bought and allowed to self-seed you will never be without it.

The second rank of eryngium begins with *Eryngium variifolium*. The flowers are less exciting, more green than blue and just as prickly, but the mounds of marbled silver and green leaves contribute for a long time to the garden scene. *Eryngium planum* is not a bad little thing, seeding about with small blue flowers, but definitely in the second class.

None of these plants will do well unless they have absolutely full sun and well-drained fertile soil. Furthermore, except for *Eryngium giganteum*, they take some time to settle down and flower. Seed of several species is available from Thompson and Morgan. Once they have germinated, do not overwater them. They sulk when kept too long in a pot and are best planted out when young. Before falling into the beginners' trap of ordering *Eryngium proteiflorum* (sometimes listed as *Eryngium* Delaroux) be warned: it looks a fetching brilliant turquoise in the catalogue (heaven knows how many filters were used to get this colour) but it is decidedly tender and by November, when it is just starting to get the message about flowering, along comes the frost and finishes it off.

 *9 August 1992*

The Yellow Rose that Taxes

Yellow is a dangerous colour. Strong yellow is explosive in the wrong position, and gleams with such ferocious intensity that it pales all nearby flowers to oblivion. American daisies, such as brassy *Rudbeckia fulgida* 'Goldsturm', are specially difficult to place – indeed some years ago I dug up 'Goldsturm' and gave it away – although redeemed by fetching black eyes, its harsh yellow was too dominant to take. (I'm not talking about soft primrosey yellows – these intermingle nicely with softer schemes.) I then decided not to be to cowardly about yellow, and set about making a new Yellow Garden.

Put yellow next to blue flowers or foliage, and its dazzle will be cooled to an acceptable level. You can also diffuse its brilliance by planting it among drifts of silver leaves. Or, conversely, make it even more radiant by mixing it with orange flowers. 'Goldsturm' is now reinstated, in a place of honour.

I've flirted with the idea of planting the herbaceous climbing golden hop, but have been warned of its over-enthusiastic behaviour. Instead, the still-scarce climber *Dicentra scandens* drapes the north-facing wall. It too has invasive tendencies – not running at the root – but its pretty fern-like leaves and charming pale yellow locket-flowers are all-enveloping of neighbouring plants. Copious seed is set, which doesn't germinate for me, but late summer cuttings are easy.

Many's the rude remark I've made about modern roses. But 'Arthur Bell' is one of the exceptions. On a good healthy disease-resistant bush you have several tones of the same yellow all at once – the flowers vary in colour depending on their age, from the deep yellow of the buds to the pale lemon of the fading flower. Several groups of 'Arthur Bell' join another of my efforts at repetition, a series of Bowles' golden sedge, *Carex elata* 'Aurea', planted along the front of one bed. This and another favourite yellow grass, Japanese *Hakonechloa macra* 'Aureola', are still looking fresh despite summer heat. Be warned – the hakonechloa is agonisingly slow to clump up.

All-important blue foliage is provided by *Hosta* 'Halcyon' – the best of the lot in my opinion, its leaves still blue and unmarked by summer – and the sumptuous ice-blue large frilly leaves of seakale. Earlier blue flowers, Jacob's ladder (*Polemonium*) and *Geranium sylvaticum* 'Amy Doncaster', toned down a profusion of yellow doronicums and *Anthemis* 'E. C. Buxton'. Just over, *Campanula persicifolia* and *C. lactiflora* acted as neutralisers for a startling patch of orange and yellow double Welsh poppies.

Last night I had visions of two adjectives scuttling off down a drain, namely 'beautiful' and 'lovely'. They had to be tempted out again to be attached to – of all plants – daylily 'Marion Vaughn'. Daylilies or hemerocallis are the epitome of plants for the non-gardener – dull, but instant bare earth fillers, the plant equivalent of wall-to-wall carpeting. But *Hemerocallis* 'Marion Vaughn' is truly lily-like, and the size and quality of her lemon flowers unsurpassed.

Not all kniphofias or red hot pokers are red hot. Residents of the Yellow Garden are desirably pale yellow 'Little Maid' and her mother 'Maid of Orleans', 'Apricot' (self-explanatory) and other shades from egg-yolk yellow through to orange. In bloom at the same time as deep blue agapanthus, they need similar conditions – the best place in the garden in rich soil and full sun with no water shortage – they admirably complement the kniphofias. I rather like yellow and silver together, as in *Achillea* 'Moonshine', which has bright yellow flowers and silvery cut leaves, and, more subdued, *Achillea* 'Taygetea'. I've continued this theme by planting *Verbascum* 'Frosted Gold', with a river of pale grey *Artemisia ludoviciana* and marigolds running through. Tall stalwarts towards the back include blue aconitum, a super yellow helianthus like a refined sunflower, blue and mauve Michaelmas daisies, orange *Lilium henryi*, and thuggish, pretty soft yellow *Helianthus salicifolius*.

Work for the week

- Cans of water aimed at the roots of plants are more beneficial than wasteful sprinkling.

- Take cuttings of pinks, ceanothus, fuchsias, lavender, santolina, achillea, ivies, pelargoniums.

- Start making notes of plants to be propagated, divided, dumped, moved to new positions.

- Feed container plants, unless long-term fertiliser (Osmocote) is in their potting compost.

- Stake dahlias.

 *13 August 1995*

Putting Manners on the Garden

The garden is starting to annoy me. It always does in August. The magical, flowery look of a few weeks ago is rapidly becoming an overgrown muddle. Much can be done to sort it out.

I shall start with the major prune of the year. Ivies on walls, of which I have many, will be trimmed hard back, allowing time for fresh growth to appear before winter. Pruning ivies is a nasty, itchy, dusty operation, best done with secateurs rather than a hedge-trimmer. Apple trees will be summer-pruned, cutting the young growth back to about five leaves. (Don't prune leading shoots required to form the framework of the tree.)

Hardy abutilons will have their shoots reduced by about a third, to prevent windrock. As usual *Elaeagnus* 'Quicksilver', the lovely silver-leaved shrub, has started to outgrow its space, and will be pruned quite hard – this happens every year and it doesn't seem to mind.

Lower branches are being removed from the cornelian cherry (*Cornus mas*) to allow more light for spring bulbs below. (Don't go near the wedding cake tree, *Cornus controversa* 'Variegata', with secateurs, except with very young specimens to remove a surplus leader). A honeysuckle, a pyracantha, a rampant summer jasmine and an over-large fuchsia will also be pruned. The silver pear will be thinned, by removing some of its inner branches right back, and its petticoats trimmed. Lavenders and grey-leaved plants such as artemisias, senecios and santolinas are all the better for a trim now; the plants will be nicely furnished with fresh growth by October, when many silver plants look their best, and will make neat and tidy shape for winter.

Gardeners fall into two categories. The Hacker, with glazed eyes and mind elsewhere, approaches any shrub regardless, slashes it about, appears bemused at the piles of mutilated vegetation at his feet, and proceeds to the next. His opposite number is a timid woman in a neat white blouse and navy blue cardigan. Secateurs in shaking hand, she approaches a shrub, can't make her mind up where to cut, and retreats indoors.

You should aim at somewhere between the two. Stand and stare at the shrub in question. Perhaps if you removed that branch the plant would be better balanced? Would neighbouring plants benefit if you reduced its height?

Perhaps you'd be better to grow a new plant from a cutting and then discard the old one? Are you too soft-hearted? When you have two valuable shrubs, growing where there's only room for one, all you'll have eventually is two poor specimens. Decide now to remove the one you like least.

Years ago Christopher Lloyd (I think) wrote that gardens in early summer would look after themselves, so that you should concentrate on late summer flowers. I agree – if the garden doesn't look good in June you might as well give up. Plants that are looking good here now include agapanthus – in blue, white and wonderful palest grey – hydrangeas, in particular 'Annabelle', with huge globular heads of creamy flowers – fuchsias, crocosmias, gypsophila, *Lilium henryi*, phlox, dahlias, aconitums and lavateras.

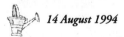 *14 August 1994*

So it's Off with their Heads

I think it was Aldous Huxley who best described falling out of love. As the person loses their magic, you start feeling guilty. Nobody enjoys feeling guilty all the time, so this gradually turns to dislike of the person who causes the guilt. There are certain plants which have had exactly the same effect on me. I remember the time I saw a new potentilla, in what was (at the time) a staggeringly unusual shade. 'Red Ace' it was, to be precise, and most desirable it seemed. (Until fairly recently, red and pink were unheard of in the colour range of *Potentilla fruticosa*, and these new colour breaks were announced to the gardening world with much trumpeting.)

It had to be obtained, and quickly at that. The flowers were eagerly anticipated, but what a let-down when they finally opened – by no means were they a dashing scarlet, more a dirty tangerine. Could it be due to the weather? The soil? Not enough water? Too much? Perhaps in time it would resemble the picture in the plant catalogue? But the following year, it looked more like its ugly sister.

I made a note in my diary – 'Dump potentilla'. Guilt set in and the plant seemed to look at me with a malevolent air each time I passed by. Soon I couldn't wait to get rid of it. Those new to gardening find it hard to dig up plants and throw them away. I have many plants on my conscience. Some were lovely plants in themselves – even the odd magnolia has left here with the bin-men. But however good a plant is, if it is not going to be happy in the limited space of a small garden, out it must go.

The golden robinia (*Robinia pseudoacacia* 'Frisia') is another plant that I used to grow. I fell in love the first time I saw it in spring, when the young foliage is a gentle shade of yellow. In late summer the leaves harshen to far too dominant a gold.

On the other hand, the delicate fern-like leaves of *Gleditsia triacanthos* 'Sunburst' remain pale yellow right through till autumn. I have never tired of this small tree – it ages with the utmost grace. Admittedly it is slow-growing, but well worth the wait.

Populus × *candicans* 'Aurora' (horrible plant, looks infected with multiple virus), *Cornus florida* f. *rubra* (heavenly, hated living in

Ranelagh, soil too limey), the variegated ground elder (lovely but wildly invasive) and *Acer griseum* (small tree with marvellous peeling bark, flatly refused to grow) all join the embarrassingly long list of has-beens (or were-heres).

Late summer is the ideal time to evaluate the garden and its plant content. If some plant is not doing well, or is not the ravishing creature you thought it was, out it must go. And if it is a geriatric plant, I'm all for euthanasia.

What you need at this time of year is a heartless friend. If you are agonising whether to remove a plant or not, it is highly irritating if somebody is making pathetic remarks in your ear like 'What a shame', 'Poor thing', 'So pretty in the spring' and so on. The Red Queen – stamping about and shouting 'Off with his head' about once a minute – would be much more useful.

Falling in love, however, is only too easy to do. Just the other day I saw a new hellebore 'Pacific Frost' – a *Helleborus argutifolius*. How to obtain this delectable plant will occupy the winter. Incidentally, if you haven't already got the Corsican hellebore, put it on your list, it is among the best of all foliage plants with beautiful, sculptured grey-green leaves which form a telling mound, and huge clusters of ice-green bell-shape flowers. A long-lasting delight for spring which, unlike most hellebores, prefers a sunny position.

 *15 August 1993*

Soothed by Agapanthus

August is quite the most horrible month in the garden. What seems to be the Irish equivalent of the föhn blows, an enervating blast of hot dry air that disturbs the plants, saps their strength, tugs the petals from already fading flowers, shrivels their leaves and brings on a general feeling of malaise to the poor gardener. The most irritating fact of all is that even when it rains, the moisture is dried by the wind almost as it falls, and the heavy mass of late summer growth prevents it soaking down to plants' roots. Whereas keen gardeners will still struggle on, glued to the treadmill of watering and deadheading, horticultural dabblers who enthusiastically gardened in early summer, buoyed by musings on the late summer climax to come, will be feeling rightly discouraged by now.

So, on a typical August day, with sharp gusts of wind and an unpleasant glare from the sun, I went round the garden to check which plants were giving a good account of themselves. The agapanthus season is at its height – there is no such thing as a bad agapanthus, and the refreshing hues of various blues and also white are just what is needed in August. The pretty creamy-yellow flower spikes of *Kniphofia* 'Little Maid' would bring about a change of heart to the most dedicated hater of red-hot pokers. No August goes by without my transplanting yet another *Aster* × *frikartii* and/or *Aster thomsonii* 'Nanus' to key positions. These two plants alone are unequalled by providing cool lavender daisies from now and on into autumn. Sedums are looking splendid – 'Vera Jameson' with dusky purple leaves with a bloom like a plum, and the little-known *Sedum populifolium* (pale pink, almost shrubby growth) are just starting to flower and there is already a pink glow on the flowerheads of *Sedum* 'Herbstfreude' (which means autumn joy). *Perovskia atriplicifolia*, the Russian sage, could not care less about a hot dry August wind, coming as it does from Afghanistan and Pakistan, where a boiling wind sweeps over the high plains, desiccating all leaves in its path. *Perovskia* has spires of flowers like little violet-blue velveteen bobbles, a charming plant for a site in full sun with impeccable drainage.

Arbiters of gardening taste profess to despise plants with variegated foliage. In general I agree with them, especially when there is a plethora of multi-coloured leaves scattered throughout a garden. But at this time of year, when all the shrubs with dreary late summer leaves – philadelphus, lilacs, forsythia, weigela and co – are looking a dusty green, absorbing the light and further increasing the drab August look, leaves variegated in cream and green of such shrubs as *Fuchsia* 'Sharpitor', *Cornus mas* 'Variegata' and *Weigela praecox* 'Variegata' add pleasing touches of light.

Those of you who already have *Anemone* × *hybrida* 'Honorine Jobert' will wonder why a eulogy is necessary on this cultivar of the common Japanese anemone. About three to four feet tall with handsome dark green leaves, in constant production of its exquisite single white blossoms for weeks and weeks well into autumn, this is a plant you have simply got to have. It may take a year or two to establish, but after that you will have it for life. 'Queen Charlotte', is a delightful semi-double in lilac-pink and very particular gardeners may search for the scarce 'Géante des Blanches' a fully double, vigorous, splendidly handsome white.

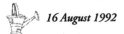 *16 August 1992*

Rare Ol' Times

Lovers of rare plants are to be found away at the end of a branch line of gardening, the types who can be heard mumbling affectionately to a sick plant. They get a great surge of adrenalin at the sight of a rarity, and a prolonged ache in the lower back that can only be assuaged by instant acquisition. Other symptoms to watch out for are wobbly knees (with one look at the heart-shaped leaves of *Cercis canadensis* 'Forest Pansy', for example), night sweats (allowing the mind to dwell on the double pink trillium) or, in serious cases, strangely itchy fingers in other people's gardens.

Why is a plant rare? Often this is because a plant seems almost programmed to die. Or because they're poor nurserymen's plants, they don't thrive for long in a pot (celmisias), look frumpish and therefore unsaleable (*Hedysarum multijugum*), or sulk off in hot weather (*Primula aureata*). Plants may also be rare because they're impossible to propagate, such as *Richea scoparia*, a Tasmanian member of the Epacridaceae, which set seed this year for the first time in 15 years. Species never regenerated from fresh wild-collected seed and cultivars that have been vegetatively propagated by division or cuttings over many years gradually lose strength and fade into obscurity. The decidedly miffy *Primula* 'Inverewe' is one such plant. It has lost the will to live.

Hardy orchids are rare because they increase very slowly in cultivation and it's illegal to collect them in the wild. *Rudbeckia maxima* is rare because, although stunning in flower, it hardly ever does. Others flower themselves to death, such as *Anthemis tinctoria* 'Sauce Hollandaise', which must be renewed from cuttings annually; strictly speaking it's perennial. Plants newly arrived on the market may be scarce now, such as the delectable *Astrantia* 'Ruby Wedding', but after a few years of propagation by nurserymen, we'll just pass by and say: 'Not that old thing *again*.'

Certain plants may only be pretending to be dead, but look so woebegone it would be a kindness to let them go to the great compost heap in the sky. A mutisia is a good example. The man from Kew had told me to treat mutisias (daisy-like climber from the Andes) just like clematis, with their heads in the sun and their feet in shade. I duly planted mine in a prime spot on the terrace. It's holly-like leaves shrivelled one by one and few of its dirty pink daisies appeared. Eleventh in the line of failed mutisias, it too had to go. In such cases, rare equals difficult.

Gaultheria sinensis is the sort of plant that enthusiasts drool over. It is a low-growing shrublet with shining dark evergreen leaves. The inconspicuous white bell-shaped flowers are followed by disproportionately large pear-shaped dazzling turquoise berries, sexy in the extreme. Reasons for its rarity? It insists on lime-free soil, shade, cool, moisture at the root; furthermore, it's tender.

Gardeners who bleat 'Where can I get it ?' and are not prepared to go further than the nearest garden centre make me sick. Some garden centres make great efforts to get hold of special plants for customers. It's now easy to import plants legally and *The RHS Plant Finder* lists 70,000 plants and where to get them. Join your local horticultural society or flower club. Haunt plant sales.

Watch the people behind the tables selling; they are the ones in the know. Helpers at plant sales get the pick; admire the sleight of hand as yet another treasure is bought and rapidly tucked away. Watch out for the wonderful pale orange double nasturtium, *Tropaeolum* 'Margaret Long'. Double flowers are sometimes sterile, with no seed set, so cuttings must be taken each September and over-wintered under glass. 'Margaret Long' is typical of a plant that would fast disappear from cultivation, were it not for the few dedicated lunatics, such as myself, who are prepared to keep it going from year to year.

 *20 August 1995*

For the Pick of the Bulbs, Buy Now

If you want the pick of spring bulbs, now is the time to buy. Bulbs are brilliantly encouraging for the hopeless gardener – even if you plant them upside down, and at the wrong depth, you'll get a reasonable show. (NB Bulbs are generally planted at two and a half times their own depth, but I find they're better a bit deeper on light soil.)

Trawling through a catalogue (all bulbs available from late August at Mackey's Garden Centre), I noticed several that are not normally easy to get. *Crocus tommasinianus* is a major weed – I have several million, all self-seeding like mad, so I can never understand why this little species shouldn't be readily available.

The leaves of the larger daffodils spend far too long dying off, so dwarf varieties are far prettier, especially for small gardens. (To clear up a muddle here: the Latin name of daffodil is *Narcissus*. What we call 'narcissi' are the late-flowering pheasant's eye narcissus, *Narcissus poeticus* var. *recurvus*). Look out for *Narcissus pseudonarcissus* 'Lobularis' (excellent for naturalising in grass), *Narcissus bulbocodium* (the hooped petticoat daffodil), 'Rip van Winkle' (the charming old bright yellow double) and 'February Gold'. This last seems a better doer than its sister 'February Silver'.

Daffodils in the garden will already be forming new roots, so plant bulbs as soon as possible. Rather than making individual holes for each, I like to prepare a 15-inch diameter hole for 10 bulbs, say six to eight inches deep, and put a good handful of bonemeal in the bottom, and place them firmly, four inches apart, before filling in with soil.

Of tulip species, there are two worthy of special mention. *Tulipa batalanii* (yellow, six inches) and *T. linifolia* (bright scarlet, pointy petals, six inches). These two have proved reliable and long-lived (15 years) on a sunny, well-drained raised bed. Lily-flowered tulips, the most elegant of the lot are listed, including 'White Triumphator', which I cannot get enough of. You can have a good succession of colour in containers by planting several tulip varieties at different levels, with a carpet of forget-me-not or violas on top.

I like 'Shirley' (white, delicately edged in purple), 'Blue Parrot' (louche, large floppity petals in lilac blue, very late), and 'Spring Green' (cream, with greenish stripes, fits well in all colour schemes).

 **22 August 1993**

Artfully Gilding the Lily

The non-gardener probably thinks that agapanthus is a lizard-hipped extinct reptile, to be seen rampaging over pre-historic plains along with Brontosaurus and Tyrannosaurus Rex. And the story of the gardener from Cork who, annoyed by garden break-ins, put up a sign 'Beware of the Agapanthus' bears witness to this assumption. It appears the notice was most effective. But in fact agapanthus (a word formed from the Greek *agape* – love and *anthos* – flower) is the Latin name for the lily of the Nile or blue African lily. Most are in bloom at the moment.

Agapanthus praecox has broad, strap-shaped evergreen leaves and beautiful large umbels of flower. This is one of the most tender species. Considered the hardiest (so if you live in the midlands stick to these) are the Headbourne hybrids. These come in every shade from white and pale powder blue to quite dark blue. I think they look more effective planted in large groups of the same colour, rather than mixing them up.

The snag with agapanthus goes like this: the first year they are planted they are busy settling down; next year they come into their own and look really good; the following year ditto; but from then on they start to go backwards. By then their roots have become a congested, heavy mass, so they must be divided or there'll be even fewer flowers thereafter.

Books recommend spring division, but certainly in warmer parts of the country early October is excellent, when the soil is still warm. You will need a sharp kitchen knife to dissect the root ball into segments with two or three nice snouts. Replant with one bucket of well-rotted manure or garden compost and a large handful of bonemeal per plant. The position you choose for them must be first class – plenty of sun, plenty of water and a good rich soil.

Now for advice on agapanthus for the connoisseur: one of the first temptations is a double one (*A. praecox* 'Flore Pleno'). I had this one for some years and came to the conclusion that it is not worth growing. It is tender, occupies valuable greenhouse space, and makes no effort whatsoever to flower. However 'Lilliput' is a nice hardy little cultivar, easily available with neat foliage and very dark blue flowers.

The different forms of *Agapanthus inapertus* are most enticing. Even to a non-agapanthus-fancier they are quite different. Agapanthus normally have flared, trumpet-shaped flowers, but the more tubular flowers of *A. inapertus* are pendulous. One of the most beautiful has deep violet blooms.

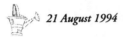 *21 August 1994*

Gravel Gardens

Yesterday I saw a wonderful lesson in how to design a tiny front garden. The site, just as unprepossessing as usual, was typically small, facing north, with only a surrounding clipped privet hedge to separate it from the street with its attendant smells and traffic noise.

Through the gate, a straight path led to the front door, nicely marked by two columns of clipped bay trees (*Laurus nobilis*) in pots. The whole of the remainder of the garden was covered in gravel (small washed pebbles or pea gravel as it is known as, not the large sharp-edged kind that makes an irritating scrunch when you walk on it.)

In the centre of the gravel was a group of pots, massed in a circular shape, not scattered about willy-nilly as you usually see them placed. Occupying the middle were standard fuchsias, a mass of pendant shocking pink and purple blossom, on woody stems three feet tall, each pot carpeted in petunias veined in aubergine purple and pale pink ivy-leaved geraniums (*Pelargonium*). There were pots of an old-fashioned strain of heliotrope, pale washy mauve but highly fragrant. (The more richly-coloured modern varieties, *Heliotropium* 'Marine' for example, have lost on scent what they have gained in colour.) Tubs filled with tobacco plants (*Nicotiana*) and white *Lilium auratum* added to the bouquet. The essential principles of design were well in evidence – good evergreen structure was provided by large tubs (filled with a lime-free mixture) containing camellias, and pots of clipped balls of box. Blue winter pansies, yellow and white polyanthus and bulbs were planned to replace the summer bedding for spring.

The whole scheme was united by lots of plants of small-leaved ivies, their stems wreathed in white and green variegated leaves, running between the pots and spilling out over the gravel. These were planted in the gravel itself. (If you are going to grow plants in gravel, clean, dig and prepare the soil as for any flower bed, rake it level, firm it by treading all over it with little shuffling steps, rake again and cover it with about three inches of gravel.)

The other day I saw another front garden, somewhat larger, that was also completely gravelled, but this time it was a sunny site, and all the plants were growing in the ground rather than pots. *Campanula portenschlagiana*, a prostrate bellflower of uncertain behaviour, far too uncontrolled to allow into a bed of choice plants, was flinging its stems about with abandon, to form pools of blue on the ground. Silvery *Artemisia stelleriana*, mats of thyme (*Thymus serpyllum*), sea pink or thrift (*Armeria maritima*), sun roses (*Helianthemum*) and *Convolvulus sabatius* with little trumpet flowers in a quite irresistible blue were making ribbons of colour. The gravel surface of such a garden acts as a mulch, conserves moisture and prevents weeds germinating.

Your average front garden contains some indeterminate bushes, a scruffy patch of grass, and the odd unsuitable rose. The reluctant owners, just as they have to polish the brass on the door, must keep this all in order: mow and edge the grass, prune, spray and deadhead the roses and so on. Might they not be better to make a gravel garden and have done with such work? The potted plants (in the first garden described above) would admittedly have to be watered, but you could well find an excuse to do it with all those heavenly scents wafting on the evening air, and as for the second garden, apart from the initial watering, you could just enjoy it – the closest you could get to a work-free garden.

 *23 August 1992*

A Classic of Colour Control

Last week I went to visit Mount Stewart, Newtownards, Co Down, one of the great gardens of the world. I've learnt more in this garden than in any other. For example, after growing plants for many years, it had not once entered my head to even think about colour and how to use it. Around fifteen years ago, after my first look at the Italian Garden, overlooked by the south façade of the house, I became a born-again gardener advising anybody prepared to listen on colour control.

The Italian Garden, begun in 1920 by Lady Londonderry, takes the form of a great parterre, the formal beds arranged in opposing colour schemes: edged in dwarf red berberis and gold-leaved thuja, and containing an assortment of vivid yellows, scarlets and orange, to the east; edged in tight-clipped blue rue and *Hebe albicans,* and surrounding plants in soft mauves, pinks, greys and blues to the west. To look down from the terrace on such a simple scheme, strong colours on one side, pale on the other, was perhaps the greatest lesson of my gardening life – although I'm not sure the thuja works as an edging plant.

Steps on one side of the Italian Garden lead up to the Dodo Terrace. Arranged around its balustrades are extraordinary stone beasts representing some of Lady Londonderry's notable contemporaries during the Great War. Beyond is the Mairi Garden, where the young Lady Mary Vane-Tempest-Stewart used to be placed in her pram. Only blue and white flowers are allowed here. 'Mairi, Mairi quite contrary' is illustrated by cockle shells around the central fountain, 'silver bells' by white campanulas and 'Pretty maids all in a row' by double meadow saxifrage. But blue and white gardens, cool and chic as they may be, sometimes feel almost too chilly.

In another great lesson, I witnessed a team of gardeners under the direction of head gardener Nigel Marshall (perhaps the finest in these islands), who has been there 25 years. A large area of the woodland garden was being prepared for a new planting of the giant Himalayan lily, *Cardiocrinum giganteum.* They were working into the soil a rich mixture of leaf mould and stable manure, fully 12 inches deep – no skimping with two miserable inches of peat at Mount Stewart.

To the west is the square Sunk Garden, designed by Gertrude Jekyll mainly on a theme of blue, orange and purple, surrounded by a raised wall covered with a stone and timber pergola. Here I learned how to cope with the unholy trio of loud orange lilies, 'Enchantment', 'Destiny' and *Lilium tigrinum*, by putting them with purple and blue. A useful half hour may be spent investigating the progress of the mature climbers draping the pergola – I've so often been seduced by a climber, only to find it's too vigorous for the space I've chosen.

A step up from the Sunk Garden, in the Shamrock Garden, is a startling Red Hand of Ulster – a giant hand-shaped bed in the paving planted with blood-coloured flowers and foliage.

After a morning examining the different areas near the house – I haven't even mentioned the Spanish Garden or the Memorial Glade – you will need a restorative lunch before setting off for the lake and Tír na nÓg, the private family burial ground. During the last three years, Nigel Marshall has been developing an area near here for South African plants in particular, such as kniphofias, agapanthus, watsonias and osteospermums. Most are wild-sourced plants direct from Kirstenbosch Botanic Gardens in Cape Town. Nigel told me that this area is looking good right now, and you can view a new acquisition, *Elegia capensis*, similar to the mega-rare *Restio*. 'Around five feet tall, a bit like a mare's tail. A spectacular foliage plant. Very ornamental – I'm pleased with this.' Few great gardens manage to combine such strong design, formal and informal, while also holding a tantalising collection of plants.

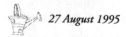 *27 August 1995*

Support your Local Dahlias

You have been warned. That dahlias require staking is a truth universally acknowledged. I can't seem to get this into my co-gardener's head. He always thinks the dahlias won't collapse. Perhaps I should let the wind have its way with them – as a lesson you understand. One of the more distressing gardening operations is trying to raise a dahlia from the horizontal to the vertical. Weighty plants even in their youth, by September dahlias are a mass of leafage, their great succulent stems ever likely to topple. Efforts to heave them once more into an upright position only result in a sickening snap, followed by bouquets of redundant dahlia.

Discussion is ongoing as to whether dahlias should be lifted and stored for winter (received horticultural practice) or left to take their chance in the ground. (Somebody told me last week that he didn't have a shed, so he kept the Bishop under the sofa for winter, and it seemed to work for him.)

Washy pastels may well be divine in midsummer, but they bleach out in harsh August light. Autumn demands glowing, brilliant colour of plants such as dahlias and crocosmias. Crocosmias are related to the common montbretia, naturalised in Ireland (*Crocosmia* × *crocosmiiflora*), but have far superior funnel-shaped flowers in a rich colour range. 'Solfatare' (smoky-bronze leaves and soft apricot flowers), 'Firebird' (glowing, orange-red, a larger plant altogether), 'Lady Hamilton' (pale yellow, very discreet), 'James Coey' (deep scarlet) and 'Mr Bedford' (also known as 'Croesus', clear light orange) are among the best. 'Star of the East' is superb, with very large orange flowers, flared wide open. I've gone off the much admired 'Emily Mackenzie' – her flowers are admittedly handsome but they are annoyingly splashed with reddish-brown.

'Rose Seedling' is a bit special (connoisseurs will note that it isn't mentioned in *The RHS Plant Finder*) with deep rosy-salmon flowers and a yellow throat. I understand this cultivar originated at Mount Usher, County Wicklow. Crocosmias need plenty of moisture, sun and good drainage, as they come from damp habitats in their native South Africa.

People are terrified of the colour orange. It is an extraordinarily stimulating but dangerous colour, with a high dazzle factor that needs careful handling. Until recently, I could hardly bear to look at it. But now I've organised a small garden within a garden, specially for orange flowers: there's lots of cooling blue (agapanthus, *Aster* × *frikartii*, campanulas, violas, cupid's dart, blue-leaved *Hosta* 'Halcyon' and *Clematis* 'Perle d'Azur') and lots of yellow *Anthemis* 'E. C. Buxton', *Hemerocallis* 'Marion Vaughn', yellow lilies, doronicum and the excellent, bright yellow small grass, *Hakonechloa macra* 'Aureola').

There's already light orange *Lilium henryi*, double Welsh poppies, and an abundance of orange and yellow pot marigolds (*Calendula*). The more I see of this common old plant, the more I like it. Astonishingly simple to grow, it sows itself and blooms almost all year. The petals may be sprinkled on salad – even an Iceberg lettuce may aspire to the heights of lettucedom if garlanded with marigolds.

 **28 August 1994**

Divide and Conquer

What you need at this point is an attack of divisionitis. There is more than one reason for dividing a plant. It could be that you like the plant so much that you want more of it. Or, as is the case with most herbaceous plants, if left *in situ* too long, they start to deteriorate, stop flowering well, have used up all the goodies in the soil and need shifting to a new position.

And don't think that it only happens with you, it is inevitable in all gardens – autumn chaos is an annual event. Approach the plant as if you mean business, with a no-nonsense attitude, the sharp kitchen knife, trowel, fork, spade, bucket of compost or old manure, bonemeal and watering can. Starting with everything to hand there'll be no need to dither around putting the job off.

A hosta would be satisfying to start off with. You can move hostas about any time of the year, and they don't object to being chopped up *en route*. Rather than planting them in winter, where you can't see what you are doing as there's nothing above ground, by moving them now you can see what effect you'll have for next year.

Dig up the hosta using the spade. By looking under the leaves, you will see how the plant is made up of several sections. Using the kitchen knife, chop these cleanly through. Rather than making lots of individual planting holes to receive them, prepare a complete patch of ground, working in the bucket of compost (more than one if necessary). Sprinkle the area with bonemeal. Using the trowel, make the holes, insert the plants, water liberally, stand back and admire.

This week I've been dividing primulas, campanulas, hellebores (*H. orientalis*), alliums, celmisias, some veronicas, violas, heucheras, astrantias, *Geranium phaeum* and many alpines. Obviously phlox, Michaelmas daisies, eupatorium, crocosmias and the throng of late-flowering perennials should wait until late October.

Autumn – the earlier the better – is an excellent time for division. There are still many weeks settling-in time while the soil is still damp and, more importantly, you can see exactly what you are doing, with regard to height, spread and colour.

I like to take the plant to its new position before dividing it up and prop it up against a fork to see what it looks like. But after dividing you should chop off the top foliage (to, say, four inches from the base) so as not to put too much strain on the unestablished roots.

 *29 August 1993*

Some Essential Translations

Those starting to garden often have far too much respect for gardening books. Presumably it makes gardening decisions easier, if one is directed to sow seeds before the dew has dried on the morning of 15 March, preferably on a rising moon, and to lift and store the dahlias in the second week of October. But remember that the majority of gardening books, written from south-eastern England, have to allow for such diverse climates as those of Cornwall and Aberdeen. In order to cover themselves they have to adopt too conservative an approach.

Also, some of the phraseology of gardening books confuses beginners and needs to be translated. 'Pricking out' for example, should be explained lest the imagination goes off in the wrong direction; it means to lift seedlings from the pot in which they have germinated, and transfer them to larger pots or seed-trays to give them more room to grow on. 'Damping down' means to slosh water about on the greenhouse floor on hot days, thus immediately lowering the temperature, and increasing the humidity. It is the best way of all of keeping down the population of red spider mite.

If you are congratulating yourself on not having red spider in the conservatory, I can assure you that you have. Although they are invisible to the naked eye, the results of their activities can be seen by looking at the plant's leaves, which have a mottled, yellowish air and the plant will be looking disgusted with life. If you look at the back of the leaves with a magnifying glass, you will see colonies of minute, pale brown, plump, spider-like insects going about their business of non-stop sap sucking – the tiny oval flecks are their eggs. Another sign is the copious silk webbing which the mites spin. Hot, dry atmospheres and lack of sufficient ventilation are the very thing the pest enjoys most. Modern conservatories are sheer nirvana to the red spider – it wouldn't do to get the carpets and fancy furniture wet, so they are rarely damped down. Spraying the plant's foliage several times a day will much reduce the breeding rate. If you have any pot plants that are looking really sick, put them outside for the next three weeks, rain and cooler autumn weather will refresh them before winter – it will certainly put the mite off sex for a bit.

Imagine 'a riot of colour'. It sounds as if a serious disturbance of the peace is taking place, the scarlet flowers fighting the shocking pinks, the bright oranges indulging themselves in wild revelry behind the hedge, loud clashes and bangs as the magentas join the fray, and a few poor whites cowering under a bush. What a scene! Very nasty.

I have to admit there is a small riot going on in the garden here, and I'm afraid there is little I can do about it. It is a matter of a pink Japanese anemone (*Anemone hupehensis* 'Bressingham Glow' to be precise). When I say pink, it is no delicate shell pink, not a bit of it, it is the most difficult pink to fit into the garden – blackcurrant fool with a dash of carmine.

Unfortunately a double Welsh poppy has seeded into the same patch, and masses of cheery orange double flowers are waving from the middle. I like both plants very much. But it is like inviting two friends to dinner that one likes individually, but together they are a disaster.

The last bone of contention is the matter of 'twiggy peasticks' (bushy branches, such as those of hazel, used for the support of culinary peas). You will often see these recommended in gardening books for staking herbaceous plants. Twiggy peasticks implies that one is the owner of some vast demesne, equipped no doubt with a hazel coppice. How nice to be able to say one morning 'Just popping down to the coppice,' instead of down to the shops.

 *30 August 1992*

September

The Future Looks Rosy

I t's early morning. There's a heavy dew and I'm out in the garden inspecting the roses. September roses, all the more precious as we won't see them again until next June, are looking rather good, despite the extraordinary sweaty summer heat. 'Perle d'Or' is covered in little peach-pink buds, like sugar ones on wedding cakes – ideal for buttonholes for elderly bachelors. They unfold to light apricot floppity flowers. 'Perle d'Or' makes a bush about four feet each way and may need a thoughtful prune now. This and other roses with Chinese blood often send up sappy growths from the base that become a mass of flower in late summer. The usual rules about deadheading such growths – 'cut to just below the second leaf below the faded flower' – doesn't apply here as there don't seem to *be* any leaves, until you get way down into the bush. You may have to cut to a dormant bud instead (a little mark like a brown line going half way around the stem).

Instead of raving on about 'Perle d'Or', I should tell you about 'Heritage'. I nearly didn't buy it, because the name annoys me. ('Make your home more stately – plant a Heritage rose!') But after years of waffling on about the romance of the old roses, I now declare that there's no rose more romantic than 'Heritage', born in 1984, courtesy of David Austin. The flowers are cup-shaped, the petals deliciously folded around each other. The colour is the melting shade of pink found on little sea shells, deepening towards the middle of the flower. The foliage is healthy, the bush neat, the flowers lightly scented. Its raiser says its fragrance is reminiscent of lemon (he's trying to be different – it smells quite plainly of rose). 'Gertrude Jekyll' (does a week go by without my mentioning her illustrious personage?) is another David Austin rose, splendid in purple-crimson, similar to 'Mme Isaac Pereire', but with modern hybrid vigour. These two, plus the butter-yellow 'Graham Thomas', are perhaps the best of David Austin roses. If they have a fault it is that their habit is unreliable – they suddenly extend an alarmingly long shoot from the base, completely upsetting the balance of the bush. What to do? Sorry I can't advise, but mostly I cut it off, muttering 'Can't have this nonsense.' Apparently David Austin roses have this habit world-wide, a gardener from San Francisco just told me that there rogue shoots can be 12 feet in the air.

My friend Rosemary Brown, who grows many wonderful roses, says that the only two Austin roses she's never had luck with are 'Chaucer' and 'Wife of Bath' – they were too prone to blackspot and their growth was weak and spindly. For some, 'Blanc Double de Coubert' is a favourite, but others insist that the flowers are too Persil-white. It's one of the rugosas, which are all good doers with rich dark green leaves, resistant to disease, and super fat round orange hips. If you never intend to spray, feed or prune a rose again, try one of these.

Now for something special, namely 'Bengal Crimson', a form of *R. chinensis* with single flowers. Many Chinese roses were originally known as Bengal roses because of their having reached gardens in India prior to being introduced to Europe. All *R. chinensis* hybrids are said to be tender – ideally it should be planted near a sunny wall. Mine's in the open, and it has never been without a flower since February. 'Bengal Crimson' is inexplicably scarce. 'Madame Caroline Testout' is a mass of full-skirted pink flowers, 'Souvenir du Docteur Jamain' is looking a bit peaky (more potash recommended) and 'Hermosa's buds are looking mildewy. The two apricot lovelies, 'Lady Hillingdon' and 'Mrs Oakley Fisher', are looking a bit worse for wear, but still producing the odd flower. 'Cornelia' is as good as ever – I didn't let her get squashed by foxgloves this year.

Work for the week

Plan major re-shuffling, making copious notes on what to move to where, what to get rid of, what needs dividing. Prune over-grown wall-shrubs that are robbing the light of plants beneath. Make notes of successful container combinations for repeating next year.

Continue taking cuttings of argyranthemum, verbena, pelargonium, fuchsia, santolina, artemisia, senecio, lavender, penstemon. Start dividing early-flowering perennials, hostas, hellebores. Cut back alpines and tidy rock gardens, topping up gravel or grit on surface. Top-dress peat beds for ericaceous plants and shade-lovers with 75% peat, 25% lime-free soil.

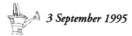 *3 September 1995*

How to Remain a Cut Above

I'm extraordinarily nice to people I don't like. It's much the same with plants. I find it almost impossible to get rid of a plant I've tired of. I may well be thinking 'beastly thug', but to tear it up would make me faint with guilt. A plant, after all, is a living entity. The best way to avoid guilt is to take cuttings. You end up with a dear little pot plant, with no thuggish tendencies, which you can give to a plant sale.

Learning to take cuttings properly is a great confidence booster. You can brandish little asides such as 'brought it back from the Canary Islands/Tokyo/Outer Mongolia in my sponge-bag', or 'pinched it from a vase of flowers at the ... hotel' (insert name of world-famous hotel).

I believe rooting powder is a load of nonsense. Cuttings will root if taken at the right time of year, at the right size, and if given the right conditions. Rooting powder is like a placebo – use it if it makes you feel better.

Late August or early September is a great time for taking cuttings. Cuttings taken now benefit from the extra warmth of earliest autumn. By rooting your own tender plants such as fuchsias, verbenas, pelargoniums, argyranthemums, helichrysum, salvias and alonsoas, you'll save money by not having to buy them again next year. (We'll gloss over the minor matter of heating the greenhouse/conservatory for six winter months.) You'll also be able to propagate your favourite harder-to-find cultivars. Already nearly rooted are the first batch of penstemons, some deutzias, weigelas, hebes, ivies and a hydrangea or two.

I'm not giving you the usual story about how to take cuttings. It's enough to mention some reasons you may have failed with cuttings. Not making the cuttings firm enough is a major reason for failure. Too large a pot is a mistake, as the volume of soil is too great and the cuttings are likely to rot. Don't be over-kind to the cuttings by giving them a rich potting mixture. A lean peat/sharp sand mix encourages the cuttings to put our roots in their search for nourishment.

Pinks, lavenders and silver-leaved plants – artemisias, santolinas, *Anthemis cupaniana* – dislike the humid conditions of a propagator or polythene bag. Pinks can be rooted outdoors in finger-deep trenches filled with sand. Keep them sprinkled with water on hot days. Plump, young, un-flowered shoots from the centre of violas root well using the same method. Pelargoniums also prefer airier conditions and are the only plant that is better if the cuttings are left lying around for a few hours, thus allowing callus (or scar-tissue), to form at the end of the cutting – an important first stage in the rooting process.

Last year, in an effort to save space under the glass, instead of potting the rooted cuttings before winter, I waited until spring. The resultant pots of starvelings, their few remaining leaves home to every whitefly in south Dublin, were very slow to recover. I won't try that again.

 *4 September 1994*

Vegetables with Frills

Decorative vegetable gardens are the height of fashion, you know the sort – *jardins potagers* or miniature Villandrys, with box-edged paths, espaliered fruit trees and regimented rows of vegetables. Frilly red-leaved lettuces are planted alongside plain green ones, with neat rows of parsley and chives, ruby chard and red-leaved spinach, cabbages, cauliflowers, carrots and any other vegetable you care to choose, the whole making a pattern of edible leaves and roots.

If you haven't got room for one of these delightful flights of fancy, consider instead the various vegetables that are highly decorative in themselves, seakale (*Crambe maritima*) for example. Gertrude Jekyll used it in her herbaceous borders and she mentions it on four occasions in *Colour Schemes for the Flower Garden*.

Its leaves are beautiful, pale, duck-egg blue with undulating edges, up to 18 inches long – and the heads of white flowers are honey-scented. It looks amazingly good planted with the blue grass, *Elymus magellanicus*, silver-leaved artemisias and pale pink erigerons. The blanched stems form a succulent early spring vegetable: darkness is essential, so in winter place a mound of peat over the crown of the plant, cover with a bucket with a large stone on top to stop it blowing away. The shoots will gradually elongate and when they are about six inches long, cut them off cleanly, steam and serve with melted butter.

I cannot understand why globe artichokes *(Cynara scolymus)* are not in every garden. Apart from being good to eat – if you can bear to harvest the buds before they expand to great blue thistles into which bumble bees rush to bury themselves, the leaves are exceptionally architectural in winter forming handsome mounds of much cut silvery leaves. A marvellous foliage plant, not often recommended possibly because it isn't fully hardy in colder climates than ours, it likes a sunny, sheltered position in soil enriched with compost or well-rotted manure.

Fennel (the herb, *Foeniculum vulgare*, as opposed to Florence fennel) is a thoroughly nice plant, especially 'Purpureum' where the leaves and stems are flushed dark maroon. Strongly aromatic, smelling of aniseed, the leaves can be chopped and added to salads or cooked with fish and the dried seeds are also used for flavouring. Admittedly the flowers, umbels of yellowy-green, are not in the first flight of flowering plants but the leaves, shining, silky and very fine are unsurpassed, specially when drops of moisture are caught in them after a shower or a heavy dew.

The smallest garden has room for some runner beans – the old-fashioned sort I mean, with the scarlet flowers, the winding stems and a taste to die for. The modern bean, however brilliant it may be at non-stop production of perfectly matched pods, is not in the same class regarding taste. Nor for that matter are those funny little beans that arrive by air in winter – they must be a dream for the shops as they take a suspiciously long time before they start to shrivel at the tips. Heaven knows what peculiar rays have been passed through their limp green bodies.

I am at the moment doing some very complicated manoeuvres to try and find space to plant some scarlet runners. This involves taking out an ailing apple tree, shifting some lily-of-the-valley, dumping a lavatera, and walking round in circles trying to fit in a daylily, a large group of pink chrysanthemums and countless different bulbs.

The last on your list of edible little treats to arrange for yourself if you haven't got a vegetable garden are wild strawberries (Chiltern Seeds if you cannot buy them as plants). They will make an attractive edging to a flower border, or will seed around in part shade or in gaps in paving slabs. They will flower and fruit in their first year if started off early in warmth.

 *6 September 1992*

Don't Forget Your Shovel

In the early morning mist, I'm standing around in the Dublin mountains, surrounded by shovels, buckets and large polythene bags. From a distance it looks like I'm burying a body. I'm frantically inventing an explanation as to what I'm doing in case somebody appears. 'The way to improve soil is by the addition of humus,' advise the gardening books. First catch your humus, as Mrs Beeton might say, for the getting of humus, and indeed of many essential garden supplies, is a grey area.

Many's the time I've been rootling under a beech tree gathering leafmould. Or standing on a river bank with a large polythene bag, scooping sand. Going round playing fields picking up cowpats is not beyond me, and I still remember the fright I had when disturbed by a string of racehorses on a sheep-dropping raid on the Curragh.

Manure is a wonder. Shit it may be, but it is the most exquisite shit you can get, made of innocent things, like hay and grass. Dilettante gardeners might wrinkle up their noses but true gardeners swoon at the sight of a pile. Manure and garden compost are unrivalled as soil conditioners. Neither is rich in plant foods, but both work miracles by making light soils moisture-retentive and by loosening up heavy soils. If you can only get fresh manure, don't worry – make into a neat stack, put a polythene cover on top to stop rain leaching the goodness out, and it'll be ready to use in three months or so. Mushroom compost I'm not so keen on, but it's light to handle.

'Get the soil right,' I blithely announce to new gardeners. If they've got as far as asking me what to do, it's probably too late – there will be plants stuffed in all over the place making soil improvement more complicated. Or worse, the house is newly built, and the surrounding soil has suffered the attentions of builders. Land recently vacated by builders is usually in a shocking condition, so compressed by heavy machinery that all the air is squeezed out of it. Often existing topsoil has been scraped away and the subsoil has been decorated with a thin icing of peat, bark or imported soil. Stick in a finger, and there's a cement-like pan a few inches below the surface. Solid as a carpark.

It is possible to make this into good soil, but it will take time and a great deal of effort. 'Working the soil' is a typical gardening euphemism: the soil graciously allows itself to be sweated over – you do the work. Topsoil, such as there is, is usually dark and easily crumbled. Subsoil is paler and comes in horrible sticky lumps. Don't mix up the two types, subsoil is mostly infertile. Tackle a small section at once. Dig a small trench, putting the topsoil to one side. Break up the subsoil with a spade or pickaxe (wear strong shoes if your aim isn't good). Work manure or compost into subsoil. Dig a trench alongside, throwing topsoil onto subsoil in first trench. Repeat process.

I've had several conversations with people in despair about their gardens. I explain that all gardens look a mess in September and all owners are disgusted. Soil must be worked in established gardens just as much as in new gardens, specially in neglected borders. Don't depress yourself: mark out an area that can be dealt with in one day or weekend. Between now and Christmas deal with the garden piecemeal, taking out all herbaceous plants and keeping the roots moist by putting them into damp peat or buckets of water. Throw out unwanted shrubs and dig carefully round the rest. Compost summer bedding plants. Dig area, adding compost or manure. Divide and replant herbaceous plants. Fill any gaps with bulbs. Water well.

 *10 September 1995*

Chop, Replant, Water and Admire

'Divide in early autumn,' announces the book. To haul a plant out of the ground and chop it up into little bits is a terrifying thought to a beginner. For a start you don't know what sort of roots you're going to find. The easy ones are the fibrous sort, like matted hair, easy to tease apart and rapid to re-establish, typical of many herbaceous plants such as phlox or Michaelmas daisies. The worrying sort are the great fleshy roots of peonies or veratrums, bringing thoughts of surgeons and operating tables to mind.

I defy you to kill a hardy geranium, whatever you did to it, so get together a garden fork, a bucket of compost or manure, secateurs, trowel, watering-can, bonemeal and two kilos of determination, approach the nearest one and have it out of the ground before you (or it) realise what's happening. Chop off some of the top leaves so as to see what you're at. Either pull it into pieces or cut it into sections with the secateurs. Work the manure or compost into the soil, sprinkle with bonemeal, replant the portions about nine inches apart, water and admire.

Most gardeners find it impossible to plant a decent big patch of the same plant; they are busy creating vividly spotty effects. A sense of order among this confusion is best supplied by planting wide groups of hostas or other low-growing foliage plants such as pulmonarias, bergenias, omphalodes, epimediums in shade or *Stachys byzantina*, catmint, anaphalis in sun. Large groups mean lots of money, or lots of division, so take your choice.

Now to the worrying sort of division. In theory peonies can remain *in situ* for ever; in practice this doesn't always work. What used to be a perfect spot with rich soil and plenty of light may well have turned into dense shade, the only sign of the peony being a woebegone leaf. Steel yourself to the fact that division is inevitably accompanied by the painful sound of breaking peony root. (By the way, the peony I moved in May, against all the rules, is in excellent order.)

The most disconcerting plants to divide are those from which long, woody, rootless bits fall off as you dig them up – bergenias and heucheras for example. Simply stuff the rootless bits back very firmly into the soil up to the leaf rosette, then stamp on the soil around them for good measure. You will of course, have prepared the ground with the requisite bucket. Should you be so lucky as to own a celmisia (New Zealand daisy) and be so bold as to want to divide it, now is an excellent time.

My black veratrum is being elbowed out by a large white phlox so I'm gathering courage to divide it in October. Most herbaceous plants can be fiddled around with throughout winter, although grasses and slightly tender plants must wait for spring. This week I've also been dividing toothworts, brunneras, hellebores, campanulas and an exceptional new hardy geranium, *Geranium phaeum* 'Samobor', in which each leaf is heavily zoned in deep chocolate. Collected in 1990 in what is now Croatia, it is widely available.

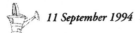 *11 September 1994*

Driven Up the Walls

The problem with wall shrubs is that they don't obey orders. You want the pyracantha to grow to eight feet precisely to hide a neighbour's washing line, but not to spread out so far it squashes the abutilon. I have occasionally seen pyracanthas trained as espaliers with the branches tightly trained to horizontal wires; to copy this, books suggest clipping back after flowering and tying in new growth in late summer. But most pyracanthas fast become dense prickly thickets.

Unless you're very strict with climbing roses, they too will get their own way, gaily romping to the top of the wall, and flowering in great profusion where you can't see them. The trick is to catch the young stems at just the right moment, which is often in early autumn, when the growth is neither so soft that it snaps off at the base, nor so mature that it's too rigid to bend. Pull the stems gently into as near a horizontal position as possible, and the rose will be stimulated into producing lots of new shoots at the leaf joints, thus more flowers where *you* want them. We've just dealt with 'Madame Grégoire Staechelin' in such a way.

As for *Clematis armandii*, I will get the better of it yet: after planting, it promptly shot 20 feet up my best south wall in one summer. 'I'll fix you,' said I, and cut the plant down to three feet the following spring. Before the young shoots knew what was happening, I trained them sideways. The plan was a temporary success, and the clematis was decently clothed in the lower regions, but this summer it got its own way again. Possibly the answer is to plant a bulging shrub at its feet.

Myrtles are one of my first choices for a warm, sunny wall. I love them for their glossy green leaves, for their fragrant white blossom, but most of all for the way they mature into small trees of great character. *Myrtus apiculata* (now *Luma apiculata*) in particular has beautiful cinnamon-coloured flaking bark, like suede to touch. All make good long-term tub plants and you can train the small-leaved *Myrtus communis* subsp. *tarentina* into a good standard (ball on a stick) far more quickly than you can box.

A pleasant plant is rather like a pleasant person. On the few occasions you notice them, you remark 'how nice,' and pass on. *Abelia* × *grandiflora* is one such. I've grown it for 20 years, on a sunny five-foot wall. It unfailingly blooms in summer and early autumn in a vague sort of a way, with clusters of pinkish-white flowers on graceful arching foliage. Much more dashing and far more noticeable, is *Abelia floribunda* with larger, tubular crimson-purple flowers. Needless to say, this is much more tender. Whoever named these two abelias got it wrong, for *grandiflora* has the smaller flowers and *floribunda* has fewer of them. Most wall shrubs require their allotted space to thrive. But the white potato vine or *Solanum jasminoides* can be let loose among other climbers without harming them. If it gets above itself, give it a major hack to within three feet of the ground in spring. The everlasting pea, *Lathyrus latifolius,* also requires little room. For lime-free beds, the Scottish flame flower or *Tropaeolum speciosum* will entwine itself without harm to host shrubs. *Eccremocarpus scaber,* the glory vine from Chile, a fragile little climber that flowers the same year from seed, will provide a little extra colour, at no cost in space, to permanent wall plantings.

Work for the week

- On the first wet day go round the garden centres and get the pick of the bulbs. Daffodils in particular must be planted immediately, but I wait until late November when the garden's tidy before planting tulips. Look out for super decorative onions, *Allium cristophii* and *A. hollandicum.*

 *17 September 1995*

The Plastic Bucket – Don't Leave Home Without One

Earlier this summer I was interviewed for New Zealand television. I sat on the sofa for what they called the 'D and M bit' (or 'Deep and Meaningful' session), in which I was expected to give a pompous discourse on My Philosophy of Gardening, Closeness to Nature, Appeal to the Five Senses, and so on. So rattled was I by the lights, and so transfixed by the quality of the interviewer's make-up (the refined curve of the eyebrow was almost too much), that I could think of little to say – meaningful or otherwise. But, on reflection, I think it all rests (my theory of gardening – not the make-up) on the use of the plastic bucket.

Neither size nor colour matters. I use both sizes, with a particular preference for the large black sort that farmers use. Old-fashioned galvanised buckets are too heavy and make annoying clanky noises, thus advertising my position in the garden.

No plant ever goes into the ground here without the addition of the contents of a bucket. Buckets of peat for shade-lovers, buckets of gravel and sand for plants that need good drainage, buckets of compost and manure for greedy plants, buckets of fresh topsoil for primroses and violas that become soil-sick, plus infinite combinations of all these ingredients; each recipe is made up on the spot to suit the plant in question. You won't understand all this performance if you have a new garden created out of old pasture-land, where the soil is still virgin, uncorrupted by regular cultivation, where as yet there's been no build-up of pest and disease. But here any plant that's looking off-colour is taken out and replanted with a fresh bucket of suitable mixture. If you're prepared to excavate and replace eight to 10 bucketfuls, you can even avoid Specific Replant Disease. To illustrate the quantity of goodies I'd dig in a minimum of eight black buckets of manure before planting an area say 1m × 2m, and feel mean at that.

The bucket is also much in demand when it comes to top-dressing. Umpteen buckets of gravel have been carried around the garden in the last few weeks for top-dressing the alpine beds. After such attention the beds look smart, the drainage is improved around the plants for winter, and the seeds of annual meadow grass are restrained from germinating. Peat beds, easily infested with pearlwort, loathsome little weed, can be effectively cleaned up by scraping off the top inch of the surface and replacing it with a few buckets of 75% peat and 25% lime-free soil. Buckets of old potting compost are used anywhere round the garden where the soil is looking slightly sunken and over-compacted. Wood anemones that have become congested and worked themselves towards the surface are all the better for a bucket of leafmould over their heads. After all, that's just what they'd get in autumn if they were growing in the wild.

I cannot recommend more highly the use of the plastic bucket. I rarely move round the garden without one. As a mixture of work-ethic and laziness, if there is such a combination, the secateurs and trowel are usually in the bottom of it, thus saving numerous trips to the shed. You can use the bucket as a travelling ashtray, or even as a hat if it starts to rain. Well may your grand gardeners profess to using a Sussex trug. These look wonderful in glossy magazines, placed ever so casually in the middle of the decorative vegetable garden, with a scattering of rose petals, a dew-drop or two, and a serendipitous bumble-bee. Apart from that, trugs are heavy and totally unsuitable for real use. To me, the plastic bucket is the supreme gardening accoutrement, to which I'm very attached. I may well go out to dinner carrying it one day instead of my bag.

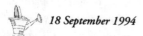 *18 September 1994*

To Design a Conservatory, First Live in One

If I had my way, all designers of modern conservatories should be transmogrified into a plant for a week, and then try living in one of their creations. Today's conservatory, although perfect for people, as a home extension, is more a concentration camp than a place of conservation for plants.

First there is the matter of humidity: people would not relish sitting in the steamy jungly atmosphere that a plant enjoys – rheumaticky aches would set in. So, people rule OK, and the humidity level is kept comfortably low. Second, I have yet to see a modern conservatory with sufficient ventilation. Even a short blast of winter sun can send the temperature soaring.

A hot, dry atmosphere is just what red spider mite, a sinister invisible enemy, particularly enjoys. The results of the mite's attentions are obvious. Leaves become yellowish-looking, desiccated, blotchy, mottled and eventually they fall off. One way of dampening red spiders' ardour is to maintain a moist atmosphere, by swilling the floor (whole cans at regular intervals), and by drenching the plants' leaves with water. Another problem is that red spider rapidly becomes immune to whatever insecticide you're using (malathion, Sybol), so it pays to keep changing the product. Conservatories, from a plant's point of view should be constructed so that the security of the house doesn't depend on all windows and doors being shut every time you go out. The furniture would have to be burglar-proof, and waterproof as well. But your reward would be healthy, happy plants.

Perhaps the only way to get this message through to a conservatory designer is to lock him into one. Choose a hot day, leave no water, and by the time his baggy designer trousers start to wilt, he should understand how a plant feels.

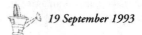 *19 September 1993*

Not Just a Heap of Soil

This week I must apologise for having to clear up various gardening muddles. The first, by request, is the matter of 'compost'. This throws beginners to gardening into confusion due to multiple use of the same word. It is used to describe the mixture of vegetable matter in a compost heap. 'Compost' can be a noun, an adjective, a verb or even a swear word, when shouted threateningly at the dog. But it also means something entirely different, ie all kinds of mixtures in which seeds can be germinated and plants grown in pots. These can be soil-based, or soil-less. Up to recently the soil-less types were based on peat, but now that the use of peat is considered almost heretical in many countries, experiments are being conducted to find a greener medium, based on coir (fibre from coconut husks), shredded bark, sawdust and so forth.

Now we get on to muddle number two: the John Innes one. In the 1930s the John Innes Horticultural Institute in Britain carried out experiments to find out the ideal mixture in which to grow plants. They came up with a potting mixture made from seven parts loam, three parts peat and two parts coarse sand. To this was added John Innes base fertiliser in various strengths. People are confused by gardening books referring to 'John Innes' without making it clear whether it is the potting compost they are referring to, or the base fertiliser (which is a good, well-balanced fertiliser that I often use in the open garden for feeding plants generally).

'Loam', one of the components of the John Innes potting mixture, needs further explanation. A mixture of sand, clay and decayed organic matter, loam in gardening terms means good, fibrous soil. Ideally the best loam for potting is made by stacking the top layer of a meadow, cut a few inches thick. The turves are laid upside down in a heap so that the grass and its roots decay for a year before use.

Bought John Innes composts very much depend on the quality of loam used. Whether you are using soil or soil-less compost, it also matters a lot how long the mixture has been in the bag, for if they have become stale the added fertiliser therein may have become inactive or even harmful to plants. So I usually mix my own, using a slightly modified potting mixture, six parts bought topsoil, three parts damp peat and two parts horticultural sand. Being an inveterate over-waterer, I also have a mixture for young rooted cuttings, alpines and small delicate plants: one part bought topsoil, one part damp peat, and one part mixed horticultural sand and sharp grit, which gives that extra drainage.

Another all-time gardening muddle is the matter of autumn crocuses: these are in fact bulbs of the genus *Colchicum*. In autumn one forgets what a pain their leaves were in mid-summer, lying round in an untidy fashion and spoiling the look of the June garden, but now all is forgiven as their plump flower buds erupt from the bare earth. You may well see them for sale in garden centres, starting to flower whilst still sitting in their cardboard boxes. Rescue them by all means, but do not plant them in a position that will be too obvious next summer. *Colchicum speciosum* 'Album' is perhaps the most beautiful, with white goblets of rare purity amongst autumn flowers. Not often mentioned are their shining green leaves, which look good all winter.

Kaffir lilies or *Schizostylis* are just starting too. They come in crimson, pink and white. You might think the white sounds infinitely desirable, but sadly it has squinny little flowers. However, there is a superb pink in 'Sunrise', to my mind the best of the lot, with large flowers and satiny petals. Kaffir lilies come from South Africa and like the sun, plenty to drink and rich food. On thin Dublin soil they should be divided every spring.

 *20 September 1992*

Cork Climate Works Magic

Even the blackbirds are bigger in Cork. Plants grow wonderfully well down there, tender shrubs waxing fat in the milder climate. Notable in the three gardens I visited were tempting, exciting pittosporums with fancy foliage. The leaves of 'Deborah' are sweet and small, variegated in pink, cream and green – you'd almost expect to see them glacéed in sugar on the top of an iced cake; 'Silver Magic' has small, feathery, delicate leaves, also variegated; whilst 'Irene Paterson' has black stems, the bush giving a wonderfully creamy effect in winter. These are all tender cultivars of the ubiquitous *Pittosporum tenuifolium*, the worthy but medium-boring shrub used as a hedge in many gardens, redeemed by tiny chocolate-purple flowers, exquisitely fragrant of honey.

I met a grove of myrtles – not of the common myrtle of wedding bouquets, *Myrtus communis*, but of *Myrtus luma* (now correctly known as *Luma apiculata*). This shrub or small tree has bark of incredible beauty, cinnamon-coloured, with the texture of expensive suede, evergreen deep green leaves and white flowers with yellow anthers. This is all the better for being planted in a group, for the lower light level causes the trees to be drawn up, thus displaying their beautiful trunks to advantage. I adore this plant, but my specimen is agonisingly slow – no doubt the Cork climate is more like that of its native home in Chile and Argentina. I've never seen a better stand, even in the wild, than that at Rochestown Road.

I also met a young specimen of the climbing dicentra, *D. scandens*, lovingly referred to by its owner as Dotey Pet. Dotey Pet was sitting smug against a warm wall, all of two foot high, masquerading as a shy and delicate creature, almost demanding a chaise-longue to lie on.

Later that day we saw Dotey Pet in its true colours, romping up a large conifer, rampaging over nearby shrubs and giving a joyous wave as it set off for the water garden – a climber with attitude if ever there was. Despite such immoderate behaviour, this is an unusual and pretty plant, with fresh green, fern-like leaves and clusters of flowers like pale yellow lockets. Copious seed is set with me, which has never yet germinated, although cuttings root readily.

Disgusted as those in colder gardens will be at not being able to grow without protection such tender delights as *Astelia chathamica* (gleaming platinum spiky leaves), *Lophomyrtus* 'Tricolor' (a confection in pink) and the rich purple form of *Dodonaea*, there's no reason not to copy an excellent planting association I saw: *Fuchsia magellanica* 'Tricolor', *Sedum* 'Herbstfreude' (often known as 'Autumn Joy', which is what the name means), pink nerines and dwarf blue Michaelmas daisies – simple, easy to grow and a charming idea for autumn.

I also saw *Coprosma* × *kirkii* 'Kirkii Variegata' (a New Zealand shrub quite hardy in Dublin) cleverly used as ground cover, its stems of little variegated leaves forming a pool of bright cream. Thank you to all those in Cork who planned such a great time for me.

Back home in Ranelagh, I noticed a poor mahonia I'd forgotten about. 'Not waving, just dying' it seemed to say, its few remaining leaves almost smothered by Dotey Pet. My specimen of the Pet has gobbled up three clematis and is all set to tackle a honeysuckle, apart from the unfortunate mahonia. The dicentra is only herbaceous, and vanishes to the ground in winter, but now is the time of year to make radical decisions about certain plants. Does their beauty warrant thuggish behaviour? If not, out they must go.

 *24 September 1994*

Tips for the Reluctant Gardener

This week it is the turn of those who secretly hate gardening. The golfing gardener is a contradiction in terms if ever there was one. So apart from mowing the lawn, what we need are some utterly foolproof plants. Total neglect is *de rigueur*. A must for the reluctant gardeners are nerines (*Nerine bowdenii*). The longer you leave them in the same place the better they do. The one proviso is that you plant them in full sun – a nice dry spot at the foot of a sunny garden wall would be ideal. Nerines are very odd bulbs. Once established their aim in life is to climb out of the soil and make a small mountain of bulbs piled on top of each other. Don't worry – they'll bloom even better. You'll get lots of credit for a good show of nerines with no work whatsoever, but if the spirit moves, you might divide them every ten years or so.

Japanese anemones. How can you believe that anything quite so lovely as *Anemone* × *hybrida* 'Honorine Jobert', the exquisite white one, could be such an easy good-natured plant? Apart from requiring neither staking, spraying, feeding, nor water, it will grow in the sort of miserable area where nothing much else will grow. These anemones are about three to four feet tall, start flowering at the end of July and go on till late October. Note that 'Prinz Heinrich' and 'Bressingham Glow' are easier to find in the garden centres than 'Honorine Jobert', probably because they are easier to propagate. Both described as 'deep rose pink', to my mind they are a prissy sort of pink and not in the same class as the others.

Many hardy geraniums (perennial plants as opposed to those grown in greenhouses, which are in fact pelargoniums) are brilliant plants to put in and forget about. *Geranium endressii* produces its cheerful pink flowers in any old corner, smothers all weeds in its path and blooms for six months non-stop. *G. clarkei* 'Kashmir White' has large white flowers veiled in pale purple. A good selection of geraniums as well as Japanese anemones (including the elusive Honorine) can be found at Hardy Plant Nursery, Ridge House, Ballybrack, Co Dublin.

A marvellously easy, forget-all-about-it shrub would be *Fuchsia magellanica*. This is the species naturalised in Ireland and it is just as happy in suburban captivity as it is in the hedge in Kerry. To prune or not to prune is entirely a matter of choice and the golfing gardener will no doubt choose the latter. *F. magellanica*, from Chile and Argentina, has a range which extends right down to Tierra del Fuego, thus it withstands considerable cold not to mention ceaseless wind. The foliage of its cultivar 'Versicolor' is quite beautiful, a mixture of cream, jade and pale crimson, a superb complement to the little red flowers with purple skirts.

26 September 1993

October

Final Blaze of Glory

I have been making notes of plants that add excitement to autumn. For most of the year *Morina longifolia* looks exactly like a large, shiny-leaved, dangerously prickly thistle. This unusual plant is now in flower, with two-foot stems decorated with whorls of white tubular flowers. Hours have been wasted by plantsmen having arguments as to whether they have the white or pink form but they are one and the same – it is just that after pollination the flowers turn pink (blushing with embarrassment I suppose).

I reckon the roses went on strike this year. No more sun, no more flowers. There wasn't a bud to be seen in August, when the second flush should have been at its peak. Only now, in late September, have they decided to make an effort. 'Perle d'Or' is a mass of buds. The creamy-apricot flowers are of the exquisite archetypal rose-bud shape, of button holes and eighteenth-century wallpaper designs. About four feet high, this is an excellent rose for the small garden, with pest-resistant dark green foliage and a tidy habit. There is an on-going muddle between this rose and remarkably similar 'Cécile Brünner', which has flowers that are distinctly pink rather than apricot. 'Bloomfield Abundance' further confuses the situation: I understand that this rose is distinguished by its longer sepals (the little green leaf-like bits directly behind the flower).

Cannas are rarely discussed. They make me think of long, slow Victorian dinners around silver *épergnes* laden with hothouse grapes. Beloved of nineteenth-century tropical bedding schemes, cannas disappeared from fashion with the demise of the head gardener and his hothouse. But however late they are to flower, such defiant flamboyance in autumn is endearing. One of mine is blessed with luxuriant large leaves richly flushed in purple (*Canna indica* 'Purpurea'), from which melting crimson flowers with floppity silk petals have just emerged – in the nick of time, for within a few weeks the fleshy roots must be dug up and potted and stored out of frost's way, kept barely moist till spring. Other tender perennials – argyranthemums, pelargoniums, certain salvias and fuchsias etc – should by now be under glass (either in the form of cuttings or as dug up, potted parent plants).

Bugbane is the common name of an autumn charmer, *Cimicifuga racemosa* 'Purpurea' (listed in *The RHS Plant Finder* as *C. simplex* Atropurpurea Group). Expensive to buy and slow to increase, this has dusky purple foliage in summer and slender tall stems bearing long bottlebrushes of creamy, highly-scented flowers at the moment. I've only divided this once in ten years, and this was out of greed rather than necessity. Part shade and a moist soil required.

I nearly forgot toad lilies. These are the best possible plants with which to impress people. They have an air of being difficult, whilst in fact they are astonishingly easy in moist soil, in sun or shade. Herbaceous perennials, they have shiny neat basal leaves and fascinating, almost orchid-like, spotted flowers on 2–3 foot stems which require no staking. Toad lilies (or *Tricyrtis*) inspired Reginald Farrer to write '... wried by perversity into an almost Aubrey-Beardsley freakishness of outline and heavy waxen texture and livid sombre colour of putrid pinks, freckled and spotted ...' Still, I reckon my clump is often visited by hopeful toads, dying to be turned into princes. Connoisseurs will want chrome yellow, maroon-spotted *Tricyrtis macrantha*. Very desirable.

This week start planting spring bedding. Rivers of forget-me-nots along path edges will self-sow from year to year. The jewel-like colours of the new strains of pansies and violas are irresistible – use them for making carpets on top of newly-planted bulbs. And on sunny path edges you can't go wrong with the old cottage garden cliché – purple aubrieta, golden alyssum and white candytuft.

 *2 October 1994*

The Great Autumn Tidy

There are a number of different approaches to the Great Autumn Tidy. It all depends on discipline, and probably relates back to potty training. One method is to shut the door, and forget all about the garden until next April. (I suspect the gardener who adopts this approach had a funny sort of nanny.) Margery Fish, a renowned but formidable lady gardener of the 1950s, must have had a similar upbringing, for she believed that you should wait until the old stems of herbaceous plants were so seared by winter that you could knock them down with a tap of a foot.

But watching the garden slowly collapse into a soggy mess is not for me. Ideally, one should patrol the garden daily, secateurs in hand, and cull any obviously withered old stems, leaving those that are still green. The exceptions are plants which, in death, are at their most decorative, a prime example of which is the teasel.

Teasels, naturalised in many Dublin gardens, are confusing plants for beginners – baby teasels have leaves like a large primrose, except they are covered in prickles. The leaves on the flower stems are intriguingly cupped, to the extent that they will collect enough water for small birds to drink from. The spiny egg-shaped flowerheads, on four-foot stems, are filmed with lilac when in bloom. For gatherers of useless but fascinating information, it appears that the inventor of the velcro hit upon the idea when a teasel head hooked on to his trouser leg and refused to dislodge.

An on-going argument ensues at this time of each year with my co-gardener (an inveterate tidier who had an old-school nanny) about whether or not teasel skeletons should be removed. But, sparkling with frozen dew after a cold night, they are one of the joys of winter. Anyway, it is essential to leave at least one plant to drop seed and ensure continuity.

Another biennial (a plant which flowers in its second year and then dies) is honesty, or silver dollar plant (*Lunaria annua*). This will settle into any old corner, providing a much-needed patch of purple or white in early summer. The seed-heads are rounded, silvery and satiny in texture. You may consider this description way OTT, because to show their true beauty each seed-head has to be unwrapped from its brown outer casing – a slow, but contemplative operation.

Other plants to leave untidied for the sake of their winter silhouettes are sedums – alive with butterflies at the moment – astilbes, some alliums, love-in-a-mist, phlomis and clematis. Giant oats (*Stipa gigantea*), the best of all possible grasses, has learned to grow old gracefully and will be a star of the winter scene through till next March.

Don't let summer linger too long in containers. Summer bedding plants should be on the compost heap, to give winter pansies, polyanthus, forget-me-nots, stocks, bachelor's buttons and so on a chance to settle in while soil is still warm.

 *3 October 1993*

Gladioli: Leave them in the Vase

Driving along yesterday I passed a garden that had a startling effect on me. Rather too startling to be precise. The house was surrounded on all sides by red and white gladioli, planted alternately. Scarlet and white, scarlet and white, up and down went their regimented rows, making stripy patterns this way and that, except the flower spikes were no longer standing to attention – for the modern gladiolus is one of the best examples of bad designs about. The unopened spikes are all very well, when tightly swaddled in cellophane packages in the flower shops, but allowed out in the garden proper – oh dear!

When the first flowers open at the bottom, there is still a slender stem of buds above, and the plant just manages to stand up straight. But as further buds open, the spike becomes increasingly top-heavy, until as the last and uppermost flowers expand, the stem has no chance whatsoever and starts leaning over at a drunken angle. Whilst the buds are comparatively neat and inviting, the fully opened flowers look distinctly blowsy, and when they are also battered about by the recent blustery weather, they are a bedraggled sight indeed.

The first time you grow these gladioli (everyone tries them once) you may decide that you cannot have all this leaning about, and you must give them a bit of correction, so you tie each stem firmly to an individual bamboo cane. Then, if anything, the effect is even worse. All in all, the man-made gladioli hybrids (he has been tinkering about with them since 1823), are a disastrous garden plant and should remain where they belong, in vases of water on hospital bedside tables.

But one of the parents of the modern hybrids is as unlike them as you can imagine. Its name is *Gladiolus papilio*, an appealing, modestly coloured plant whose graceful stems support curious, hooded flowers.

The petals are washed and stencilled in lilac, with splashes of lemony-green inside. Unlike the aforementioned hybrids, which must be laboriously dug up and protected against the winter frost, this plant can be left in the ground.

If you already own this lovely plant, you may have encountered one or two snags with it: it is inclined to run about and vigorously increase itself at the expense of flowering. If this has happened, dig up the corms in spring, replenish the soil with compost and bonemeal and replant the largest corms only. It requires sun and not too dry a position, as do many other South African plants.

Those of you (especially with Dublin gardens) who don't even know what a gladiolus is, may well have one already – that magenta-flowered plant that seems to be all over the place and which flowers in June. This is *Gladiolus communis* subsp. *byzantinus*, from the Mediterranean. Well, it certainly hasn't noticed any climatic difference in Dublin – in fact it has become naturalised in my garden and seeds madly around. Agreed, it does look quite nice for about three days, but then looks a mess for weeks while it is dying off. If at this point you decide you've had enough of it and try to dig it up, some of the corms (or surrounding cormlets) are sure to be left behind.

The way to get rid of it, I've discovered, is to catch it early in the year, say about February, when you first notice the green spiky leaves, for at this stage it won't have got its roots down and the corms are easy to tweak out. (The same applies to bluebells in the wrong place.) If you only have one or two, and want to encourage more, just let it set seed.

To please one of the prettiest gladioli of the lot, 'The Bride', you need a warm garden and well-drained soil. A delightful little thing, one of the few hybrids that retains all the grace and charm of the wild species, it flowers in June and is excellent for picking.

 *4 October 1992*

At the Bottom of the Garden

A garden feature can be anything from an antique marble statue to a well-placed pot of box. They are important elements of design, and garden seats, sundials, birdbaths, pots and urns all draw the eye towards an inviting shady spot under a tree, or act as a focal point at the end of a long alley. Each should enhance its particular site. However humble, they provide emphasis, their stillness contrasting with the living plants around them.

We can't all have a Gothic folly or distant hermitage (the career of travelling hermit to stately homes was popular in early days, the only requirement being a serene disposition and a decent bit of sackcloth), but I once saw a most successful feature, costing nothing at all. It was a gnarled piece of driftwood, bleached by salt water, over which trailed a variegated ivy with small leaves.

Gnomes (fishing or otherwise) and concrete bunnies, doggies, kitties and piggies are also features, and after a tour of the local garden centres I should report that the market in winsome ladies is booming: they come in all sizes, with varying degrees of simper. I also saw what appeared to be a dead pig in a bikini. The choice is limitless.

Some really nice Vietnamese pots had great style, and I imagined how good they'd look planted with a deciduous azalea (or Japanese acer if you could find a sheltered enough spot). They were made of pottery, about 22 inches in diameter, and glazed on the outside in subtle watery greens and blues.

Handsome, large Grecian terracotta jars, like those used for oil, with a soft, antique-looking finish would look wonderful planted with spring-flowering clematis, such as *C. alpina* or *C. macropetala*, tumbling down the sides.

The reason I'm so concerned about the colour of statues, pots, seats and so on is that you don't want these to be too obvious, shouting out 'Look at me, I'm the new feature.' Ornaments should look as if they've always been there. Try painting new ones with a solution of yoghurt, manure and water, to attract mosses and algae. Vehement arguments take place between gardeners about whether garden furniture, seats and such like, should be painted white or not. My opinion is that you can get away with white close to the house, such as on the patio, but elsewhere in the garden white is too prominent.

Ironcrafts (Hill of Ward House, Trim Road, Athboy, Co Meath) make excellent-quality garden furniture, all based on old designs. A wrought iron Gothic seat and their 'Tara' seat made of timber laths, with intricate metalwork sides in cast aluminium, would grace any garden, large or small.

 *9 October 1994*

Best of the Bulbs

Most beginners know only one daffodil, 'King Alfred' by name. A brasher flower would be hard to imagine, so large and gold he dominates the garden scene in April, and then proceeds to drape his dying leaves over nearby plants until June. I soon tired of him. 'Mount Hood', equally large, at least has the virtue of being white, but was also banished after an interim period in disgrace behind some shrubs. Large daffodils are no better swaggering around in large gardens – their big trumpets seem too man-made. Much more appropriate, especially in a wilder setting, would be the old scented May-flowering *Narcissus poeticus.*

Little daffodils are quite another matter. Look out for 'Hawera' (a jonquil with sulphur-yellow flowers) and 'Rip van Winkle' (a bright little double yellow). The hooped petticoat daffodil, *Narcissus bulbocodium,* makes up its own mind whether to flower or not – I suspect it prefers a position that is not too dry. If you can get seed of *N. rupicola,* do. Only four inches high, it is an adorable miniature.

Tulips, although programmed from birth to behave in regimental fashion, are invaluable for filling up gaps in the flower border. Wonderful bulbs for overcrowded gardens, you can wait till late November before planting them, when you'll easily find a space. Parrot tulips, so dashingly vulgar, with their striped frilly petals, demand a formal setting close to the house. You might not recognise the lady tulip, *Tulipa clusiana,* so far removed is it from the glossy hybrids that breeders have been tinkering with since the seventeenth century. A delicate little thing, it has two-tone little flowers in pale red and cream. It is naturalised in southern Europe although native to northwest India, so, as you would expect, it likes plenty of sun and good drainage.

Erythroniums or dog's-tooth violets are undeniably lovely flowers with their marbled leaves and pendant flowers, recurved at the tips. Not the same as other bulbs, they hate being dried out, and are best bought as growing plants in spring. They like partly shaded woodland conditions and well-drained soil enriched with peat and leafmould, in a place that doesn't dry out in summer. Try and plant bulbs in drifts, more as they would be in nature, rather than in tidy circles with one in the middle. Bonemeal is always an acceptable fertiliser, but on poor soils well-rotted compost (not manure) is good, provided it is worked into surrounding soil and not in direct contact with the bulbs.

 *10 October 1993*

Plan of Action for Next Autumn

At this time of year, disillusion sets in, the best laid schemes have gone awry and it seems that the beautiful garden for this year exists only in the imagination. So here are three key ways to improve matters for next autumn.

The first is to include some repeat-flowering roses. Agreed, hybrid teas and floribundas (now known respectively as large-flowered and cluster-flowered) are still doing their stuff, but if you only like the old-fashioned sorts, you must be very particular when choosing them, for most only have one glorious midsummer flowering. Today climbing 'Madame Caroline Testout' is covered in deliciously pink cabbagey roses, looking just as good as she did in June. The heady scent of 'Madame Isaac Pereire' wafts on the air as she presents her second flush of voluptuous purple-pink flowers. 'Souvenir de Saint Anne's' (an Irish rose, a sport of 'Souvenir de la Malmaison') has been in flower for weeks and will potter on till Christmas. 'General Schablikine' is regathering strength for a late October presentation.

Poor 'Jacques Cartier' *would* be producing its scented, tender pink double flowers, if it wasn't planted in the wrong place – a dry spot too near a wall. I cannot wait to move it to a better soil in a sunnier position and will do so in a few weeks. Even old rose bushes transplant remarkably well. Without fail cut them back to about 12 inches to an outward-pointing bud, neatly trim any damaged roots, and prepare the planting hole with two buckets of well-rotted manure or compost and two handfuls of bonemeal. (Remember it is no use digging up a rose you dislike and replanting one you do in exactly the same spot. Specific Replant Disease causes the original rose to poison the soil for the new rose, which will languish indefinitely.)

The second way to improve the look of your autumn garden is to include plenty of summer plants that bloom on into autumn, such as penstemons, osteospermums, fuchsias, verbenas *(including *V. bonariensis*), *Aster × frikartii* 'Mönch' and *A. thomsonii* 'Nanus', violas (provided they have been deadheaded) and *Erysimum* 'Bowles' Mauve'. Worth special mention in this category is *Geranium × riversleaianum* 'Russell Prichard'. From May to October it sends out ever-lengthening slender greygreen stems copiously sparkled in shocking magenta flowers. One of the parents of this hybrid is *Geranium traversii* from the mild Chatham Islands off New Zealand, so plant it in a sheltered, sunny spot. There is some dispute as to its other parent: some say the Pyrenean *G. endressi* and others our native *G. sanguineum*, the bloody cranesbill. Whatever its pedigree, 'Russell Prichard' should be in a book of records under Longest Flowering Season.

Another contender for inclusion under the same heading is *Potentilla nepalensis* 'Miss Willmott'. This is a little herbaceous plant from western Nepal, with strawberry-like leaves and cherry-red petals with finely etched veins and black velvety middles. The flowers positively glow on dull autumn days.

The third and obvious way to improve your garden in autumn is by leaving plenty of space for plants that truly belong to autumn, such as nerines, asters, boltonias, colchicums, *Cyclamen hederifolium*, dahlias, chrysanthemums, schizostylis, sedums, toad lilies and so on. *Salvia uliginosa*, just coming into flower now, is pure bright blue, a scarce flower colour at all times but specially so in autumn. *Uliginosa* means 'growing in marshy places' but it manages fine on dry Dublin soil. A lanky salvia, floppity in growth, fond of leaning on nearby plants, its azure spires of blossom are immensely refreshing when most other plants are slowly winding down.

 *11 October 1992*

Autumn Gardeners Sing the Executioner's Song

The autumn blitz is in process. Heads are rolling. But I think I'd learn a lot from one of those 'How-to' books on assertiveness – how can businessmen sleep at night after multiple sackings, when I find it difficult to dig up one clematis?

The case of the clematis goes as follows: some eight years ago a white *Clematis montana* was planted to grow up an apple tree. It did a fine job, flowering at apple blossom time, mingling its flowers with those of the apple. Enchanting. It continued to grow. A nearby honeysuckle, itself no mean grower, is now struggling for light, as are two ivies, a climbing rose, plus a cluster of shade-loving bergenias and hellebores, now barely surviving in the gloom beneath the clematis. We have encountered the typical dilemma of all gardens, always noticeable in autumn.

There is a non-existent word, which urgently needs to be coined, meaning 'one plant must die in order to save a dozen'. I can think of numerous applications for it. I think *Clematis montana* a wonderful plant, but the game of gardening is all about getting the best possible value out of the smallest space. So, the executioner now appointed, I'm avoiding the clematis for the time being and walking round the garden the other way.

Note number 870 has been reached in my gardening notebook. 'Re-do corner under yew,' it announces. The time comes when it's easier, and better gardening, to take out every plant, dig and manure an area and replant, rather than fiddling around re-doing small patches. This bed is under next door's huge yew, so a major dig should give the new plants a chance against the competition of the yew's roots. The new scheme is in part of the yellow garden, so I'm going for a gold-variegated holly as the linchpin. Underplanting will include perennial yellow foxglove (*Digitalis grandiflora*), a low-growing gold-leafed campanula 'Dickson's Gold', and Bowles' sedge, *Carex elata* 'Aurea', a well-behaved neat plant, quite different to Bowles' golden grass, *Milium effusum* 'Aureum', which is madly pretty in the spring but soon becomes a mess.

I noted on a visit to a friend the excellent use of *Argyranthemum* 'Jamaica Primrose'. This is a tender, non-stop flowering, yellow daisy (you should have cuttings in by now). *Anthemis* 'E. C. Buxton', another yellow daisy, did marvellously well in early summer, but let the side down later. Next year the anthemis will be treated as an annual – as soon as it fades, out it will come, and pots of 'Jamaica Primrose' will be popped in instead. Miss Jekyll was always cheating and sticking in tender plants – cannas, heliotropes, begonias, you name it – why shouldn't I?

You should be asking yourself serious questions now: next year's garden depends on it. Which areas need a complete overhaul – taking everything out, digging, manuring and replanting? Does the arrangement of plants please you? Perhaps the bed needs some more large leaves (bergenias, hostas), some more spiky leaves (phormiums, yuccas, irises). Are the plants growing well? Have you got enough good evergreens for winter? What about mahonias, hollies, *Viburnum tinus* or sarcococcas? These latter are rather neglected plants, with shiny, intense deep green leaves, and tiny, boring flowers with a wonderful scent that carries on the winter air.

By the way, the clematis got its own back. The executioner arrived in lashing rain. Mud slurped over everything – garden paths, tools, clothes. But later – after two hours of path washing (and three goes of the washing machine) – the plants released from the gloom beneath the clematis have just seen the sun for the first time.

 *16 October 1994*

Finding Objects of Desire

The gardening bug, once caught, can only get worse. Akin to compulsive gambling, the desire to acquire more plants turns into an obsession. Although it may recede in summer, when the garden's full to bursting point, empty spaces appear in the autumn, so the sight of a new plant may cause immoderate excitement.

The very idea of lusting after a plant seems strange to new gardeners, who are excluded from what seems to be the secret society of senior gardeners, who operate private deals in rare plants. The garden Mafiosi are a dedicated bunch of plant enthusiasts, to be recognised only by the acquisitive gleam in their eyes. Venturing rarely to the garden centre proper, you may see them there briefly, gliding past the plant tables, occasionally prodding a pot with a grubby finger. They only go on wet week days – avoiding busy Saturdays as they have no wish to discuss their plant collections with lesser fry, and, of course, no true devotee would waste a sunny day in the garden centre.

But remember, these steely-eyed godfathers of the gardening world have all come through the ranks. At many a plant sale they have eagerly offered to hump boxes of plants, make tea, or stay late and sweep up. They have attended umpteen lectures and listened respectfully to gardening doyennes as they laid down the law on matters horticultural. They have visited other gardens at every opportunity, all the while making copious notes. They've accepted every invitation – to morning coffee, lunch, tea or indeed no refreshment whatsoever – provided there was a chance to see the garden. For once inside, opportunity knocks, and desire goes into overdrive.

An acquaintance used to say on garden visits 'I come to admire and not to acquire.' This charming lie sows the seeds in the mind of the garden owner that you would like something. The next step is to hover beside a particular plant, and say 'What is this called?' This immediately implies that you haven't got it, and should jog its owner into action. If this doesn't work, try 'Is it easy from cuttings?' The owner is then torn between boasting how simple it is to root from slips, so it would be churlish not to give you some straight away, or muttering 'Wrong time of year,' and chivvying you along.

But garden networking is difficult if you don't yet know a wide circle of gardeners. And the aforementioned Mafia will surely intimidate the beginner. So, if you detect symptoms of the bug about to attack, get up off your ass, bypass the hierarchy, launch into the attack. Search every local garden centre weekly and invest in the *The RHS Plant Finder* (Dorling Kindersley). So no more bleating, please, that you can't find the object of your desire.

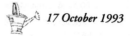 *17 October 1993*

Lose Friends but not Nerines

Unless you garden in total shade you simply must grow some nerines. Autumn-flowering bulbs from South Africa, the most usually seen is *Nerine bowdenii.* You may have noticed them in other gardens – the lily-like flowers, in a clear, pale, shocking pink, out at the moment. Very easy to grow, provided you give them well-drained soil in full sun (under a south wall in cold areas), lovely for picking, and once they are planted you can forget about them for years.

In similar vein to *Nerine bowdenii,* but even more desirable, *Nerine undulata* is a far more refined little thing, each petal of the pale pink flowers crimped and frilled. Their slender stems and delicate blooms have surprising stamina against heavy autumn rain and remain in bloom for a full four weeks, a patch of them forming a haze of pink.

Just as in real life, in the gardening world there are those that do the giving and those that do the taking. Each year in early October I am sharply reminded of the latter, when *Nerine undulata* comes into flower. I had a friend (notice the past tense) who was possessed of such a formidable strain of acquisitiveness when it came to plants, that I did not dare to invite this person to the garden during October. (May too was a dangerous month, when a fine camassia in the most delectable shade of blue, was the star of the garden.)

Anyway, at first our erstwhile relationship went well, as I soon became acquainted with the rules of the game: the idea was that I would give the person any plant they fancied in *my* garden and they would return the compliment. No sooner was a note taken of a desirable plant in Ranelagh than off it would go to its new home; the snag was, there were few plants in my friend's garden that I didn't already possess. This somewhat one-way system of friendship prospered until October. Then my one and only bulb of the nerine flowered for the first time. One look at this plant and you would see why to part with it would be unthinkable. Out of sight, out of mind seemed the only course to take. So, inventing numerous excuses, muttering 'nothing in flower – garden in horrible mess – early frost has blackened everything, etc,' I just managed to avoid confrontation.

Sixteen years on, from that one bulb, there is now a group of 31. I must have given away at least a dozen over the years. Some visitors to the garden stand and gaze at a plant and politely refrain from asking for it, but one can sense how much they long to own it. There is a lady dimly at the back of my mind, I think she was called Mrs Do-as-you-would-be-done-by, a character from *The Water Babies*. Anyway, she must have made a lasting impression as, knowing what it is like to want a plant desperately, in certain cases I have weakened and dug one up.

 *18 October 1992*

The Trees are in their Autumn Beauty

Recently I went to Mount Usher Gardens. I went alone, so nobody was gossiping in my ear, shattering the silence of a still autumn day. Except for the mild chattering of rooks high in the trees and the buzz of a tired wasp, the only sound was the scrunch of my feet, scuffling through fallen leaves on gravel paths. Warm, damp air wafted beneath the tree canopy, bringing fragrant, mushroomy smells of decaying vegetation, mixed with the scent of bonfire smoke.

Red-hot pokers, their glorious autumn torches vivid in the low sun, grew close to *Enkianthus perulatus*, a beautiful little lime-hating shrub from Japan, its neat leaves now intense blood red. Trees on the Japanese maple walk nearby were beginning to blaze, the sun shining through their dazzling crimson foliage, the shadows on the grass beneath patterned with scarlet. These small trees at Mount Usher (forms of *Acer palmatum*) are wonderful specimens, rarely seen in such beautiful maturity.

Another outstanding shrub (not for autumn colour but for its bark), was *Rhododendron barbatum* from the Himalayas. Its branches are as many-hued as tie-dyed silk, in maroon and deep apricot, biscuit and rusty brown, with a satin finish, wonderful to touch.

The artery of the gardens is the river Vartry. You can sense its watery presence wherever you are. Mesmerised by its still, dark pools, you can stand on one of the suspension bridges, and watch the reflections of gunnera leaves, their giant umbrellas making mysterious liquid shadows.

Walking along the riverbank you encounter many special plants, such as *Disanthus cercidifolius*, a Japanese shrub of fussy temperament, for lime-free soil and a sheltered position. A member of the witch-hazel family, uninteresting flowers appear in autumn, just as the foliage turns brilliant claret-red. A gem for the lime-free garden, but a heart-break shrub for limey suburbia. The leaves of *Fothergilla major*, also allied to the witch-hazels and likewise a lime-hater, were just on the turn to golden yellow.

Autumn colour is a fickle moment to catch – on the same tree you can see graded colours, all the different stages from summer green through yellow and apricot, with some leaves already flaring crimson. *Nyssa sylvatica*, the Tupelo tree from North America, was at just such a heavenly stage, the grass beneath it radiant with colour.

Draped over a tree on the riverbank walk was *Vitis coignetiae*, too large for all but the most extensive pergola or bank. Its huge leaves were dying a slow and splendid death, hanging in great festoons, backlit by the sun, or scattered on the path in pools of defiant brilliance.

New to me was *Euonymus bungeanus*, a remarkably pretty small tree. The leaves were a luminous light yellow. Elegant and fluttery, they seemed suspended like graceful ringlets. Presumably an ancient specimen, its branches were almost completely clothed in silky mosses and lichens.

Mount Usher is a great Irish garden, owned by Mrs Madeline Jay. John Anderson is the head gardener. You can go there in March for the great pink magnolias, in May for the rhododendrons, in August for the eucryphias, or any time at all for the renowned collection of eucalyptus. But perhaps this garden is at its best on a still day in autumn, where you can both marvel at the collection of rare trees and shrubs in their autumn colours, and find a little of the rarest of commodities – silence.

 **23 October 1994**

The Curse of the Vine Weevil

'It just died.'

I like this remark, for it absolves the gardener from blame, as if the plant, out of sheer bloody-mindedness, died in order to spite you. Daphnes are fond of dying. I'm on my second *D. cneorum* and *D. arbuscula*, fourth *D. retusa* and fifth of the delectable *D. petraea* 'Grandiflora'.

The thing about daphnes is that they don't die overnight – they go into a sulk. It starts with one twig. You think nothing of it. It happens again. You prune it off. Some weeks later, ditto. Then it comes to the stage that whenever you look at the plant, another branch has yellowed. Eventually you can stand it no longer and remove the offending object. (Such an affront, one's garden littered with dead daphnes.)

Only *D. bholua* goes from strength to strength, with a scent that carries half a garden away and is also sniffable at close quarters. I have made a note to replace *Daphne × burkwoodii* 'Somerset' (easy, pink, spring). This had the grace to live for ten years before a respectable death of what I assumed was old age.

One invisible cause of death is explained thus: the plant starts life in its nursery, in perfect conditions for rapid growth, its peat-based compost filled with fertilisers so nourishing they are as mother's milk to the roots. On being planted in the garden, the roots refused to be weaned from the original compost and are reluctant to sample ordinary garden soil. This was brought home to me yesterday as I was dividing two newish plants, an astrantia and a pulmonaria. Both root-balls were a congested tangle and only the occasional root had chanced life in the surrounding soil. And, despite an incredibly wet autumn, this mass was dry in the centre. Whilst herbaceous plants will eventually get going, when this happens to trees and shrubs, not only are the roots unable to cope with dryness at the root, but also the plant can never establish as it is grossly unstable.

'The lads got it,' is the verdict on many a cause of death. 'Lads' is an upside down euphemism, for it refers to the vine weevil, all of whom are female. The adult vine weevil is a nondescript small greyish black beetle with a short snout. This is used for biting neat, half-circular portions out of the edges of leaves. You can tell within minutes of entering a garden, whether the 'lads' are present: just look at the bergenias, and the tell-tale bites will inform you. (Note: One of the mores of polite gardening behaviour is never to comment if you *do* notice – it's like mentioning somebody's grubby kitchen or noticing a rat in their yard.)

The larvae of the vine weevil are slightly curved, creamy-white grubs with pale brown heads. They attack favourite plants such as cyclamen, camellias, rhododendrons and fuchsias. No member of the primula family is safe. Limp-leaved primroses given a tweak will often reveal that they have virtually no roots, and a gang of grubs feeding on what's left. Rules for controlling vine weevil: dig up and investigate all suspect plants, examine the roots, wash them out in a bucket of water, move to another part of the garden. Change potting compost in containers at least once a year. Adopt a policy of extreme cleanliness, as piles of leaf litter in sheds and greenhouses are ideal hidey holes for adults. (There is a form of biological control available, which is effective, but requires a reasonably high temperature to operate.)

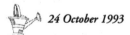 *24 October 1993*

Pruning is the All-Time Hoax

A request came the other day for a piece about pruning. Impossible to cram it all into this week, but here is Pruning Part 1.

The more I've thought about it the more I've come to the conclusion that pruning (with a few notable exceptions) is the all-time hoax. The secrets of the ancient art of pruning have been carefully guarded by generations of head gardeners, who had to justify their existence during the winter months. (Nothing better for convincing an employer that work was in progress than the distant sound of clipping and chopping.) Agreed, the pruning of fruit trees is somewhat specialised, but outside the orchard it is quite in order to adopt a different approach.

Pruning is an operation designed to make those new to gardening feel thoroughly intimidated. Have you noticed that gardeners with notions always seem to have secateurs to hand (or back pocket)? I once knew a lady gardener who, when she sat down to lunch, laid her secateurs on the table beside her knife and fork. This was not because she wanted to use them as an implement for cutting up her dinner, but as a unique form of horticultural sabre-rattling.

Pruning, to keep a plant vigorous, healthy and well-balanced in shape, is largely a matter of common sense. The trouble is, beginners are inclined to turn into a jelly at the very idea of cutting a plant. It is a most unconfident hand that holds the secateurs. Even if you do something quite outrageous, the chances of actually killing the plant are slim. The first rule is to cut out any dead, damaged, diseased or weak wood, which will only use up the plant's energy to no purpose. (In this climate you can do this entirely when it suits you.) An important point is to keep a close eye on a young tree: make sure that it has only one leading shoot – you don't want to breed a two-headed monster.

You will read that some shrubs flower on wood formed the previous year. I could never understand what this meant until I learnt the hard way. Why, each April, was the whole district alive with yellow forsythia whilst my own bush was a boring lump of green leaves? Indeed it was so uninteresting that as soon as it put on some new growth (which I didn't realise would bear next year's flowers), I immediately chopped it off. It was only when I forgot about it one year that it became a bright splash of yellow the following spring. So, if you own a forsythia, cut out the branches that have just flowered in May. (I've since decided that there are enough forsythias in the neighbourhood without having one here as well.)

Slightly later flowering, but requiring similar treatment, are deutzias, philadelphus and weigela. Immediately after flowering (late June or so) cut out all the branches that have just bloomed. This prevents them becoming a congested, shapeless mass of overcrowded shoots, allows all their strength to go into supporting the young growth and lets in light, air and sun to ripen next year's wood.

Another group of plants that are pruned very hard in spring are fast-growing, late-flowering shrubs that bloom on the current year's wood, such as *Buddleja davidii*, caryopteris, *Hydrangea paniculata*. This is to prevent them becoming too tall, to keep them compact and, in the case of the buddleias, to enable the flowers with attendant butterflies to be closer to eye level.

The other point to hammer home is that very few plants actually need pruning (hard to understand when you see those grown in the vicinity of public lavatories where, regardless of species, all shrubs have been turned into a blob). But a thoughtful snip, provided you remember that you are dealing with a living plant, may not only improve its appearance but also enable more light to reach neighbouring plants. And, to achieve total rejuvenation of an ancient berberis or lilac, prune to within a few feet of the ground. Hang on till spring before doing this.

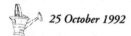 *25 October 1992*

The Full Box Set

So plain, so green and so infinitely satisfying: I cannot say enough good things about box (*Buxus sempervirens*). I love it in pots, I love it used as an edging and I love it used in pairs to announce an entrance or exit, to different bits of the garden. In summer box makes a soothing background, controls escapades of bright colour and gives formality to exuberant plantings. But it is in winter that the intense green of box is invaluable. For small hedges in the smallest gardens the dwarf cultivars such as 'Myosotidifolia' and 'Suffruticosa' are best – they don't mind being clipped indefinitely to under a foot high. Any time of year will do for planting and moving box, except when it's actually freezing. Sun or shade is equally acceptable. Any type of soil will do, provided there is good drainage.

I was lucky enough to obtain two plants of a very small form from an old garden in Tipperary. I pulled them to bits and turned them into cuttings, which rooted outdoors in a little trench in the shade, the soil around them made very firm. From those two plants I now have enough box to edge a small parterre if necessary. Box needs clipping once a year, around July. It's worth putting down sheets of polythene beforehand, and on no account clip in wet weather, as the little leaves stick to everything and are a nightmare to pick up.

I was recently asked whether it was worth taking a present of an elderly box hedge. I suggested a new hedge would be quicker to make, using young plants. As soon as you disturb an old hedge it annoyingly separates into different scruffy plants. But old portions of hedge are excellent for making into topiary shapes. They can be formed into cylinders, sphere cones or pyramids comparatively quickly.

Box shapes are not cheap to buy – the wonderful curlicues imported from Belgium are well over £100 – but there's a good way to make a box ball yourself: buy five cheap plants, plant four in a square roughly 10 inches apart, with one in the middle, and clip. You should have a recognisable ball within a year. When planting box cones, remember that they'll become old and fat over the years, so allow plenty of space.

Topiary is living sculpture, allowing the gardener to indulge in flights of fancy, by creating fantastic birds, beasts, corkscrews, chess figures, lollipops (balls on sticks), giant eggs in egg-cups, mushrooms or plainer geometric forms, such as obelisks or cylinders. Simple shapes such as balls or cones are best for small areas.

For making complicated figures, a peacock for example, yew should be trained over a wire frame or wire netting squeezed into shape. Portugal laurel, bay, holly (both plain and variegated) and privet are other options for topiary. I'm particularly fond of topiarised holly: the shears twitch every time I pass my large specimen of 'Golden Queen' – perhaps it should be turned into a cylinder?

An important note here on the subject of yew: the Irish yew is totally unsuitable for topiary as it's too fastigiate (upright) in habit; the ordinary English yew (*Taxus baccata*) must be used instead. Irish yews that have become obese with age can only be restored to a slender column by removing every second outer branch as low down as possible, and then tying them in with plastic-coated wire, so as not to chafe the branches. On no account take out the middle of the bush, thus leaving nothing left to tie the outer ones to.

I'm making a small Green Garden. It should be a relief for the eye in the summer and a pleasing spot for winter. The paved, rectangular space will be surrounded with a box hedge and have a round carpet of dwarf box in the middle, set on gravel, and surrounded by a square of box hedge. Growing in occasional gaps in the paving are going to be foliage plants. These will only be green – absolutely no variegation, nor glaucous tones – just plain green – crested hart's tongue ferns, lacy *Cystopteris fragilis*, shiny *Bergenia stracheyi* 'Alba', London pride, lady's mantle and sweet woodruff. The only flowers allowed will be modest white or green except for spring, when there'll be blue chionodoxas and scillas.

 *30 October 1994*

A Rose by any Other Name

Flowery ghosts abound, some benign, some otherwise. The generous spirit of Mr Bowles (1865–1954) is always with us, in the form of his wallflower *Erysimum* 'Bowles' Mauve', never without flower. In the less benign category is *Dianthus* 'Mrs Sinkins', named last century for the matron of Slough Poor Law Institution. Her scent, though hauntingly delicious, still brings cold corridors and cold soup to mind. The shade of Lawrence Johnston, the creator of Hidcote, has many different guises – *Lavandula angustifolia* 'Hidcote' perhaps the most ubiquitous. But his campanula 'Hidcote Amethyst', although often sighted in choice collectors' gardens, is such a ghostly, lonely mauve it is nigh impossible to blend with anything else.

The rose 'Madame Caroline Testout' was christened in honour of a French couturière in 1901 who, adept at courting publicity, persuaded Pernet-Ducher (the celebrated rose breeder) to name a rose for her. Still voluptuous, magnificent in her second blooming, she shines on despite the chill of autumn nights.

You may have wondered about Miss Jessopp, as in *Rosmarinus officinalis* 'Miss Jessopp's Upright' (note, none of your Ms in the nineteenth century): the upright rosemary is a fine plant commemorating a Sunday school teacher (rejoicing in the Christian name of Euphemia) that haunts the best of gardens.

Alice Artindale must have had a delicate constitution, for the delphinium named in her honour is so prone to mildew that one wonders if she herself suffered from consumption. 'Some flowers seem to gather to themselves a special aura of romance,' says Alex Pankhurst of this rare plant in her excellent book *Who Does Your Garden Grow* (Earl's Eye Publishing). But the double flowers of *Delphinium* 'Alice Artindale', though infinitely covetable, have an eerie effect when dusted with powdery mildew.

As his home was right next door, Augustine Henry stalks this garden regularly. A customs officer and plant collector, among the many good plants he introduced was *Lilium henryi*, from the limestone hills of China (1889). In the wild, this gorgeous light orange lily, faintly spotted with maroon inside, grows only a few feet, but here, due no doubt to his benevolent spirit, it reaches fully seven feet.

At dusk this evening, pottering out of the shadows, you may even see the shade of David Douglas, come to inspect his *Limnanthes douglasii*. The cheerful yellow flowers of the poached egg plant belie his untimely death in 1834 in Hawaii, mangled to death in a pit dug to trap wild animals. And if you hear a faint rustle in the bushes, it could only be the poet Thomas Moore, come to savour the perfume of the Last Rose of Summer, *Rosa chinensis* 'Old Blush'.

 *31 October 1993*

November

Plants and a North Wall

I am often asked to suggest suitable plants to clothe a north wall. First, the north wall in question needs to be qualified. Is it fairly low, relatively light and bright, with no invading tree roots nearby (in which case you have considerable scope), or is it a high north wall, casting much shade, in which case the choice narrows?

The secret of planting near walls (of any aspect) is the preparation of the planting hole. People have the vaguest ideas about what this consists of. Some think that all they have to do is make a little scoop (you could hardly call it a hole) exactly the same size as the plant's container. They then wonder why the plant fails to grow. The soil near buildings is often so poor and rubbly that no plant has a chance. Therefore excavate a hole preferably three feet square and two feet deep – you may need a pickaxe for this. Break up the soil at the bottom of the hole and refill with good soil from another part of the garden, lavishly mixed with compost or well-rotted manure (two to three bucketfuls), several handfuls of bonemeal and two handfuls of general fertiliser.

Hydrangea petiolaris, the climbing hydrangea, is often recommended for a north wall. It really does thrive in such a position. When it actually starts to do the thriving is another matter. Depressingly slow to begin with, I didn't look after mine properly and it sat and looked at me for years, refusing to grow in any direction, let alone up the wall. Eventually I started to give it fertiliser, copious amounts of water and a thick top dressing (three buckets) of well-rotted manure. Now well-established, it requires little attention save annual applications of manure. A self-clinging climber, it makes its own way up the wall by means of aerial roots. The creamy-white summer flowers are sweetly scented (a fact I have yet to see mentioned in gardening books) especially on warm evenings after dark.

Another plant that has proved most successful on my north wall, lighting up the area in winter, is a thoroughly ordinary plant, *Euonymus fortunei* 'Silver Queen'. It has evergreen leaves, nicely variegated in green and white, and insignificant greenish flowers in spring. It too is slowish to begin with, but conversely it is always tidy and well-behaved, so you are not presented with a major hacking job after a few years.

231

But suppose you wanted something with really good flowers? Easily organised by planting a clematis to grow through it. I didn't choose one of the large-flowered climbers for this position (they are too fussy and liable to wilt) but *Clematis macropetala* 'Maidwell Hall', a spring-flowering kind with dark blue double flowers. The two plants are totally compatible, like in the very best marriages, where neither party wishes to dominate the other. The euonymus leaves are interwoven with indigo blue of clematis in April and late summer presents a charming secondary display, when the euonymus is draped instead with fluffy silvery-clematis seed-heads.

Pyracanthas are often suggested for north walls. Apart from their creamy flowers in summer followed by orange-red berries, it is their dark evergreen leaves, excellent in winter, for which they are desirable.

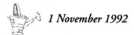 *1 November 1992*

A Passionate Affair with the Flowers of Romance

November is a month for daydreams. Instead of worrying about the unspeakable mess outdoors, let the leaves gather into soggy congregations, draw the curtains, sit down by the fire, and plan a garden of romance.

Romantic gardeners are in constant opposition to those with tidy minds. The latter, desiring order at all costs, can see gardens in strictly formal shapes only, viewing each bit of the garden as an architectural problem with an architectural solution. Scent and colour become also-rans. He patrols the garden (it's invariably a 'he') snatching at weeds, muttering about imperfections of the lawn, emitting a constant grumble about the untidiness of plants.

The romantic gardener adores plants for themselves alone, and considers them for their evocative connotations as well as for their individual beauty. The romantic gardener, busy thinking up outrageous and delightful schemes involving wild expense, thinks nothing of planning for pergolas, ruined temples and flowery meads. There must be lavender hedges, bowers draped in honeysuckle, and old roses in glorious profusion – damask, gallica, bourbon and moss – with the old-fashioned colours – amaranth, mulberry and damson.

To stir the imagination, beauties such as 'Souvenir de la Princesse de Lamballe' are included (commemorating the governess to Marie Antoinette's children, lynched by a furious mob on her way to the guillotine); Thomas Moore's 'Last Rose of Summer' – *Rosa chinensis* 'Old Blush'; 'Cuisse de Nymphe' (as plumply pink as you'd expect); and the sweet briar or eglantine, *Rosa rubiginosa*, beloved since civilisation began for its perfumed leaves. The apothecary's rose, *Rosa gallica* 'Officinalis', is another rose of great antiquity and you must have 'Rose d'Amour' (also known as St Mark's rose), a good shrub with clean foliage and clear pink flowers over two months or more.

In the shade, lily-of-the-valley, bluebells, violets and wild strawberries colonise with blatant abandon. Drifts of Queen Anne's lace (known as cow parsley by the more prosaic) display umbels of delicate creamy flowers each May, mixed with fragrant white poet's narcissus, *Narcissus poeticus*, the last of all the daffodils to bloom.

The heavenly pink tree peony, to be found only in old Irish gardens, grows in remembrance of Maria Edgeworth (1768–1849), who wrote: 'My peony tree is the most beautiful thing on Earth – 19 flowers will be in full blow next week. Poor dear Lord Oriel gave it me and his own is dead and he is dead. But love for him still lives in me.' (Lord Oriel had given her a piece of the first tree peony to be imported from China.) The romantic garden is full of such delicious sadness.

For spring, there will be bulbs such as crown imperials (*Fritillaria imperialis*) which were introduced to cultivation prior to 1590, and madonna lilies (*Lilium candidum*). This is the lily you see in early Italian paintings of the Annunciation, the loveliest of all lilies, despite being afflicted with in-built virus. They say the madonna lily prefers to grow only in cottage gardens, and pines away when moved to more lavish conditions.

Plants with biblical associations abound – Jacob's ladder, Solomon's seal and of course the 'lilies of the field', now said to be *Sternbergia lutea*. This little bulb, of the same family as the daffodils, is just coming into bloom, with flowers like large bright yellow crocuses and strap-shaped deep green leaves. It must have a warm sunny position and good drainage.

Some rare antique plants have been in cultivation so long that they have lost vigour. One such is fair maids of France (*Ranunculus aconitifolius* 'Flore Pleno'), reputed to have been brought to England by refugee Huguenots. The flowers, in May, are enchanting double white buttons.

 *4 November 1994*

Near to the Madding Crowd

It isn't often I get a chance to review television, so here goes. I first heard mention of *In an Englishwoman's Garden* (a series screened over the last few weeks by the BBC), when a friend remarked she had seen a programme. A rather tiresome woman and not much of a garden, she reported. The first programme I saw was on Nancy Lancaster, one of the founders of Colefax and Fowler, interior decorators to the upper class and would-be members thereof.

Opening picture of a lawn, upon which was the topiary equivalent of a chocolate whirl. To the left was one of those natty seats on wheels, like a wheelbarrow, gleaming with white gloss paint. Next, dawn in the garden at Hasley Court dewdrops and all. An elderly butler equipped with a tape recorder appears. He wobbles along the path in the mist, his duty to tape the birdsong so that it can be played back during his mistress's breakfast.

Next shot, ceremonial preparation of the said breakfast. Nancy Lancaster appears, looking wonderful in yellow. She is well into her 90s. Nobody but her, who has enormous style, could have conceived the birdsong idea. She whizzed around the garden in her wheelchair, wearing a black beret. Then a few nice shots of the garden. Needless to say there were masses of box, old roses, topiary and good vistas in every direction. It positively seethed with good taste.

Next, a large party of visitors arrives. They are being shown round by the new owner of Hasley Court (apparently Nancy Lancaster has sold the house but has a life interest in the garden). It appears that the makers of this series were more interested in the visitors to the gardens than in the gardens themselves. A fascinating social comment in itself, these visitors were almost sickeningly keen: 'You too can be a middle-aged groupie,' they seem to be saying, as they plunge from their coach, cameras and notebooks at the ready, rushing along the garden paths in their sensible shoes, macs over the arm, a cry of delight at each corner.

Another programme included a visit to Mrs Merton at the Old Rectory, Burghfield. I went there myself one March and was very taken with the garden, the massed planting of hellebores and pulmonarias being exceptionally good. In the programme we saw little of the garden, but an enthusiasm of visitors. One of the groupies, complete with straw hat, treated us to an earnest explanation as to why the middle-aged take to garden visiting. Another, having achieved the prize of actually conducting a conversation with Mrs Merton, was positively slavering. And the sales tills jumped.

 *7 November 1993*

Getting to Grips with Leaf Control

Leaves. It seems they will never end. Immediately you tidy them up, along comes another lot, fluttering down and swirling about, clogging up gutters and drains and forming damp little heaps all ready for somebody to slip on. I don't know whether worms eat fallen leaves (they certainly eat fresh ones) or if they use them as ventilation shafts. Notice how quickly leaves become half buried in the soil, as worms drag them down to their burrows. Much harder to dislodge at this stage, one of the keys to easy leaf control is to keep leaves on the move until you get a chance to pick them up.

Regular raking is the traditional method but a blowing machine, used regularly, will so disturb the leaves they have no chance of settling into sodden, less easily moved heaps. Blowing machines, the ultimate answer to hoover envy, must have been specially invented for men. For a start blowing machines, like hoovers, can be left with the engine running, to give an impression that work is in progress, whilst the operator may be sitting down reading the paper. Suburban man may not be so far removed from the cave as you think – he can make loud war-like noises with his blowing machine or compost crusher and he can make fires all summer with his barbecue – I dare say fragrant wafts of roasting wild pig is not unlike that of burnt sausage.

Lazy man will no doubt choose the sort of blowing machine that sucks the leaves up into a bag. Apart from pandering to his hoover envy, he thinks this type of machine will make life easy. Sensible man will get the non mickey-mouse type machine, admittedly very expensive, which only blows the leaves. Having hunted the leaves round the garden and collected them up into heaps you can either put them in an enclosure made of four stout posts surrounded by wire netting or put them in a large polythene sack, such as peat is sold in. You then tie up the top of the bag, and then charge at it several times with the garden fork to allow air to enter the bag, and store until leaves have become nicely rotted.

The best leafmould is made from oak or beech leaves. Plane and sycamore take for ever to rot down – leave these and evergreens such as laurel, holly and privet out of the mixture, as well as pine needles, which are too acid and take too long to decay. Small amounts of fallen leaves can be put on the compost heap, well mixed in with everything else, but larger quantities are best rotted down on their own. You can let the leaves stay put on large areas consisting mainly of trees and shrubs and they will rot down to feed the soil and allow the blackbirds good places to rootle for worms. The most likely worm you will see on the surface of the soil is *Lumbricus terrestris* and you may even hear it nosing about among the leaves.

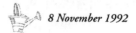 *8 November 1992*

Rockeries Rear their Ugly Heads

Leafy, muddy, bedraggled November. A negative month in the garden at the best of times, I spotted some gardens the other day that made me feel even gloomier, not a million miles from Palmerston Park, we might call them the result of the Palmerston Park School of Gardening. Graduates of this particular school have an unerring eye for the unsuitable. How else could you describe a fine, red-brick Victorian family house equipped with a minimalist Japanese garden in the front?

Or perhaps a collection of phormiums, all different, with a predominance of the more colourful cultivars, the sort with the garish stripes? One single phormium may well be used as a brilliant focal point. But just imagine an indiscretion of phormiums rampaging through the autumnal gloom of Dublin 6.

Early this century a new gardening craze came to boiling point, namely the construction of rockeries. Alpines, wild plants from the mountains of Europe, became all the rage, much inspired by the writing of Reginald Farrer, who travelled extensively, discovering plants and then describing them in extravagant language. Rockeries mushroomed in the suburbs, many more akin to a rock bun with currants sticking out all over than a natural outcrop of stone.

Farrer, well-known for his argumentative disposition, was memorably scathing about one rock garden in particular, that of Sir Frank Crisp at Friar Park, near Henley. It was constructed out of concrete and slate, with caves, ice grottoes and a mock Matterhorn with bronze chamois atop. One can only assume that Sir Frank Crisp is the inspiration behind certain gardens today.

The important rule about rock garden construction, ie that the stones should be laid so as to imitate the natural strata of rock, was rarely adhered to in those days. Farrer described one in 1918 thus: 'The plan is simplicity itself. You take one hundred cartloads of bald, square-faced boulders. You next drop them all about absolutely anyhow; and you then plant things among them. The chaotic hideousness of the result is something to be remembered with shudders ever after.' Quite. Most of these rockeries of yesteryear have thankfully crumbled away. Meanwhile, a new generation of gardeners is busily re-inventing them, following the formula as Farrer describes above. They are often to be found in Dublin front gardens, where for some inexplicable reason, you will find a large mound of soil, liberally decorated in a random fashion with lumps of granite. Further embellishments include a wide selection of different plants – trees, shrubs, herbaceous plants and otherwise, usually only one of each, planted very close together. Perhaps the person who first remarked 'And what on earth is that?' had just spotted one of these essays in horticulture.

Lastly, there seem to be two interpretations of 'organic' used as a term in gardening. Firstly, 'organic' describes the admirable philosophy of never using chemicals and recycling all vegetable matter. Secondly, you can have what's known as an 'organic' shape in garden design, ie an irregular wavy-edged shape, of a path or bed, strongly reminiscent of a kidney, liver or even an appendix. There's a lot of it about these days in Dublin 6.

 *14 November 1993*

Winter Winners

Will it grow in a container? The answer is yes. Provided you are prepared to look after it, you can grow any plant in a container, from roses to bamboos, from water lilies to monkey puzzles. But remember: the plant is totally dependent on you for water, rainfall is never enough even in winter. (The only possible exceptions are sedums and sempervivums, which will manage without attention, provided you use a gritty, well-drained soil mix and position them in full sun.)

Most gardeners cannot bear to rip out summer bedding plants when they ought to, which is the end of September or early October, thus allowing spring bedding (wallflowers, stocks, winter pansies and so on) plenty of time to settle in whilst the soil is still warm. But the recent gales and frost will have finished off the last of the petunias, argyranthemums are looking bedraggled and even fuchsias, struggling on in sheltered corners, are looking the worse for wear. I cannot imagine spring without wallflowers, but these should have been planted by late October.

There is no need to change all the existing soil in the containers, just the top eight inches or so – rich feeding is not required by winter bedding plants, it would encourage too much leaf at the expense of flowers. Either use a bought ready-made potting compost, or mix up your own from six parts of topsoil, three parts of damp peat and two of horticultural sand.[4] Buy some tulips at the same time and plant them beneath the pansies – these are the only bulbs that will stand late planting without next year's performance being affected.

---

4. See page 6 for up-to-date mix.

Box (*Buxus sempervirens*) is unsurpassed for use in containers and is long-lived in such cramped conditions. Its particular shade of green is pure delight in winter.

An amusing invention is to make a kind of box soufflé: take a large terracotta pot; do not fill it quite as much as usual with soil mix (say three inches down from the rim) and closely plant it with small box bushes all over. Clip them neatly into a very shallow dome, which rises no more than three inches in the centre (from the level of the rim). My pair of box soufflés may not be much to look at in summer, with many other colours to compete with, but in winter these two bright green vegetable puddings are in a class of their own.

Other evergreens that are long-term successes in a container are camellias and rhododendrons (lime-free soil mix please, and never let them dry out). For good architectural shape, try spiky-leaved cordyline, yucca and phormium. Handsome *Fatsia japonica* with large glossy palmate leaves and all ivies would do well in shade as will sweet box (*Sarcococca humilis*), a little unassuming plant, with nondescript flowers and a powerful honey scent on warm winter days. Variegated hollies or small euonymus such as 'Emerald 'n' Gold' would make a cheerful patch in a dull corner, especially if surrounded with cream pansies and blue primroses. I hesitate to recommend primroses, since the brazenly coloured modern hybrids are a travesty of the original wild primrose (a delicate charmer in pale yellow with a hint of green), but the blue ones are quite nice.

Sun is the prerequisite for a grouping of herbs in pots. Even in winter they can look good, with their contrast in shape and leaf colour, if you choose, say, rosemary, purple-leaved sage, bay, lavender and myrtle. Myrtles in pots, by the way, are the last word in chic interior decoration, trained as a standard into a lollipop shape, like a ball on a stick. Very *House and Garden*.

 *15 November 1992*

OK, Answers to those Tedious Questions

My gardening career began in the 'Doubts and Difficulties' department of *Amateur Gardening*, in Covent Garden, London. The magazine was under strict union control, and chapel meetings of the print union or the NUJ were held almost daily. The only escape for those of us in 'Doubts and Difficulties' from the umpteenth letter 'Why has my busy lizzie died?' was to take refuge in the Ladies. We could hear the head of the department, Pecksniff personified, furiously pacing up and down outside, but even he hadn't the courage to try and get us out. We invariably discussed how to achieve extra minutes either end of tea-break time, and succeeded in negotiating, to the outrage of Mr Pecksniff, for 20 minutes pre-lunch and 20 minutes after-lunch official tidying-up time (extra in wet weather) – all to take place in the privacy of the Ladies.

The very same question that haunted me then 'What do I do about moss on the lawn?' still has the same effect on me – I feel weak with boredom and want to go and hide. But today, on this dreary November afternoon, I shall do my duty and look it up in the books for you.

The Essential Gardener by Dr Stefan Buczacki (Sidgwick & Jackson): 'One lawn weed ... causes gardeners more anguish and concern than any other. I would cherish a pound for every time that I have been asked how to rid a lawn of moss ... Actually, to kill moss is not difficult. Any of the modern selective moss-killers will do it, although none I think is more effective than lawn sand. But assuredly the moss will return unless it is possible to correct its underlying causes. Moss will thrive when the grass is closely mown, when the lawn is shaded and poorly drained and the grass is not fed ...'

The Gardening Year (Reader's Digest) remarks stuffily: 'moss ... the presence of which is an indication of bad physical conditions, such as waterlogging and compaction of the turf, and indicates that attention should be paid to better drainage, aeration and general management.'

Miller's *Gardeners Dictionary* by Philip Miller (excellent fellow, always to the point, no messing) (Dublin, 1732): '... the rubbing of the Moss will signify little, for the Cause not being removed, the Effect will not cease, but the Moss will, in a short Time, be as troublesome as ever.'

Exactly. May these comments finally lay to rest the question of 'moss on lawns.'

Another question which sent me dashing for the Ladies recurred without fail in the November postbag – the one about botrytis. Only last week I was congratulating myself that I didn't have this particular fungus disease. Suddenly, the greenhouse is full of it. You'll see a fluffy grey mould on plant parts; the puffs of dust that fly off when you touch it are spores setting out to infect other plants. The best prevention is to meticulously remove dying leaves, and go easy on the watering. When in doubt, don't. Most plants are having their winter rest, there's little root action, and the last thing they want is to sit around in a puddle; houseplants, ditto.

Having dealt with the tedious aspects of the month, let's consider the few true flowers of November. *Nerine flexuosa* 'Alba' has white lily-like flowers, similar to the more robust common pink nerine of September, but with delicate, undulating petals. Give it your warmest possible well-drained spot at the base of a sunny wall. Another delightful plant, infinitely valuable for producing fresh flowers in the autumn sea of destruction, is the old chrysanthemum 'Emperor of China', a pale and lovely thing, wan in the low November light, with drooping heads of silvery rose pink.

 *10 November 1994*

Don't Fear the Rose

When I started to garden I found the subject of rose pruning highly alarming. Gardening books were full of little diagrams of 'the correct cut' and the 'wrong cut' with much mention of 'the outward-facing bud'. Armed with the secateurs, I would approach the rose, gaze at it in a worried fashion, see no sign of any rosebuds, and weakly put it off for another day.

In the gospel according to the most ancient books on gardening, it has been decreed that roses shall be pruned in the springtime. What we in Ireland forget is that most gardening books originate in London, and have to lay down a law which covers them for rose pruning in northern Scotland as well. (In Aberdeen pruning is delayed until March.)

I like to prune roses in November for several reasons: you can create more light for surrounding plants; the tidier you can get the garden now, the less there will be to do in spring; the leaves are going to drop off anyway, so you might as well cut them off before they do; many roses should have their stems shortened now anyway, to prevent wind-rock; lastly, by cutting off and/or picking up any leaves with the tell-tale signs of blackspot (self-explanatory) you are preventing the spread of disease. All surplus rose wood is removed in autumn and even in the event of a hard winter all you'll have to do in spring is a minor tidying down to the first undamaged bud.

Now to the angle of the cut. The bud, by the way, looks like a small knob and is found directly above each leaf. By observing which way the leaf is pointing, and making a cut directly above it, you can encourage a new shoot to grow in that direction. Hence the instructions about the outward-facing bud. The idea is to get the plant to spread out its new growths, instead of forming a congested tangle in the centre.

Now to the bit that matters: regardless of the type of rose, take out all damaged, weak, twiggy or dead wood. Then take out some of the oldest wood right down to the base. I needn't go into long explanations about which this is, common sense will tell you that it is the gnarled, darker-coloured wood as opposed to the fresher green shoots. As a rule of thumb, shorten any too young, thin shoots – a thin shoot will never produce good flowers, if any. Next, yank out, ie pull rather than cut, any suckers from the base, easily recognised by the fresh green, suspiciously healthy leaves. The paradox of rose pruning is that pruning invites growth and suckers are better weakened by pulling rather than cutting.

Old-fashioned roses that only flower once, such as 'Madame Hardy', 'Céleste' and 'Charles de Mills', had a major deadheading that amounted to pruning immediately after flowering in July. For continuous flowering types such as 'Madame Isaac Pereire', 'Souvenir de St Anne's', prune as in the previous paragraph, taking out dead, old and weak wood and lightly shortening other shoots. Species roses grown for their hips, such as *Rosa moyesii*, don't prune, except for dead wood.

 22 November 1992

Make Light of Winter's Dark Shadow

The garden is littered with tea-cups abandoned in icy showers. Muddy trails lead along the paths, up the steps to the front door, and through the house to the phone. Leaves swirl fitfully, undecided where to settle. Hands are chapped.

The only thing I envy the seriously rich (apart from real linen sheets), is the space to make a Winter Garden. Only to be visited in midwinter, this would be hidden by high walls and paved in mellow sandstone. There I would sit, in the low sun, beside a malachite table, eating Gentlemen's Relish sandwiches and drinking jasmine tea. Unseen gardeners would work overnight, bringing fresh pots of white hyacinths and paperwhite narcissi.

There would be an ancient specimen of wintersweet in the centre, huge tubs of camellias, mimosa on the south-facing wall, witch hazels galore, countless hellebores and carpets of *Cyclamen coum*. The rare, Christmas-flowering daffodil 'Cedric Morris' would be there by the hundred. *Lonicera fragrantissima*, the December-flowering honeysuckle, would scent the air.

Witch hazels (*Hamamelis*), long admired by Gardeners with Taste, have a major drawback. When their bare branches are wreathed in funny little twisted, fragrant flowers, they are indeed special, particularly if seen against a dark evergreen background. But their summer leaves are second-rate; blood will out, they are first cousin to the ordinary hazel. As for the winter honeysuckle, dreamy as its flowers may be, its summer appearance is moth-eaten, the leaves a dullish green. These two shrubs would be all the better hidden away in the Winter Garden proper.

For those of us with only a Winter Corner, *Viburnum farreri* is essential. A sprig in a warm room invites the nose to a swooning scent of heliotrope. A native of China, apparently common in Chinese gardens, it has clusters of light pink flowers, appearing in succession from November on. Soil and aspect are of little concern.

Rubus thibetanus, a type of bramble, has prickly stems around five-foot tall, which have an almost opalescent, silvery-white bloom, very pronounced in winter. I have it underplanted with a carpet of black-leaved *Ophiopogon planiscapus* 'Nigrescens'. Rather sophisticated, don't you think? *R. cockburnianus* is similar, the stems just as decorative, but a plant better used by country landowners for pheasants to hide in – it's too invasive for the small garden

Would that designers of Christmas cards knew a Christmas rose when they saw one – in some cases they portray a white Japanese anemone instead. The true Christmas rose, *Helleborus niger*, has pure white flowers, sometimes ageing to pink, with golden stamens. Flowering time is variable; some forms don't flower until February. The size and quality of the flowers also varies, some flowers are cup-shaped with beautifully rounded petals and others are squinny little things. *H. niger* prefers a heavier soil than mine and certainly likes good living.

But hellebores of the *H. orientalis* type, ravishing plants to the last, are easier to please. The flowers, the first in bloom now, come in heavenly colours, including smokey purple-black, crimson, yellow, pink, white, and numerous different shades of purple. Every December I cut off all the old leaves, an important part of preventing the spread of fungus disease, which distorts the flowers and leaves with blackish spots.

Winter gardens have a magic all of their own. Ordinary things, when illuminated by a low winter sun, are suddenly transformed. A withered herbaceous stem, fallen leaf or even a stray pebble suddenly becomes a thing of mystery when attached to a long dark shadow.

 *27 November 1994*

Plants that Earn Pride of Place in the Greenhouse

Plants almost need a reference to qualify for a permanent home in my greenhouse. Many is the plant that has been given its cards for growing too big, or not contributing enough to the flowery effect.

But, apart from a short period during which I experimented with other climbers, *Jasminum polyanthum* has always been given a place of honour. On warm spring days its heavenly scent fills the greenhouse, overflowing through cracks in the windows and seeping out under the door. Until now I never doubted the law laid down in gardening books – *Jasminum polyanthum* must have frost-free conditions. But last week I saw a wonderful specimen growing outside on a south wall. This is the jasmine you sometimes see in flower shops, trained around a wire hoop; it adapts quite well to bright living room windowsills; you could give it a rest outside in summer, repot it once a year and keep it hard-pruned. Growing in a border of soil in the greenhouse, it is never fed and only watered when I remember to do so. A vigorous climber, it will soon take over unless you give it a serious hack after flowering about May. You needn't get involved in soul-searching about whether you should cut it above or below a leaf-joint or whether to take out old or new wood, just shut your eyes and chop the whole thing down to within three feet of the ground.

The highlight of the greenhouse year is in autumn, when the Chilean bellflower, *Lapageria rosea*, is in full glory. It ascends by means of twining, flexible stems, clothed in prominently veined, leathery, evergreen leaves. The flowers are large, pendulous, rose-pink bells, flared at the rim and voluptuous to touch – exquisitely cool and waxy. It needs lime-free soil, cool conditions and plenty of water – not the plant for a hot conservatory.

Tips for this week

- Plant tulips (daffodils should all be planted by now).
- Continue dividing herbaceous plants, but leave all grasses, kniphofias, and any plant you suspect is tender until spring.
- In cold areas lift dahlias, cut them back, stand tubers upside down in a shed so that the ends of the stems can dry out. Store in boxes in a frost-free place with a light covering of peat. During winter, check occasionally and remove any pieces of rotten tuber. If they've dried out too much, soak in water to plump them up. Dahlias in milder areas, including Dublin, should be left in the ground, with a thick mulch (6 inches) of peat above them.
- Continue tidying up leaves. Don't let them collect on top of small alpine and herbaceous plants.

- Under glass, take precautions against botrytis (a grey mould) by picking off all dead leaves.

 *28 November 1993*

A Landscape Dotted with Errors

There it was, a ceanothus, an all-time sunlover from California, planted in deep shade underneath a fully-grown beech tree – a sure sign that the owner had had a visit from a landscaper. The remainder of the area under the beech consisted of one berberis, one cotoneaster, one *Viburnum tinus*, one mahonia, one pampas grass, one variegated privet, one *Rubus tricolor* (I cannot understand the name of this plant, there is nothing tricolor about it, it is a very ordinary green all over), one weigela, one philadelphus, one *Jasminum nudiflorum*, one potentilla (shrubby), one euonymus (variegated), one griselinia, a nondescript deutzia and a poor, sad rose 'Blanc Double de Coubert'. Scenes of such disgraceful planting abound.

Disgraceful for two reason, firstly because none of these plants is ever going to thrive in such a position. (Dry shade is one thing, and there are plants that can cope, and cope quite well. But the shade of a fully mature beech is quite another matter. Early bulbs, such as snowdrops and perhaps the hardy autumn-flowering *Cyclamen hederifolium* would be appropriate, but best of all would be a simple carpet of moss.) Survive they may, but thrive they will not.

Secondly, all plants above are perfectly respectable in themselves, but the choice of one of this, one of that and one of the other shrub do not add up to a garden, just a totally senseless muddle, an uncoordinated hodgepodge, like a Christmas pudding of plants with umpteen different ingredients to start with, plus a box of Smarties. It is easy to see how it happens, the scenario goes as follows: a young couple, both working full time, have just finished doing up the house. They haven't had a minute to think about the garden, the evenings are drawing in, they call in a landscaper.

To justify the expense the landscaper presents them with a long list.

The couple are bewildered but impressed by the string of Latin names – they haven't a clue what all these plants are, but surely something with 'Superba' at the end of its title can only live up to its name?

The problem is intensified by the time of year. Gardening renovations are often undertaken during the winter. The garden owners are out at work, and when they come home they must be able to see something for their money. Thus you will see plantings where evergreen shrubs predominate, very good for instant customer satisfaction, as the new site is dotted all over with green leafy mounds. Over-planting of evergreen shrubs, ie more than a third of the whole selection, will lend a rather leaden, heavy look in summer. (Be warned these remarks apply to all plantings, whether in sun or shade.)

Underneath conifers it is virtually impossible to grow anything. The position is seriously dry and shady throughout the year. But under the shade canopy of large deciduous trees (other than beech), plants such as bulbs will have almost completed their life cycle as the tree comes into leaf. And under small deciduous trees, enough light filters through to the bed beneath, especially under trees with airy foliage, such as *Gleditsia* or silver birch. One plant in particular is a star customer for doing well in a dry, shady position: *Euphorbia amygdaloides* var. *robbiae*. It will smile at you from the poorest, dryest soil. It has deep dark green rosettes of leaves and lime green flowers. They begin to form soon after Christmas and they very slowly expand, looking pretty all the while, until they are fully out in April. Marvellous for picking, a few bits will turn a bunch of supermarket daffodils into a bouquet.

 *29 November 1992*

December

Penny, Knee-Deep in Expertise

P enelope Hobhouse was in Dublin last week to launch her book *Penelope Hobhouse on Gardening* (Frances Lincoln). Unlike other gardening gurus (my opinion of whom is best left under the bench in the potting-shed), she is a real, hands-on gardener – no namby-pamby gloves for her. Penny is an internationally famous garden designer and lecturer, and among the elite of gardening writers. It gives me great satisfaction to tell you that she is Irish, born in Derry.

For 14 years, Penny was in charge of Tintinhull, a heavenly National Trust garden in Somerset. In the new book, using Tintinhull as a model, she explains her ideas on design, planting and practical matters. I already have a Leaning Tower of Pisa on the coffee table, made up of gardening books full of impossibly beautiful flowerbeds, with little information as to how to set about making one. This book, however, contains watercolour planting plans, that are easily understood, of all the beds at Tintinhull. Now there's no excuse not to get one and copy them.

I used to imagine that gardening princesses spent more of their time in social pursuits rather than in the muck-spreading department, but this book contains pictures of Penny knee-deep in a heap of mushroom compost, planting out seedlings with mud-caked fingers, plus many more informative pictures of step-by-step sowing, pruning, mulching and so on. Very refreshing.

It is also a beautiful book, and considering the quantity and quality of the photographs (the magical, misty, early morning sort by Andrew Lawson), it isn't expensive. Penny has now left Tintinhull to start a new garden of her own. She has a lifetime's experience of making gardens and looking at plants, so I was itching to ask what it was going to be like. Apparently it's going to be rather like Tintinhull in structure, 'but planned so there's lots of flowers for the next 10 years. I love growing annuals from seed, for flowers for now. Later, when the energy runs out, the whole thing will become a sort of green and grey evergreen jungle.'

Evergreen shrubs are her passion: 'I like the texture and shape.' When pressed to name particular ones: 'Olearias, I adore them, osmanthus, phlomis and *Bupleurum fruticosum*.' I looked in the book for further persuasion about olearias (having always been half-hearted about them): '[Olearias] remain much neglected because they are temperamental, disliking fierce sun – they die of sunstroke – but needing light.'

Mrs Reiss (who made Tintinhull, mostly during the 1930s and 1940s) was an enormous influence. 'She used plants in such an architectural way – I have absorbed her sense of scale and structure and learned the importance of repetition in planting to prevent the restlessness produced by too much variety.'

Penny has designed gardens for such diverse climates as Texas, Maine, Michigan, New York, Italy and Germany. 'I love doing gardens where I have to learn a new vocabulary of plants.' Was there any one plant that could be used everywhere? '*Verbena bonariensis* – such a wonderful plant.' (In colder climates this would be grown as an annual.)

Some years ago I went to see Penny at Tintinhull. Amid an amazing whirl of activity, she was in control of two word-processors (two books at once?) the fax, the telephone, garden visitors at the door, the toaster, the coffee machine and the breakfast conversation. So I asked if her life would now become more tranquil?

'I plan to go to the USA every two months instead of every month,' she replied. I asked which of her numerous books she likes best. *Plants in Garden History* gives me much satisfaction – that's the book I'm proudest of – but I think I like this newest book best.'

So do I.

 *4 December 1994*

The Good and Bad of New Zealand Plant Life

In New Zealand there is an immense, nation-wide dislike of imported plants that have naturalised themselves, ie those plants brought out by the early settlers to remind them of home – gorse and broom, clover, buttercups, ox-eye daisies and numerous examples of what we think of as wild flowers but are rudely referred to on the other side of the world as 'aliens'.

In order to support European grasses, essential to farming, vast amount of nitrogenous fertiliser must be tipped on to the land and it is the fertiliser that kills or much diminishes the local plant population. So accustomed are the native plants to a lean diet, and so rampant do the imported plants become, that in areas of heavy farming, roadside verges (although reminiscent of an Irish country lane) have little sign of native sedges (*Carex*) or the marvellous silver-leaved New-Zealand daisies (*Celmisia*). So, after a month in New Zealand earlier this year, I too began to blanch at the sight of a buttercup, choke at the sight of a field of clover and feel disgusted at the way imported plants had terrorised the local plant community.

Ireland, with a temperate, high-rainfall climate, is perhaps more suited to New Zealand plants than any other country in the northern hemisphere. Where would we be without *Pittosporum tenuifolium*, olearias or daisy bushes, silver-leaved astelias, hoherias, leptospermums and the best of the lot, the aforementioned celmisias?

But there is one plant from New Zealand to which I must return the compliment and refer to as 'alien' and that is the New Zealand flax, or phormium. Phormiums are tall spiky-leaved evergreen plants. Agreed, one phormium is an excellent provider of strong foliage contrast among a froth of small-leaved plants. The trouble starts when a garden becomes over-phormalised, with phormiums waving their alien spikes all over the place. Their rather exotic, tropical-looking leaves, may seem all very fine in summer, but in winter, when the garden palette is reduced by the low light to more muted tones, their over-bright leaves seem to emit a foreign glare.

Great restraint is required, not only in limiting yourself to just one phormium (unless you have an enormous garden) but also in your choice of cultivar. Ten years ago or so, with much trumpeting of their charms, many new varieties were launched on the market. Just imagine the leaves of 'Aurora', striped in red bronze, salmon pink or yellow or of 'Pink Panther', bright pink with startling red edges, as suitable additions to the Irish garden in winter! But there are one or two good phormiums which do seem appropriate. 'Cream Delight' seems acceptable on the dullest winter day, with leaves striped in pale cream and green. It is slow-growing, one metre high at the most, with nicely arching leaves. I have it planted next to *Euonymus fortunei* 'Emerald Gaiety', with dainty leaves exactly the same colour as the phormium, which further emphasises the contrast in leaf-shape.

Tall purple-leaved phormiums can seem very dominant in winter, with their lowering gloomy look, and those I used to grow had to go in a fit of ethnic cleansing. But if you choose one of the neat purple-leaved cultivars, such as *Phormium tenax* 'Nanum Purpureum' or 'Bronze Baby', it will make a good architectural shape in summer and still be tolerable in winter because of its size. And for a large garden, the plain green-leaved species *Phormium cookianum*, a superb foliage plant, will blend nicely with the landscape.

Now that I have given the phormium a thoroughly good knocking, with many criticisms of its exotic tropical appearance, the irony is that in fact it is a mountain plant of a coldish climate, which is found in the wild at considerable altitudes.

 *6 December 1992*

Getting to the Bottom of Botany

Botany must have been specially invented to intimidate gardeners. When the scientific study of plants began, botanists were among the few people who could read. The humble horticulturist, grubbing away in his garden, didn't get any say as plants were organised into orders, families, genera and species; if he had, things might have been different. Instead of having plants categorised into families such as Cruciferae (cabbage) or Rosaceae (rose) he would devise a completely new system of plant nomenclature, classifying such plants as *Populus × candicans* 'Aurora', the scourge of the Irish countryside, as a member of the Euthanasiaceae. In the gardener's mind this is far more descriptive than the botanist's choice of Salicaceae.

Leptinella squalida is described in *The New Royal Horticultural Society Dictionary of Gardening* as follows: 'A creeping, monoecious perennial ... leaves toothed in distal half, obtuse, yellow green with scattered long hairs ... phyllaries 6–12 green, villous.' If this horrid little creeping daisy had been put in the Euthanasiaceae in the first place, you wouldn't have to wade through all that gobbledegook – you'd know immediately not to plant it. Leptinella is so firmly ensconced in my lawn that there have been recent arguments as to whether in fact it should be in the Wanderlustaceae.

You will all know of the Ephemeraceae, known in the vernacular 'Here today and gone tomorrow' – which incorporated all daphnes, some lilies, and the wonderful chocolate-scented *Cosmos atrosanguineus*, which I cannot keep alive. Then there's the large family of Publicaceae, which live on the side of the motorways and on roundabouts, including such plants as berberis, choisya, *Lonicera nitida* and *Viburnum tinus*. The Heepiaceae would include all the ever-so-humble plants which actually enjoy being trodden on – thymes, chamomile and the tiny creeping mint, *Mentha requienii*. And it goes without saying that the most beautiful plants of all would be placed in the Orgasmaceae, thus properly describing such plants as *Paeonia* 'Joseph Rock', Himalayan blue poppies and *Paraquilegia anemonoides*.

If you cannot remember the name of a plant in the presence of a botanist, try saying 'What do *you* call this plant?' This implies that you do, of course, know the name, but the plant might have been subject to a recent change of name. It probably has. You will have noticed that as soon as you learn the name of a plant, the botanists change it, just to keep the gardener in his place.

 *12 December 1993*

Matching Plant and Turkey

The breeding regime of the poinsettia must be closely synchronised with that of the turkey. The euphorbia family is one of my favourites, but it is hard to feel anything but negative with regard to the Christmas poinsettia (*Euphorbia pulcherrima*). For a start, its brilliant (English) pillar-box red petals are a real swiz: they are not petals at all but bracts, with none of the ethereal delicacy of real petals; they are more crepe paper cut-outs, first cousins of the Christmas cracker.

The poinsettia comes from Mexico. By nature it is a shrub that can reach nine feet. Whereas turkeys are bred to have enormous breasts, the poinsettia is treated for market by being treated with chemical growth regulators (chlormequat) to induce compact habit. Should you want to keep this vegetable dwarf going for another year, reduce watering in late winter. When all the leaves fall off, cut the stems back by half, and move to a warm, shady place indoors and water sparingly. After repotting in summer, move to bright but indirect light with a temperature of about 18°. Poinsettias do not start to form their flower buds until the nights lengthen in autumn. By then you may be surprised to find that the effects of dwarfing compound have worn off, and the poor thing is at last achieving its normal height. I did once see a very old and good specimen poinsettia that had been kept going for years – it was at least six feet or more tall and twice that in circumference.

Evergreen azaleas, with proper care, can become faithful old friends, flowering regularly at Christmas time, provided you remember that their rootball must never, ever be allowed to dry out. I learned this on seeing pots of commercially grown azaleas standing permanently in trays of shallow water. Ideally, once they've finished flowering they should be moved to a frost-free greenhouse, but in very sheltered seaside parts of the country they may survive outside. In any case, move to a shady spot outdoors for the summer. Repot every second year using lime-free compost and feed occasionally with ericaceous fertiliser. Just to explain the 'ericaceous'. The Ericaceae means the heath family (ie heathers) which includes such plants as rhododendrons, azaleas, camellias, pieris and so on, none of which will tolerate lime in their soil. Special fertilisers are available just for this group of plants. Evergreen azaleas come in pink, red, magenta, white and salmon and various different shadings thereof. The colours seem to undergo changes of fashion – a few years ago you could buy nothing but magenta and now frilly petals are *de rigueur*, the frillier the better it seems.

Cruel as it seems to expose hyacinths to midwinter weather, as soon as flowering is finished plant them out. The flowers will be later in future years, and considerably smaller, but so much the better.

The florist's cyclamen has been bred from *Cyclamen persicum*, a native of the eastern Mediterranean – Rhodes, Crete and Libya. The fragrant, white, pink or mauve flowers and leaves variously patterned in silver have, over the years of hybridist's attention, produced some very fancy progeny – the flowers may be quilled or ruffled, or scattered with amazing frills. Even a medium-good gardener should be able to keep a cyclamen going. They dislike hot, dry central-heated air and cold draughty windowsills. A cool room, with plenty of light is required. Over-watering (signals are drooping leaves and the pot feels too heavy) is the most likely killer. After flowering, gradually reduce water until the pot is completely dry. Leave in a cool place for two or three months when you should see signs of new life and watering may be gradually increased. Do not wet the base of the plant, and preferably water from below, by standing the pot for a few minutes in a saucer of water that has had the chill taken off.

Study all plants closely before buying, avoid anything with a limp, sad look, or hint of a yellowing leaf. If an azalea has been allowed to dry out any time on the journey from glasshouse to shop, and a cyclamen or poinsettia has been left on a freezing pavement, they may never recover.

 *13 December 1992*

Man in the Garden – Bit of a Deadhead

Man in the garden doesn't like being told what to do. He requires careful handling, or doors bang, parties sulk behind bushes, and a major storm develops. There are certain gardening jobs he's happy to do (and more importantly be seen to be doing). Every week a great show is made of Mowing the Lawn. The day before this momentous occasion you hear him psyching up for it – speculating about weather, worrying if there's enough petrol, and anxiously patrolling the sacred turf. Probably at this very moment he's contemplating a light pre-Christmas mow.

His macho image must be preserved at all costs. This may extend to clipping the hedge, digging the vegetable patch or pruning apple trees (he considers fruit pruning an exclusively masculine skill), but as for being seen in a flower-bed, whatever next? Deadhead the roses? Indeed not. Might as well ask him to serenade you from the border (to the tune of the ad for Cornetto ice-cream) with a rose between his teeth.

His refusal tactics are boundless. Perhaps the most imaginative is the one when he agrees, disarmingly, to whatever you've suggested. Of course he will remove the dead tree/build a retaining wall/study the catalogue of new conservatories. He then sweetly explains, with teeth-gritting logic, that whereas he'd be only too delighted to dig out the dead tree, it is in fact still alive (indicates one remaining green twig), and to build the retaining wall would be no trouble whatsoever – except that it would be a visual disaster. He goes on to insist, with a heavenly smile, that the idea of a new conservatory is indeed brilliant, except there's nothing on the market with quite the olde world charm of the existing one. Distressed buildings are the height of fashion, don't y'know? With broken panes of glass? Better still.

As you see, man is master of the art of getting out of doing something he doesn't want to do – by inventing an infallible argument as to why it shouldn't be done in the first place.

Man in the garden likes to advertise his presence. The more noise he makes, the better he feels. My theory is that his passion for motorbikes metamorphoses overnight (around 30-something) into an obsession with mowing machines. They serve equally well as rattlers of tranquillity to the neighbourhood.

Around 40-something, extra virility may be added to his image in the form of a compost shredder or leaf-blowing machine. The horrendous clamour of these machines makes me think of banging of drums prior to a cannibal feast – the difference is marginal between suburban man guarding his territory with a noisy machine and primitive man brandishing his club with threatening grunts at the entrance to his cave.

After 50, he may need an extra boost. I love the ads for ride-on mowers: depicted thereon is man, now silver-haired. Astride his expensive steed (a giant toy tractor in thin disguise), he whizzes up and down the rolling lawns of deepest Surrey, turning the turf into striped dralon. The thrill of the great vroom-vroom of its motors (not to say the quivering joystick) acts as a sort of mechanical hormone pill.

Plants in the garden need buckets of compost or manure. For any hope of work out of him, man in the garden needs a daily bucket of flattery, half a bucket of compliments and a regular teaspoon of honey. The well-managed man in the garden may also need a weekly massage of his ego (particularly useful if he's proving resistant to a special job you have in mind).

 *17 December 1994*

Casting a Cold Eye on the Winter Garden

Every autumn there is the usual speculation about whether or not we're going to have a hard winter. The quantity of berries on holly and hawthorn is invariably remarked on. In my opinion a cold winter is just what's required. Greenfly have had the audacity to breed in sheltered places outside for the last decade and it's time they got their come-uppance.

Take weeds. It would be nice to think, for once, that the annual meadow grass (*Poa annua*) and hairy bittercress (*Cardamine hirsuta*) had a short break over Christmas in their non-stop breeding programme. You think you don't know these weeds? Step out to the garden and make their acquaintance: the annual meadow grass is the innocent-looking small tuffet of green at your feet and the hairy bittercress is the little rosette of purple-tinged leaves nearby with the tiny, grubby white flowers atop, and seed pods just about to burst.

A serious frost might also solve the cabbage problem. The ornamental cabbage I mean, a frilly monstrosity, the leaves a shocking combination of white, green, pink and purple. The proper place for a cabbage is on a plate of corned beef and not in a front garden.

A friend has a very small (8 × 4 feet) town garden, surrounded by iron railings, with a sunny aspect. At the moment it contains one arum lily (*Zantedeschia aethiopica*), one recently mutilated rose 'Queen Elizabeth', one *Lamium* 'Beacon Silver' and three visiting cards from a neighbouring cat. What should she do with this garden?

The soil hasn't been fed for years, so first I would dig in six large buckets of manure and 10 large handfuls of bonemeal. Then I would plant some box. I'd take out 'Queen Elizabeth' and plant instead, but not exactly in the same place on account of Specific Replant Disease, 'Souvenir de St Anne's'. I would also plant 'Pompon de Paris' either climbing or bush form, a sweet little pink rose and non-stop flowerer. Then I would plant French lavender (*Lavandula stoechas*) and the lemon-scented verbena (*Aloysia triphylla*) near the front door. I would let either *Solanum jasminoides* 'Album' or *Jasminum polyanthum* climb up the house wall. I'd then fill in with white and yellow primroses and as many tulips as I could afford. Then I would indulge in delicious indecision until the New Year about which clematis to plant to go through the plant railings. ('Perle d'Azur' would be hard to beat ....)

Tip for the week

• Sit back and do nothing until after Christmas.

 *19 December 1993*

Searching for Good Secateurs

If there is only one gardener in the house peace will reign. With two, fights are bound to break out. Having surveyed squabbles I can report that the most common cause is missing secateurs. It goes like this: one of the parties goes out to the garden. Despite three resident pairs of secateurs, there is none to be found. Searches take place in the potting shed, the kitchen drawer, the greenhouse, the bag of weeds awaiting composting. The bag of weeds is turned out. No secateurs. Irritation grows. A grumpy walk around the garden reveals nothing. Rage mounts. Then shining from under a bush, a pair of bright red handles. Thoughts of divorce recede. Tranquillity returns.

Before I discovered Felco secateurs (they of the bright red handles) I didn't care whether secateurs got lost. They were always falling to bits or losing their cutting power, and the older they got the more they crushed flower stems, rather than cut them clean. Felco secateurs are all priced at over twenty pounds, but are worth every penny. I even lost a pair of Felco secateurs in the compost heap. A sorry sight, when they emerged a year later, but after a quick wash and some oil they were as good as new.

The second most common argument about the garden concerns trowels: there are several trowels in this garden but only one I want to use: the stainless steel one (I think it is Wilkinson Sword). The wood of the handle feels like silk and at no stage during use do you get that sinking wobbly feeling that the joint between the handle and the blade is going to bend. You may well manage with a different trowel, but for me there is none other. In this case the row ensues because it is in use when I want it.

Watering cans can be another source of friction. There is something about the balance of a watering can that can only be explained by handling one. Like a teapot, there is a wide variation on how they pour. From good watering cans, such as Haws, the water comes out in a smooth stream, and lands precisely where you want it. Other watering cans are just as likely to deposit it on your foot. Or, with an unpleasant glug, they splash the foliage of nearby plants (in winter, under glass, this is a free invitation to botrytis fungus). And the roses (sprayers on the end of the spout) seem to have only two methods of releasing water, with nothing between a sullen trickle and Niagara Falls. Haws watering cans give an even spray, such as to remind seedlings of gentle rain.

 *20 December 1992*

The Ghosts of Gardeners Past

Was that a soft footfall? Or only the rustle of a leaf? You can never be too sure. Garden ghosts abound, never more so than at Christmastime.

Only the other day, I was about to dig up a sempervivum, when I thought I heard 'Don't touch that', the words coming from just over my left shoulder, accompanied by a whiff of tobacco. The plant had been given to me in the 1970s, by Miss Otway-Ruthven, the late professor of medieval history at Trinity College, Dublin, without doubt one of the most formidable women of Irish horticulture. I could almost see her standing there, resplendent in one of her tweed suits of the exceptionally itchy Harris variety – I don't think she ever wore anything else. A vivid streak of orange in her otherwise white hair bore witness to the fact that she was a dedicated smoker – this much we had in common. I remember going to have tea with her – a proper, old-fashioned tea, you understand, with scones and cake and thin bread and butter, brought in by the maid. We sat by the fire, me on the edge of the chair. Conversation was limited. Miss Otway-Ruthven was not a believer in small talk, and I was desperate for something intelligent to say about medieval history. The agonies of tea over, we withdrew outside.

In a garage at the end of the garden, seeds from obscure horticultural societies the world over were sprouting on the dimly lit, cobwebby windowsill of a Rathgar garage, in yoghurt pots, margarine cartons and other assorted containers. Miss Otway-Ruthven, albeit the most formidable woman I've ever met, complete with intimidating bulk and growling voice, had a passion for rare seeds. I've now changed my mind about digging up the sempervivum, so vividly does it recall that afternoon.

The second ghost I never actually met in the flesh. Miss Ellen Willmott is well-known for *Eryngium giganteum*, known as Miss Willmott's ghost. But you may not know *Potentilla nepalensis* 'Miss Willmott', a modest plant with cherry-red flowers still in bloom. Such innocence belies its name, for Miss Willmott was, by all accounts, thrustingly ambitious and rather unpleasant. She was known to inspect the trugs of her less experienced gardeners, picking out anything she didn't consider a weed. She is also accredited with the damning remark (made after a visit to a garden she considered poor): 'It is most fortunate that the owner is so completely satisfied with it.' Botanists now say she had no right to name the potentilla after herself, as it's only a variant of the species. Just another attempt at self-promotion.

The shade of Miss Jekyll is ever present. I hear the scrape of her boot behind me whenever I'm planting. Whispered on the wind I hear 'Quite the wrong colour,' or 'It won't do here,' followed by the tap of a disapproving stick. But some of the exalted lady's recommendations have proved more like those of her *alter ego*, Miss Hyde. For example, she was fond of the blue lyme grass, *Leymus arenarius*, a dangerous coloniser, with the intemperate instincts of scutch grass. The spiky leaves are indeed a beautiful light blue (and it makes an excellent stabiliser for sand-dunes, for which nature intended it), but I would only dare to grow it in a bottomless dustbin, sunk to the rim in the soil.

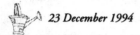 **23 December 1994**

Three Classic Books for New Gardeners

I must tell you about three classic gardening books. The cognoscenti among you will certainly have them, so this is for new gardeners who really must be told about them. One can read endless instruction manuals, in which you may discover how tall something is, what conditions it likes, what its leaves are like, what colour its flowers are, what time of year they appear, when to prune it, and how to propagate it. At the end of which you are none the wiser. What you need to know is why should you grow it in the first place?

You could say that all plants are beautiful in their own way. So they are. But for me the essence of gardening is selection. What one wants is an author who is prepared to point out the pros and cons of a plant. Christopher Lloyd in *The Well-Tempered Garden* will commit himself to saying rude things about plants, such as 'its evergreen leaves are dull at best and objectionable for a good deal of the year' (on *Garrya elliptica*) and 'a coarse looking plant' (on × *Cupressocyparis leylandii*) and 'a hideous or, at best, shapeless bush' (on the hybrid tea rose). Apart from being an A1 gardener, he writes so well he carries you along in a nice unpatronising way, talking to the reader as an equal.

V. Sackville-West's Garden Book should inspire anyone to garden. The book is a selection of Vita Sackville-West's weekly gardening articles for *The Observer*, which appeared from 1947 to 1961. A poet who was able to communicate her great love of flowers, as well as her particular philosophy of gardening, she has probably been the greatest influence on gardening this century. My own copies of this and the former book are old, dog-eared, coverless and grubby, but they were originally published in hardback by Michael Joseph and Collins respectively – I think they are both available in paperback now.

Perennial Garden Plants or The Modern Florilegium by Graham Stuart Thomas (Dent) was first published in 1976, but there have been several new editions, one recently. His descriptions of plants are so fitting and so beautifully put that after reading them no other author will suffice. He too will say precisely what he thinks, such as 'neither this nor the other species are in the first flight of plants' (on *Phyteuma campanuloides*). I'm not sure I agree with him over this plant, though. It has a long flowering season if deadheaded and is a nice violet-blue. Graham Thomas, the gardens advisor to the National Trust for many years, is an artist as well as a writer and thus the book contains many good suggestions of companion plantings, as well as his pencil drawings of great delicacy.

The above three books may not be so glossy nor full of flowery photographs as some. However, it is only when one thinks of the great quantity of gardening books, cluttering up our coffee tables, from which one learns nothing at all but can only remark 'Oh how pretty,' and turn over the page, that one realises the value of the above three books.

 *27 December 1992*

Index

263